Workers
in French Society
in the 19th and 20th Centuries

Gérard Noiriel

Workers
in French Society
in the 19th and 20th
Centuries

BERG

New York / Oxford / Munich
Distributed exclusively in the US and Canada by
St Martin's Press, New York

English edition
first published in 1990 by
Berg Publishers Limited
Editorial offices:
165 Taber Avenue, Providence, RI 02906, USA
150 Cowley Road, Oxford OX4 1JJ, UK
Westermühlstraße 26, 8000 München 5, FRG

English edition © Berg Publishers Ltd 1990

Originally published as *Les ouvriers dans la société
française, XIXe–XXe siècle.* Translated from the
French by permission of the publishers.
© Editions du Seuil, septembre 1986

British Library Cataloguing in Publication Data

Noiriel, Gérard, 1950–
Workers in French Society in the 19th and 20th
centuries.
1. France. Working classes. Social conditions history
I. Title II. Ouvriers dans la société française,
XIXe–XXe siècle. *English*
305.5'62'0944
ISBN 0–85496–610–2

Library of Congress Cataloging-in-Publication Data

Noiriel, Gérard.
[Ouvriers dans la société française XIXe–XXe siècle. English]
Workers in French society in the 19th and 20th centuries / Gérard
Noiriel : translated from the French by Helen McPhail.
p.   cm.
Translation of: Les ouvriers dans la société française XIXe–XXe
siècle.
Includes bibliographical references.
ISBN 0–85496–610–2
1. Working class—France—History—19th century. 2. Working
class—France—History—20th century. I. Title.
HD8431.N6513   1990
305.5'62'0944—dc20   89–35885

Printed and bound in Great Britain by
Short Run Press Ltd, Exeter

Contents

v

Contents

Contents

Figures and Tables

Acronyms and
Abbreviations

ACJF	Association catholique de la jeunesse de France
AFL	American Federation of Labor
BAS	Bon de l'aide sociale
BEP	Brevet d'études primaires
BEPC	Brevet d'études du premier cycle
BTS	Brevet de technicien supérior
CAP	Certificat d'aptitude professionelle
CEE	Communauté économique européenne
CEP	Certificat d'éducation professionelle
CERA	Centre d'études et de recherches d'architecture
CFDT	Confédération française et démocratique du travail
CFTC	Confédération française des travailleurs chrétien
CGT	Confédération générale du travail
CGTU	Confédération générale du travail unitaire
CIERA	Centre international d'études et de recherches appliquées
CNAM	Conservatoire national des arts et métiers
CNRS	Centre national de la recherche scientifique
CPA	Classe de pré-apprentissage
CPPN	Classe pré-professionelle de niveau
CRDP	Centre régional de documentation pédagogique
CRE-DES	Centre de recherche d'étude et de documentation en économie de la santé
CRS	Compagnies républicaines de sécurité

CSU	Centre de sociologie urbaine
EDI	Études et documentation industrielles
EDIRES	Éditions de recherches économiques et sociales
EHESS	École des hautes études en sciences sociales
ESC	École supérieure de commerce
FNSP	Fondation nationale de science politique
FO	Force Ouvrière
FTPF	Francs-tireurs et partisans français
GRECO	Groupement pour la reconstruction des cités ouvrières
HLM	Habitation à loyer modéré
IEP	Institut d'études politiques
IFOP	Institut français d'opinion publique
INED	Institut national d'études démographiques
INRA	Institut national de recherche agronomique
INSEE	Institut national des statistiques et des études économiques
JCF	Jeunesse chrétienne française
JOC	Jeunesse ouvrière chrétienne
LGF	Librairie génerale de France (livre de poche)
NJ	New Jersey
OHQ	Ouvrier hautement qualifié
OS	Ouvrier specialisé: unskilled worker
PC	Parti communiste
PCF	Parti communiste français
POF	Parti ouvrier français
PUF	Presses universitaires de France
PUL	Presses universitaires de Lyon/Lille
SEVPEN	Service édition et vente publication de l'éducation nationale
SFIO	Section française de l'internationale ouvrière
SGF	Statistique générale de la France
SMN	Société metallurgique de Normandie
SNCF	Société nationale des chemins de fer
SNECMA	Société nationale d'étude et de construction de moteurs d'aviation
SOFRES	Société française d'enquêtes pour sondage
TUC	Travaux d'utilité collective
UGE	Union des grandes écoles
UIMM	Union des industries minières et métallurgiques
ZUP	Zone à urbaniser en priorité

Preface
to the English
Edition

Following a well-established tradition in French historiography, my first work on the history of the French working class was written as a monograph,[1] but, like other researchers who have wanted to extend their horizons in order to understand the wider importance of factors applicable to a certain place or time, I very quickly found that this presented a problem. The history of the Lorraine steelworks, at the heart of the second stage of industrialisation, reflects the extent of the upheavals in the early twentieth-century working-class world (notably as a result of rationalisation of work and of mass immigration), but the connection between technological change and the shifting ethnological pattern within the working class, which has been studied with great thoroughness in the United States,[2] has never been spelled out in relation to French development. This lies behind my concern to establish whether Lorraine was exceptional in this respect or whether it was an integral part of nineteenth-century working-class history in France.

Starting from this initial question, I found it necessary to extend

1. See Noiriel (1982; 1984). In 1930 the Longwy region produced one-third of French steel.
2. With reference to the steel industry, see in particular Brody (1960); for the American working class overall, see Montgomery (1979; 1987).

xi

my inquiries ever more widely. Social history, particularly in France, suffers from the effects of a growing compartmentalisation of research, which is particularly apparent in the absence of any real syntheses. In keeping with the spirit of the series in which the first edition of this book appeared, I have therefore tried to bring together the findings of the many works published in France and elsewhere over the last 20 years, for these works have profoundly reshaped our knowledge of the French working class in the nineteenth and twentieth centuries.

A further purpose behind the book has been to put forward certain theories on the distinctive aspects of the 'moulding' of the French working class.[3] I note these briefly in order to relate them to work published since the book first appeared:

1. From the methodological point of view the primary purpose has been to stress the value of a 'long-term' approach to social phenomena. As will be shown, this has made it possible to correct the many errors of perspective observed in work that is too closely restricted to one particular period. Thus the historiographical emphasis on the nineteenth century and the sacrosanct cut-off point of 1914 so frequently adopted in postgraduate theses has led many historians to think that the question of the formation of the French working class was fully resolved in the nineteenth century – which is far from being the case. Analysis based on a long-term perspective also offers a detached historical approach missing from much sociological and economic work, yet indispensable for a clear understanding of current problems in the world of work. If it can be claimed, with Émile Durkheim and Fernand Braudel, that a society's 'unconscious' is its history, the historian is well placed to offer an insight into why social change is so often an extremely painful experience for the individuals affected, and why it usually takes place so slowly.

2. The main purpose of this book is to show that the most distinctive characteristic of the history of the French working class is its extreme instability, its heterogeneity resulting from the perpetual renewal of the sequence of rupture and breakdown which prevented – far more than in other countries – the construction of a

---

3. The emphasis on the problems of 'construction/deconstruction' of the working class explains why certain problems (for example the specific place of women in the working-class world) have not been investigated in depth despite their importance.

genuine class.[4] Consideration of the whole of French social history is essential to an understanding of this unique factor, frequently looking much further back than the 1789 Revolution. The latter, wrongly identified as a 'bourgeois' revolution, undoubtedly delayed rather than accelerated capitalist developments in French society, providing those who resisted upheavals similar to those seen in Great Britain at the beginning of the nineteenth century with the means of effective opposition. The chronic weakness of the rural exodus, a factor of inestimable importance in the overall pattern of French social history, was exacerbated by multiple employment which in the nineteenth century reached the level of a genuine 'mode of production', encouraged by the employers themselves. Since the links between various social groupings were insufficiently strong to draw workers into the factories, the factories had perforce to be established close to the villages. Although the economic dynamism of this type of French industrialisation is indisputable, it nevertheless reinforced the old pattern of separation between town and country to the detriment of any unifying progress towards a single class encompassing artisan and industrial elements of the working world. The 'revolutionary proletariat' in fact only represents the urban element, the élite of craft workers, securely anchored in its corporatist traditions.

3. The theory dominant today among historians, which denies the reality of a French 'backwardness' (particularly in comparison with Great Britain) and accentuates the diversity of patterns of industrialisation, is one which I consider untenable beyond a strictly economic point of view. As is illustrated in this book, working-class resistance in the nineteenth century meant above all that the harmful effects of industrialisation were spread over a long period; they did not reach their full strength in France until the aftermath of the First World War. The 1900–30 period was remarkable for profound reorganisation in the world of work, resulting in fresh compartmentalisation of the working-class focused round three poles. The first covers 'service' workers, particularly in transport, enjoying statutory protection and job security; they form the social base of the reforming worker movement which emerged in the late nineteenth century and dominated the trade-

4. In all countries, however, it appears that the process of the 'formation' of the working class was much more complex than first appreciated; for Germany, see Kocka (1983); and for Great Britain, Jones (1983).

union movement between 1920 and 1936. The second and third poles provide the driving force of the second industrialisation: on the one hand the mechanical and electrical engineering establishments, concentrated in the suburbs of the large cities, the home of the new élite working class, figure with new skills notably in engineering, while on the other hand there is the world in full reconstruction, the world of heavy industry in the paternalistic areas[5] of the Nord and Lorraine where most jobs require little or no qualifications, and where there is massive recruitment of immigrant workers.

The Popular Front of 1936 marks the irruption into the political area of these new worker groups which grew out of the second wave of industrialisation. The weakness of the nineteenth-century worker movement explains why – in contrast to the United States for example – the inter-war union split in France occurred not between craft-based and industry-based organisations, but at the very heart of the industrial sector, between the protected 'service' sector and that of heavy industry. The latter, under the influence of the skilled Paris metal-workers, adopted the Communist Party as the instrument of power over the mass of the working class.

The relative stability of these major industrial bastions right up to the 1960s or even the 1970s, together with the high profile of the large establishments after their workers' combativity under the Popular Front, the Resistance and the cold war, fostered a process of homogenisation and class unification unknown in earlier decades. This was encouraged by the development of new professional classifications and the statistical system of INSEE (the National Institute of Statistics & Economic Studies), which placed workers at the centre of major undertakings – one has only to think of Renault's symbolic status at that time – to the detriment of the artisan class and rural industry.

This book shows, however, that the unifying movement within the working class was too recent and too fragile to survive the fresh upheavals reshaping the whole of French society since the 1960s. Benefiting from the immense reservoir of rural manpower still available in France, for the reasons indicated above, management abandoned old-established industrial areas to set up new automated factories manned by unskilled workers in rural zones; this encour-

5. On the importance and persistence of 'paternalism' as a form of management control in heavy industry in France, see Noiriel (1988).

aged the emergence of a new generation of worker-peasants without working-class traditions, and lacking strong links with other sectors of industrial work. The breakdown of the working class has been accelerated by massive recourse to female workers and new waves of immigrants. The progressive collapse of key sectors of the second industrial revolution (mines, steel, shipbuilding, car manufacturing and so on), at its peak at the beginning of the 1980s, was a mortal blow to the worker movement, completing the breakdown of the work-force into its separate entities as it exists today.

Historical studies of the working world published since this book first appeared have in general confirmed the analysis offered here. Several referring to the nineteenth century have shown that the traditional notion of the 'defeatist' workers could not explain the formation of the working class.[6] The significance of the break at the end of the century was evident even in the old worker centres such as Saint-Etienne. It is visible among the miners, through a very marked diminution of the class's self-renewal, and here too there has been massive foreign immigration.[7] Surveys comparing France with Great Britain show that before the inter-war years the lack of trained manpower and the importance of modest rural ownership in the French working class led to management strategies unknown on the other side of the Channel, and in the absence of social security comparable to the English system the agriculture-industry symbiosis remains the solution favoured by French managers anxious to stabilise their work-force.[8] Elsewhere recent work on French communism has to some extent abandoned explanations of a political nature to confirm the close correlation between the emergence of a worker group entrenched in heavy industry since the 1930s and the success of new political forms and practice introduced by communist organisations. There is now equal emphasis on the fundamental contribution of the crisis in ancient industrial bastions to the current weakness in the PCF (French Communist Party).[9]

Recent tendencies in French social history, however, pose two important and unavoidable questions.

6. See in particular the work of Cottereau (1985; 1987).
7. See Burdy (1986).
8. See Lorenz (1987).
9. See 'Sociétés ouvrières . . .' (1987).

The first concerns the introduction of the historiographic tradition to which this book contributes, including the objective analysis of social procedures inaugurated in France by the *Annales* school (notably by Ernest Labrousse and his pupils). The swing of the pendulum in French intellectual life is customarily extreme; following two decades marked by the rule of an 'objectivist' approach combining Marxism and structuralism there is now a substantial swing to the diverse 'subjectivist' alternatives, rejecting any idea of objective class or social grouping in favour of a 'microhistory' centred on individuals and their families, whose social destinies would make any attempt at overall social classification ineffective through their specific singularity. It is certainly true that some of these works offer valuable contributions to historical research,[10] but their underlying theoretical assumptions – interaction, phenomenology, or the hermeneutics inspired by Gadamer – when taken to extremes render any debate virtually impossible.

The second question touches on a subject that is only treated briefly here: the role of the state (in its broadest sense) in the development of the working class. This book still shows too strongly the influence of the French *Annales* school. It is accepted that French historiography has developed round two currents of thought shared to some extent by areas of historical knowledge. Political history (monopolised by the Sorbonne) turned away from the world of work, too preoccupied with the life of 'great men', and in reaction against this approach the *Annales* historians developed the field of 'economic and social history', generally rejecting political history itself as unscientific – while the true prize at stake was the establishment of social history of politics.

Sociology, from Émile Durkheim to Norbert Elias via Max Weber, has nevertheless supplied a number of elements making it possible to develop this approach. The persuasive hypothesis thus arises, that the chief specificity of contemporary society derives from the immense social task of codification which ultimately affects in general terms all aspects of life in society, shaping everything right down to individual existence. My most recent work,[11] taking the problem of immigration as its point of departure, seeks to bring into focus the decisive consequences for society at large of the triumph of the late nineteenth-century nation-state. This is still

10. See in particular Gribaudi (1988).
11. Noiriel (1988a).

developing and is now, in the interests of greater precision, beginning to control the norms and practices of the world of work down to its smallest details through collective negotiations between the authorised and accepted representatives of the different groups which make up French society.[12] All this legal work is also accompanied by substantial activity – as seen in an unprecedented expansion of bureaucracy – designed to put the new regulations into practice. The great ideal of the Italian economist, Beccaria, dreaming in the mid-eighteenth century of a world where the force of law would follow the citizen 'as the shadow follows the man' is daily becoming a more tangible reality. Where workers are concerned, the progressive establishment of the welfare state illustrates the contradictory nature of the law: on the one hand there is an effective unifying principle bringing together individuals who share common interests, while on the other it represents an essential tool in the forming of new divisions within the working class (based on criteria of nationality or legal or craft status) between those 'endowed as of right' and the remainder.

The logic of the welfare state also leads to a fundamental reorganisation of proofs of individual identity, as now fully incorporated in 'papers', 'cards', 'identity numbers', etc. In complete contrast to the classic image presenting the state and the civil society as two separate entities, the intervention of the law now means that the state has a hand in the most intimate details of the individual's daily life.

Such matters, barely touched on in this book, open the way to a field of research which would undoubtedly extend our knowledge of working-class history. By including the problem of the state more closely in its considerations, the comparative approach – much developed in recent years[13] – would lead to a better understanding of why workers in different industrial countries have become more and more 'national', not only in their political activity and their material preoccupations, but also in their fundamental condition as workers.

Gérard Noiriel, December 1988

12. On this point see in particular Salais et al. (1986).
13. For example, Katznelson and Zolberg (eds) (1985) and Julliard (1988).

Introduction

The working classes in France can perhaps be defined as the social group that is always being defined by name, the exact opposite of the bourgeoisie as described by Roland Barthes: 'the class that resists all definition'.[1] At the time of the July Monarchy the subject of 'the proletariat' moved firmly to the centre of the political stage and has remained there throughout contemporary history. It might therefore be supposed that the working class had been exhausted as a subject for study and comment, that its traditional struggles and heroes, from the early nineteenth-century Lyon *canuts* striking to establish the principle of minimum wages to the unskilled workers of May 1968, via Popular Front metal-workers or late nineteenth-century coal-miners, had been fully explored.

Closer inspection of the facts, however, reveals confusion between two aspects of reality. Attention has focused exclusively on the history of the working-class movement, the world of unions and political conflicts, while the social history of the working classes has long been neglected.

Although the left in France has been the subject of many volumes of political history, there has been no general history of the working-class world since the somewhat distant date of 1927.[2]

This appears to support the view expressed by François Furet and Mona Ozouf that any society that claims revolutionary origins, particularly a fairly recent one, is likely to encounter many diffi-

1. Barthes (1957), p. 225.
2. Louis (1927).

1

culties in writing its contemporary history.[3] Marx himself asserted, fully 100 years ago, that 'the drama of the French working class lies in its great memories'.

This book was originally intended to emphasise the distinguishing features of working-class development and adaptation in France, as distinct from that of other industrialised nations, but it rapidly became clear that it was impossible to study the working class and its world in isolation from other sectors of society. In economic terms the working class is to a large extent defined by the division of labour, over which it has no control; but additionally, and most significantly, any survey of a social class must include the ways in which it is seen as a whole. As Georges Duby has shown with reference to feudal society – and his point is equally valid for the contemporary world – 'in order to orientate itself and others in the complexity of social relations, society adopts the simple classifications which constitute the governing framework of ideological structure'.[4]

Rather than starting from a generally accepted definition of the 'working class', therefore, I have chosen to outline the methods for establishing a detailed assessment of social categories. This categorisation has generally been applied, at varying periods, from outside the working class itself, with indications that this underlying approach was implicit in the historian's work.

Any survey dealing with such a vast subject has to be selective. Notes have therefore been kept to the bare minimum, and readers wishing to know more about any particular point should turn to the extensive bibliography.[5]

3. Furet (1978), p. 136.
4. Duby (1978), cover.
5. The historical anthropology of work and immigration which forms part of the content of this book is the subject of current research in the Social Sciences Department of the École Normale Supérieure in Paris.

1

In Search of the Proletariat

The French working-class world from the Restoration to the beginning of the Third Republic appears better documented and known than any other period; there are almost too many sources available to the researcher. From the 1830s onwards, proliferating statistical data and surveys offer abundant printed papers and an impressive body of archive material. Working-class literature, unparalleled in later times, gives the workers' own point of view, hence the period's rapid popularity with historians. Over the last 20 years, however, the enduring vision derived from the extensive surveys of the July Monarchy and confirmed by any history book, of a 'suffering proletariat', crushed by the industrial revolution, bound in slavery to colossal machines, existing on survival wages amid the cesspits of the great industrial cities, has been fundamentally challenged. Following François Simiand, Georges Lefèbvre and Ernest Labrousse have launched a substantial series of investigations based on the quantitative analysis of social phenomena. Starting from a strictly economic definition of social class, these studies stress an approach to the working-class world founded primarily on the enumerations and census counts of the nineteenth century and supplemented by research into wages, levels of wealth, etc., with the INSEE socio-professional classifications providing a framework for the codification of facts and data processing. Starting from the principle that 'scientifically speaking, all social history is quantitative',[1] this type of study rejected all 'literary' sources as

1. Daumard and Furet (1959).

Table 1.1 Evolution of the active population (per cent)

	Agriculture	Industry	Services
1781–1790	55	15	30
1856	51.7	26.8	21.8
1881	47.5	26.7	24.9

Source: Toutain 1963, table 60.

being too unscientific and too subjective. Through its efforts to break away from the specific and the anecdotal, the quantitative 'French school' achieved an approach to the study of the working class based on increasingly reliable tools. This chapter therefore uses these studies to outline this social group in the nineteenth century, while at the same time stressing the limitations of a too narrowly economic approach.

I. Statistics of the Working Class

A period of relative stagnation

Jean-Claude Toutain's study of the evolution of the French population after the Revolution remains the best point of departure for any comprehensive research into the popular classes.[2] Between 1789 and 1880 the working population increased from 10 million to 16.5 million, out of a total population which grew from approximately 28 million to 38 million; yet the most striking aspect of these statistics lies in the persistence of *ancien régime* proportions in the balance between principal sectors of activity. Although table 1.1 (above) indicates a reduction in the numbers of agricultural workers and a corresponding increase in industrial workers, this shift remains very limited and, significantly, it appears to falter in the middle of the nineteenth century. Between 1856 and 1881, even as industry expanded briskly under the Second Empire, the industrial population scarcely altered. It is an important factor of contemporary French social history that towards 1880 almost one worker in two was still employed in agricultural labour, while

2. Toutain (1963).

from 1840 onwards the equivalent figure in Great Britain was no more than one in four – a figure not attained in France until the 1950s.

Closer examination of statistics on the working class as a proportion of the total active working population of France confirms this impression of 'incomplete proletarianisation'. According to Pierre Léon, in 1789 the number of workers 'in strict terms', meaning those who were engaged in 'large industry', did not amount to more than 400,000.[3] At the end of the July Monarchy the first overall statistical survey estimated that there were 1.2 million workers employed in manufacturing, out of a total of 4.4 million. Artisan workers, active in what were then known as industrial technical crafts, were still by far the most numerous.

At the beginning of the Third Republic the low numbers of factory-employed workers were still remarkable. In 1881 labourers constituted 41.3 per cent of the working population, against 40.8 per cent for 'employers' and 14.4 per cent for 'employees' in the broadest sense of the term, although at that time agricultural labourers were still the most numerous, 3.4 million compared with 3 million industrial workers. It must again be stressed that most were employed in very small businesses; in the 1866 census, considered the most reliable of the nineteenth century, industry accounted for 2.8 million workers (in round figures) compared with 1.3 million employers; that is, one employer for slightly more than two employees!

Dividing the industrial work-force into major sectors of activity provides further valuable information on the characteristics of the working class in nineteenth-century France. Yvonne Crebouw estimates that 60 per cent of industrial workers were employed in the textile industry under the First Empire, and 15–20 per cent in mines and metal work. Some 30 years later the industrial survey of 1840–5 shows that out of 1.2 million workers taken on by firms with more than ten wage-earners, 700,000 were in the textile sector, i.e. 58 per cent of the total, and 120,000 in metal-work, i.e. 10 per cent; barely 2 per cent of workers in large industry were employed in coal-mining. Within the textile sector itself, figure 1.1 (p. 6) shows three predominating areas: cotton (245,000 employees), wool (144,000), and silk (165,000). Thus in the middle of the

3. Léon (1968).

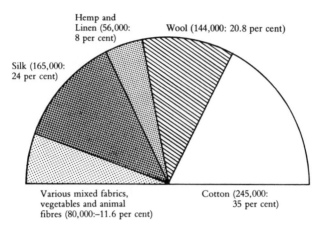

Figure 1.1 Workers in Major Textile Industry at the End of the July Monarchy (establishments with more than ten people)

Source: Crebouw 1967, page 57.

century cotton manufacturing alone employed twice as many people as the whole of the heavy-metal industry.[4]

In 1866 the textile sector was still overwhelmingly predominant, employing more than 50 per cent of the total; construction and metal industries trailed far behind, each with between 13 and 14 per cent of industrial workers, while the remaining quarter was divided between other sectors.

In addition to the numerical stagnation of the industrial work-force, it must be observed that this work-force was essentially dependent on the textile sector, the favoured area of major undertakings; out of the nine areas of industrial activity in figure 1.2 (p. 7), textiles show the greatest proportion of employees in relation to the total number engaged in the sector concerned: 93.7 per cent in 1866, compared with 6.3 per cent employers, while the building sector, for example, shows 62.7 per cent of workers for 35.8 per cent employers, and the food industry had proportionally more proprietors than employees: 55 per cent against 41 per cent.

Finally, a third characteristic of the nineteenth-century working class that deserves emphasis is the importance of women, children and foreigners.

In a total working population of slightly over 14 million people

4. Crebouw (1967), p. 57.

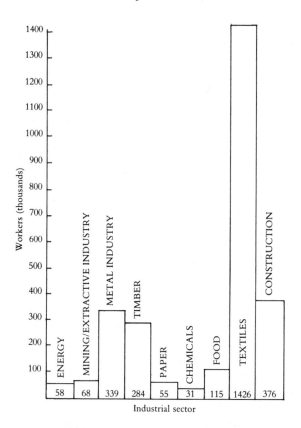

Figure 1.2 Distribution of Workers by Sector in Industry in 1866

Source: Toutain 1963, table 77.

in 1856, nearly one-third were women, a proportion which was to persist throughout the following decades. Although particularly numerous in 'services' (35.5 per cent), with many employed as domestic servants, women were also of great importance in the industrial sector; in 1866 they provided nearly 30 per cent of the total, i.e. 1.2 million women. It is also noticeable that from 1850 to 1880 the female industrial population increased in absolute terms as much as did the male industrial population. Women were particularly sought after in the clothing trade (making up more than three-quarters of the total number in 1866), textile manufacturing (45.7 per cent), and the chemical industry (more than 40 per cent).

The 1847 survey shows that women were encouraged even in large businesses, for in companies with more than ten workers there were 254,000 women and 670,000 men and 130,000 children under 14.

More precise statistics confirm that increasingly mechanised and unskilled work resulted in a greater proportion of female workers. In Mulhouse, according to Villermé, in the 'superior' sector of fabric printing with its demand for large numbers of skilled workers, a typical large firm employed 99 women and 564 men; while in spinning the proportions were reversed, with 93 men to 327 women.

The same figures illustrate the proportion of child workers in nineteenth-century industry. The employment of children was still more widespread in heavy industry than that of women, since in addition to the textile industries children were also active in sectors such as mines or metal-works which employed few women workers. Children were highly esteemed in spinning mills for their agility and suppleness, qualities that enabled them to slip under looms in motion, to connect broken threads, clean bobbins, or clear up cotton waste. In most of the country's mills children made up a good third of the work-force employed on the 'machine' side. They usually started their working life at the age of eight or nine, or even, as in the Oberkampf printed-fabric mills, at five or six, effectively acting as an apprentice to the adult worker. In coal mines such as Carmaux, they made up 20 per cent of the work-force in 1850, and still no less than 15 per cent in 1879, their physical aptitude for edging through galleries too narrow for adults being highly valued by the employers.[5]

The range and variety of the nineteenth-century working world is further accentuated by the presence of a large foreign contingent. The census of 1851, the first to include them, gives a total of about 380,000 foreigners: 30 years later France had a million immigrant workers. Most came from neighbouring countries, Belgians in the north, Italians in the south-east. Although many worked in various craft sectors (tailoring, cabinet-making, stonemasonry), it was increasingly in the great industrial concerns, the textile manufacturers of the north and the east and the mining companies, that they found employment.

Recent historical research has shown various distinct aspects of economic development in nineteenth-century France compared

5. On children at work, see Chassagne et al. (1976); also Sandrin (1982).

with Great Britain. The absence of 'take-off', a genuine British-style industrial surge, explains why the modern working class remained on the periphery of French society until the end of the nineteenth century.[6] Similarly, the rural exodus, often used as a symbol of economic transformation at the birth of capitalism, never attained in France the extent which Marx described in *Das Kapital*, referring to those millions of people 'without hearth or home' living in dire poverty, crammed into England's immense industrial cities. In 1861 only 11 per cent of French people lived in a *département* other than the one in which they had been born; in 1881 the figure was 15 per cent.

Problems of classification

These few statistical examples of the nineteenth-century working-class world are offered simply to give an outline of this social grouping. It must be emphasised that nineteenth-century statistics are generally very unreliable. In discussing Jean-Claude Toutain's study, Jean Marczewski stresses the lack of precision inherent in any attempt to reconstruct numerical statistics on the working population of past centuries, and treats Toutain's study as an additional item for debate. In the course of using these figures as though they were primary truths for econometric calculations, such scruples have been forgotten: hence the importance of social history aimed at showing up what is arbitrary or contradictory, and the stakes at risk, concealed by past classificatory terminology.

Technical imperfections in nineteenth-century statistical procedures should be considered briefly as a first step.

Although the Act of 22 July 1791 required census forms to include questions on employment, it was not until the 1840s that the first industrial and professional enumeration worthy of the name appeared, a development resulting from the creation in 1833 of the SGF (the French general statistical institute). All regional historical theses on the period, however, underline the shortcomings of this first attempt. The industrial survey carried out from 1839 to 1844, and published between 1847 and 1852, dealt only with those actively employed, and among them only those employed in workshops, ignoring the (larger) number employed in industrial trades

---

6. Principal sources: Lévy-Leboyer (1968), and, more recently, O'Brien and Keyder (1979).

and crafts. Pierre Lévêque quotes a number of firms of the 'industrial' type in Burgundy (such as the small boat-building yards along the Canal du Centre) which were omitted.[7] In the Lyon area some of the mayors responsible for collating data at a local level thought that 'printing' concerned paper, while others took it to refer to fabric.[8] How accurate is a national résumé carried out under such conditions? These divergences have added relevance because perceptions of social conditions vary from one survey to another. Research into occupations for the 1840 industrial survey having shown up all the difficulties of such an approach in contemporary France, later census counts enumerated the number of people 'who were provided for' by each occupational activity; the concept of 'the active working population', as defined at the time of the 1851 census, was thus partially abandoned until 1866, when the 'active/inactive' distinction was at last clearly defined. To this can be added all the problems of subdivisions. The best example is undoubtedly that of fishing, classed with food industries (in 1861 and 1866), or with transport (1876 and 1891), sometimes with agriculture, sometimes in a section of its own. The numbers employed in this section were not great, but it demonstrates the fluctuations resulting from different methods of calculating total worker numbers. There are many other examples; Pierre Pierrard states that in Lille, at the time of the Second Empire, basket makers, hairdressers, theatre employees and railway workers were all classed in the 'industrial' sector;[9] this does not take into account such borderline categories as, for example, 'finishers' to small-scale Paris industries, considered by Jeanne Gaillard as 'legally speaking, registered employees, but in actual fact self-employed',[10] and enumerated under one or other heading depending on the census. And then there are the unemployed: it is not known whether census figures included or excluded them before 1896. Wives of farm labourers were sometimes counted as 'active' and at other times as 'inactive'.

This goes some way towards explaining the sometimes considerable distortions shown by contemporary statistical data on the world of work. Philippe Vigier notes that at the end of the July Monarchy the numbers of silk workers in the Hautes-Alpes varied,

7. Lévêque (1983), vol. 1, p. 186.
8. Lequin (1974), vol. 1, p. 4.
9. Pierrard (1965), p. 6.
10. Gaillard (1977), p. 431.

according to the sources used, between 3,000 and 8,000,[11] and, if we are to believe Claude Fohlen, the accuracy of figures relating to those employed in the textile industry was scarcely any greater some 20 years later. According to some sources, the embroidery trade in Beaujolais employed 20,000 people: according to others the correct total was 100,000. There are similar doubts as to the numbers employed by the 'works' in Cholet, or in Amiens, etc.[12]

In such circumstances it is easy to comprehend the problems faced by the historian trying to assess the evolution of the work-force over a given period. Considerable distortions develop rapidly, rendering comparison impossible and opening the way to entirely contradictory interpretations. In Georges Duveau's opinion the numbers of artisan workers in Paris fell during the Second Empire – but this view is vigorously challenged by Jeanne Gaillard, who shows that the statistical variation reveals no appreciable sociological change but simply illustrates a shift in the norms of classification used; for example finishers are no longer included with 'proprietors'.[13] Similarly, as there is reason to believe from the economic dynamism experienced at that time, the question remains open today as to whether France's industrial population increased under the Second Empire, or whether it actually diminished, as Georges Duveau has claimed on the basis of François Simiand's minutely detailed calculations.[14]

The reader should be aware, therefore, that reassuring charts with handsome sets of figures often conceal unrewarding and laborious attempts to harmonise very disparate data. Jean-Claude Toutain, for example, undertook a considerable amount of work to establish a more 'logical' set of occupational classifications for the nineteenth-century census returns. Concierges, who appeared under the heading of 'banking', are moved to the 'domestic' category. Butchers and abattoir workers move from the food industry to commerce, while those employed in making starch, potato flour, and vegetable oils move from the chemical industry to the food industry. As with other similar undertakings, such reclassifications are based on criteria drawn up by INSEE (the national institute of statistics and economic studies) after the Second World War.

11. Vigier (1963), vol. 1, p. 107.
12. Fohlen (1956), p. 187 *et seq.*
13. Gaillard (1977), p. 430.
14. Duveau (1947), p. 197. The proportion of industrial workers in the active working population dropped from 29.07 per cent in 1856 to 25.93 per cent in 1876.

The question now arises as to whether it is legitimate, from a scientific point of view, to apply today's analytical standards to the interpretation of yesterday's social structures. In fact, as has been shown in recent work carried out by INSEE researchers, it is not possible to confront the 'science' of modern classification with the 'irrationality' of nineteenth-century demarcation. In searching for unskilled workers and managers in the social structure of the last century the historian runs a strong risk of foundering in anachronism.

This point touches on a problem illustrating the need for the multi-disciplinary approach to history. Rather than desperate attempts to assess former categories of classification in terms of late twentieth-century standards, an anthropological approach can help the historian by indicating the need to recapture the relevant logic and modes of thought underlying the development of nineteenth-century classification. It is essential to understand why the questions, 'What is being made?' and 'How is it being made?', have become confused in industrial surveys, and also to study in greater depth the criteria adopted in classifying production work, criteria based on a naturalistic distinction not far removed from primitive notions of the differences between 'animal', 'vegetable', and 'mineral'.[15]

Without embarking here on proofs, which remain to be formulated, it may be stressed that one of the essential causes of variation between nineteenth-century census counts and those of our own time is that the social conditions under consideration are often very different from those of the present day. The concept of the 'active working population', for example, remained vague for a long time partly because in the popular classes, as will be discussed in the next chapter, individuals were often very much less entrenched than nowadays in a single occupational activity. Oberkampf, proprietor of Europe's largest printed-fabric business, wrote in 1813: 'I give the number of persons whom I employ without indicating their occupation because there is too much diversity and frequent change from one occupation to another.' A police report 30 years later commented on the same phenomenon concerning a Marseille plasterer: 'He is self-employed as long as he has work, and is employed by others as an unskilled workman when he lacks

15. INSEE (1977) indicates the attitudes of INSEE researchers. G. Thuillier had already focused on this problem; referring to the Nivernais region, he comments, 'The vocabulary and administrative classification of earlier times require a full-scale study' (Thuillier 1966, p. 76).

personal custom.' William Sewell, who quotes this document, remarks that marriage certificates and census forms of the period giving the individual's occupation rarely indicate whether he is engaged as 'proprietor' or as 'employee', adding: 'Perhaps we should not worry too much about a distinction which was evidently not very important in contemporary eyes.' The same social realism is still dominant in Paris 20 years later,: 'Where the status of being an employer ended or began was a matter on which citizens under the Second Empire had no very clear notions', stresses Jeanne Gaillard.[16] Such examples demonstrate how inappropriate are the categories of fundamental Marxism, at least where nineteenth-century France is concerned.

II. Different Facets of the Working World

The difficulty of making a statistical definition of the French nineteenth-century working class resurfaces in any attempt to establish the unity of this social group, apart from its economic status and its integration within the world of work.

The proletariat

The greatest emphasis on the place of the proletariat at the heart of the nineteenth-century working class has come from Marxist historians. Jurgen Kuczynski, to whom we are indebted for a massive study on the development of the working class in western nations, maintains that it is machinery that defines the proletariat. The worker's low rates of pay prevent him from purchasing the means of production, rendered ever more expensive by scientific and technical development and demanding the investment of enormous capital sums. The result in nineteenth-century France was a fundamental break with the *ancien régime*, where in general the workman owned his own tools. 'Owning nothing beyond his own capacity for work, producing goods in which his personal possessions had no part to play, the workman depended for his living on the functioning of machinery which was the concern not of himself but of its owner.'[17]

16. Gaillard (1977), p. 132. See also Chassagne et al. (1976) and Sewell (1971).
17. Kuczynski (1969), p. 50.

The statistics quoted earlier show that until the end of the nineteenth century the true French 'proletariat' was of little importance in numerical terms. Intensive study of large-scale surveys dating mainly from the July Monarchy also proves that although this statement is accurate and irrefutable, it is in fact more contradictory than it first appears.

Grievances ascribed by contemporary observers to the industrial revolution may all be grouped under two broad themes: the ill effects of mechanisation on workers' jobs, and the destitution affecting the disinherited masses who left their roots and moved into the great cities.

Contemporary observers were greatly struck by the sudden irruption of machinery into textile work. Until the middle of the nineteenth century, however, mechanisation in France affected only one particular occupation on a large scale – that of spinning. Spinning machines were invented in the eighteenth century and improved steadily thereafter; they meant ruin for the rural spinning women who were typical of the *ancien régime*. Large establishments could be set up, using the power of water and then of steam to drive mechanical looms. The first complaint concerning these new inventions was that they removed all interest from manual work. Dr Villermé, author of what is certainly the most impartial and profound survey, states that 'with the mechanical loom it is the machine that creates and the mechanism that imposes the rhythm. The loom is not the worker's tool but the master's machine, which dictates the pace. The loom requires supervision: one loom, then two, then several'. No one has described better than Michelet the worker's subjugation to his task when set to work with machinery: in the great spinning and weaving sheds 'the phrase that resounds incessantly in your ear is *don't stop, don't stop, don't stop*, the automatic rumbling which shakes the floor'. He adds later:

> The work of the independent weaver was much less onerous. Why? because he could dream. Machinery makes no allowance for dreaming, no loss of concentration. It's impossible to slow down for a moment unless you hurry to catch up afterwards. The untiring hundred-spindle shuttle no sooner moves down the loom than it comes back to you again. The hand-weaver weaves quickly or slowly, just as he breathes slowly or quickly; he operates as he lives; the loom obeys the worker. There, on the other hand, the worker must obey the loom, the creature of flesh and blood whose life varies with the moment must submit to the inflexible steel creation.[18]

This gave rise to the sentiment that was widely shared until the middle of the nineteenth century and spelled out by Étienne Buret: 'Mechanical employment increases the number of unskilled workers; unskilled workers are preferred by this type of industry, which favours their work above others.'[19] The fact that the use of machines encouraged proprietors to concentrate their labour force in vast establishments lies behind the many complaints concerning the 'confinement' of workers within their factories. This led Villermé to comment:

> They reminded me of the many conscripts whom I have seen in past times overwhelmed by homesickness, far from the familiar haunts of their childhood. Obviously the extremely limited horizons of the factory floor, which do not suit everyone, are particularly unsuitable for those who until they reached a certain age were always out of doors, surrounded by the great spaces and infinite variety of the countryside.[20]

This strikes the observer as particularly disturbing because the simplification of work which resulted from the use of machinery meant that women and children were most frequently employed in these mechanised workshops. There is eloquent testimony in the autobiography of Norbert Truquin, born in 1833 and employed from the age of seven in a woollen factory in Amiens. After a 6.00 a.m. start, 'work in the factory ended at 9.00 p.m., but we did not leave for another quarter of an hour, at the sound of the bell. . . . To be even slightly late meant being fined, and a third offence brought dismissal with a bad reference which made it impossible to find other work in the same area'.[21]

While philanthropists inveighed against the long working day demanded of these children, which often extended to 14 or 15 hours, Adolphe Blanqui's survey of workers in the Rouen textile industry shows them particularly critical of the introduction of piecework wages; this system seems to have increased considerably under the July Monarchy, accelerating the pace of life still more because worker's pay depended henceforward on the speed at which they worked.[22]

18. Michelet (1974), p. 99.
19. Buret (1840), vol. 2, p. 35.
20. Villermé (1840), vol. 1, p. 223.
21. Truquin (1977), p. 50.
22. Démier (1982).

As well as providing the workers' uncensored point of view through the forms which they filled in themselves and which have been preserved, this survey by Adolphe Blanqui evokes the heavy physical burden of factory work. The workers complain of 'stiffness', of 'exhaustion due to the fatigue of work' which was considered a 'permanent and genuine illness'. Three-quarters of the cases of serious illness in Rouen were lung conditions related to unhealthy workshop conditions. Villermé considered this particularly relevant where raw cotton was being worked.

> The dust there settles on the workers, dirties them, sticks closely to their woollen clothing, to their hair, eyebrows, eyelids, ears, nostrils, beard, anywhere where there are hairs to retain it, so that they look very strange when they are at work. And then they absorb it through the nose, the mouth, the throat, and apparently right under the deeper breathing tracts.[23]

The result was the high incidence of lung inflammation and tuberculosis in this section of the populace, illnesses aggravated by the very high workshop temperatures (34°–37°C) demanded by contemporary spinning techniques. Other sectors of heavy industry presented hazards which were sometimes even greater. Coal-mines, for example, became more deadly as they spread further under the earth. In the Nord 15 deaths were officially recorded between 1842 and 1858 as occuring during the removal of pit-props alone. In 1867, 88 people were killed in an explosion at Blanzy, in Saône-et-Loire, and worse was to come. The great metal-work establishments were also prone to industrial accidents – steam-driven machinery could explode, gearing systems mangle and mutilate, overhead loads fall and crush, in addition to industrial illness caused by inhaling toxic vapors. During the 1860s the hospital in Saint-Sauveur, Lille's most populous district, admitted 100 workers every year suffering from lead poisoning.[24]

Apart from the harmful effects of concentrating workers in factories, nineteenth-century observers emphasise the damaging effect of uncontrolled urbanisation following industrial development; although not on the same scale as in Great Britain, several French cities suffered a violent population explosion. The population in Paris, for example, grew from 500,000 in 1800 to one

23. Villermé (1840), vol. 2, pp. 209–10.
24. Pierrard (1965), p. 154 *et seq.*

million in 1846 and two million in 1879, a fourfold increase in the capital's population in the space of three-quarters of a century. The much smaller city of Mulhouse experienced spectacular growth, doubling its population in 25 years (1801–27), with immigrants representing 87 per cent of this increase. The growth of Saint-Étienne was even more pronounced, with its population increasing sixfold between 1801 and 1866.

This concentration underlies all the problems of rootlessness generally described in the 'urban sickness' language most vividly employed, in the case of France, in Louis Chevalier's survey.[25] The shortage of accommodation forced newcomers to crowd together, sometimes lodging several families in one room, using any available space such as cellars, attics, and sheds. Paris was the unchallenged capital of furnished rooms where single men moved in temporarily or as long-term immigrants, sleeping in dormitories containing perhaps dozens of beds. The crisis became so acute during the 1850s that thousands of families were reduced to this type of dwelling, normally the preserve of the unmarried. Rootlessness was also apparent in poor furnishings. In the cellars of Lille, for example, Villermé drew up a rough inventory: a few tools, an earthenware oven, occasionally a stove to battle with the cellars' persistent dampness, straw mattresses instead of beds. Many Mulhouse families slept on bare straw, with a packing case for storage, and a table with a few chairs or a bench. Potatoes and soup provided three-quarters of the daily nourishment for many people.

Promiscuity, lack of sanitation, malnutrition combined with the effects of work on their health – all these elements contributed to the colossal mortality rate prevalent in the more populous districts. Quite apart from the great cholera epidemics, such as that in 1832 which resulted in the death of several hundred thousand Parisians, infectious diseases flourished in such favourable conditions; every year working-class districts were ravaged by typhoid, meningitis, tuberculosis and syphilis. At the end of the Second Empire the death rate in Lille was 33 per 1,000, compared with 25 per 1,000 for France as a whole. In the most heavily industrial quarters of the city, Wazemmes and Saint-Sauveur, the figures are even more eloquent: 70 per cent of the population died before reaching the age of 40, with children under five making up half the annual

25. Chevalier (1978).

Table 1.2 Wages in the Rouen Textile Industry (average of 22 companies)

	Workers		Employers	
	minimum	maximum	minimum	maximum
Men	1.92	2.76	2.18	3.35
Women	1.08	1.36	1.25	1.53
Children	0.50	0.75	0.57	0.95

Source: Démier 1982.

number of deaths. Stillbirths, already running at 2.5 per 1,000 in 1851, increased further and attained the rate of 3.1 per 1,000 in 1868.

As unskilled newcomers these rootless workers received the lowest wages, which increased their problems with poor living conditions. The diversity of methods of payment, the fact that employment was still very irregular, the vast variation in wages according to region, grade of work, or circumstances, make it impossible to calculate the average wage; the numerous studies of this topic are generally misleading. For example, table 1.2, which has the advantage, rare for the period, of bringing together data from both workers and employers, shows the low average rates of pay for industrial workers in Rouen. It also demonstrates the strong internal hierarchy favouring men, who earned four times as much as children and twice as much as women.

These figures, however, appear optimistic when compared with the data shown in other surveys. Villermé has established an average for the same period of two francs per day for men, one franc for women, 45 centimes for children between eight and twelve years old, and 75 centimes for adolescents between thirteen and sixteen. It must be remembered that the total lack of security of employment, a fundamental condition of the time, represented a considerable diminution of this income. Wage rates might be cut ruthlessly in times of crisis, or the number of hours to be worked might be reduced without compensation. A recession in the economic climate usually resulted in substantial unemployment. In Lille, for example, 60 per cent of the textile workers were 'out on the street' during the 1844/5 crisis; in Rouen the figure was three-quarters of the work-force. This insecurity was aggravated by the general lack of any contract of employment; Blanqui reports the remark of a worker he questioned in Rouen, that work lasted only 'as long as the worker suited the master, and as long as the master suited the workers'.[26]

The slightest unforeseen contingency could therefore plunge such workers into destitution. 'Just suppose a third child, unemployment, some misfortune, lack of savings, habit, or simply a single chance extravagance, and the whole family would find itself in dire straits, in terrible destitution; they had to be helped.'[27] Acute poverty, occasional or chronic, was a constant fact of life for the industrial working class at this time. Public assistance, philanthropists, charity benefactresses, all were keenly sought for their services in times of crisis. In 1830 one-sixth of the population of Lille was recorded as 'indigent', and in 1849 the proportion in the Saint-Sauveur district reached 42 per cent. Paris recorded one destitute person in just over every 11 inhabitants in 1831, and still one in 17 in 1869.

This picture also requires mention of what contemporary surveys called 'moral destitution'. Rootlessness and the breakdown of the traditional family which followed the influx of single men into the great cities were among the fundamental causes underlying a certain type of proletarian outcast life, marked by violence, fighting, alcoholism, and a high incidence of cohabitation and irregular liaisons.

'Social breakdown' was also indicated by a reduction in group activity, particularly in religious activity. In the Lille district of Saint-Sauveur, favoured by Belgian immigrants, only 1,500 people attended Easter services out of a population of 18,000. Religious attendance in Paris was very limited in such districts as Belleville or Montmartre, where the population was increasing enormously. Naturally the 'dechristianisation' of the working classes had many other underlying causes, as shown in convincing detail in Pierre Pierrard's recent book, but the industrial upheavals presented the church with a challenge to which it was for a long time unable to respond, for the very reason that traditional religious structures were firmly anchored in the rural world where they had first blossomed.[28]

26. Démier (1982). See also Villermé (1840) and Pierrard (1965), p. 6 *et seq.*
27. Villermé (1840), vol. 2, p. 14. Statistical studies indicate that only a tiny proportion of the working class left any inheritance before the end of the century. See Codaccioni (1971).
28. Pierrard (1984), particularly pp. 28–35. The pattern of social ties disintegrating in urban life can be given for Paris. One out of every five corpses deposited in the

A limited phenomenon deliberately exaggerated

There is little to be gained from a more detailed description of the workers in large mechanised establishments. Many writers have emphasised the most squalid aspects of the nineteenth century, and to dwell on this section of the working classes in order to match what has been written about Great Britain would be to give a distorted view of working-class reality in nineteenth-century France; indeed the most clear-sighted observers from the days of the July Monarchy onwards have alerted their readers against such exaggeration. Michelet is one observer who did not allow his criticism of mechanisation to interfere with a fair evaluation of the phenomenon. In his eyes the rootless proletariat represented no more than a minimal fraction of the working class: 400,000 individuals, or one-fifteenth of those engaged in physical labour. Hence his rage when faced with populist surveys: 'Here are your artists' models . . . whatever is bizarre, extraordinary, monstrous, that is what you are seeking out. . . . You go around with magnifying glass in hand, searching in the gutters, finding Heaven knows what in the way of dirt and squalor, and you offer it up to us: Triumph, triumph! We have discovered The People.'[29]

As with the statistics shown above, the historian must therefore examine most scrupulously the terms of structure of nineteenth-century surveys before adopting their conclusions. This general study cannot undertake such an examination, but some comments are relevant concerning the motivation of so many scholars in their studies of the working classes at the time of the July Monarchy.

It was at this time that 'the proletariat' first appeared on the French political scene. 'The workers' became a subject for comment after the 1831 and 1834 revolts of the Lyon silk workers, not only because of the militancy of the skilled urban élite but also because all those sectors of society hoping for Louis-Philippe's downfall saw the proletariat, with its revolutionary history dating back to 1789, as the perfect instrument for overturning the régime. The majority of surveys undertaken at this time are therefore innocent of any scientific intent to establish social truths. Indeed, as Arthur Dunham was well aware a long time ago, 'surveys on the

---

morgue at the beginning of the Second Empire remained unclaimed: see Gaillard (1977), p. 222.

29. Michelet (1974), p. 152.

French work-force were mostly inspired by utopian idealism and ferment'.[30] It is undoubtedly one of France's most distinctive features for studies of this nature that research into the working class, from the beginning of the nineteenth century to the latter part of the twentieth, has almost always been subordinated to political aims, and objective knowledge of social reality has given way to works of denunciation. To quote Michelet again, 'They exaggerate the evils so that we will the more eagerly rejoice in the blessings foretold by their theorising.'[31]

An understanding of this passion for 'the proletariat' requires recognition of the sociological context of the early decades of the nineteenth century. Traditional social structures were profoundly disturbed by the Revolution and the Empire; to those known as 'the 1830 generation', born after the Congress of Vienna, the future appeared completely unimaginable. One example was the 'over-crowding of the medical corps', a major problem for the July Monarchy which induced M. Orfila, dean of the faculty of medicine in Paris, to suppress health services and thus reduce the number of practitioners by half. As Jacques Léonard said of the medical profession in 1848, 'Surely it is they who speak out loud and clear in the name of the wretched', playing a very active role in the February Revolution, working out a complete plan of action which included, notably, a whole network of 'local medical societies' aimed at maximising rural medical care so as to increase the potential clientèle.[32] Contemporary medicine, still caught between

30. Dunham (1953), p. 154.

31. Fresh surveys assessed the working-class world under the Second Empire, but with changing political winds they are generally concerned to 'refute' surveys dating from the July Monarchy. In Levasseur's eyes the famous revised statistics, which supposedly gave ample 'scientific' evidence of the harm done by manufacturing, showed on the contrary the positive effects of industry on the nation, since the height of new military recruits increased more over 20 years in a textile-working *département* such as the Seine-Inférieure than in the rural Vendée. Similar comments appear in Reybaud and Audiganne's work: see Audiganne (1860); Levasseur (1907); and Reybaud (1977).

32. Léonard (1981), p. 179 *et seq*. The struggle was made more difficult because the doctors' actions conflicted with the prejudices of superstitious popular culture; in the Limousin area, for example, a barren woman 'should touch the lock of Saint Leonard in order to become pregnant. A woman suffering in childbirth should put her husband's nightcap on her stomach'; quoted by Corbin (1975), vol. 1, p. 622. Town life had matching customs, as in Lille where workers gave wine to children with measles, while a cure for meningitis was to put the beak of a live pigeon into the patient's anus: see Pierrard (1965), p. 142.

'knowledge and capacity', was also faced with distrustful public opinion which complained of the gap between aims and achievements, particularly after the great cholera epidemic of 1832. Medical activity therefore tended to be directed towards origins, the causes of illness, and in particular standards of public hygiene. The very recent discovery of a statistical correlation between mortality rates and social amenities provided a legitimate scientific basis for demographic studies and statistical surveys which helped to compensate for the shortcomings of medicine itself. This was the reason, according to Quételet, for the multiplicity of calculations aimed at establishing a causal link between the physical stature of conscripts and the destitution resulting from industrialisation.

Similar links could be proposed in relation to barristers without briefs or notaries without clients who at the time, according to a contemporary journal, 'swarmed like locusts in Egypt'.[33] The social standing of writers likewise underwent a profound transformation in the early decades of the nineteenth century. Gradually the patron of the *ancien régime* gave way to the present-day public, forcing the writer to conform to the demands of the open market. During this period before the establishment of the democratic political system with its parties and official leaders, the thinker—writer came to the fore as the voice of the people; he identified himself with 'the common man', as, for example, in the case of Eugène Sue.[34] Under such conditions, as Eugène Buret remarked naïvely in his survey, 'description alone is not enough, there must be judgement'.

Then there was the contribution of those who were nostalgic for the *ancien régime*, all the swifter to denounce mechanisation because it was an opportunity to rehabilitate earlier political powers. Count Chamborant was one for whom industry 'puts an end to the

33. Extract from the journal *Le Peuple Souverain*, quoted by Mazoyer (1938). The author adds that there were at that time approximately 40,000 notary's clerks for 9,871 lawyer's offices. Even those who found a place had to chase after clients, agree to all sorts of reduced fees, and dabble in intrigue. A barrister with three years of expensive study and five years' apprenticeship could hardly hope to set up his business before the age of 27. 'In order to become known, he had to offer his services free. . . . If unsuccessful he would doubtless try, like so many others, to make his way in writing, in journalism, or in politics, risking more painful disappointments.' In the author's opinion the Republican party owed its dynamism under the July Monarchy to this youthful vigour demanding both universal suffrage and competitive entry to the professions.

34. Thiesse (1980).

suzerainty of the sword, which was not without its moments of glory, in favour of the serfdom *of the machine* [his emphasis] which demands no fewer human victims'.[35]

The gloomy picture of the proletariat sketched by the disciples of social catholicism was another consequence of their political strategy. In 1848 their leader, the Comte de Melun, one of the instigators of the 1841 law limiting children's employment, admitted openly that his activities on behalf of the working classes resulted from his wish to 'take over socialism'.

Apart from the strictly political context of the structure of these studies it is important to remember the continued existence of a certain literary tradition which sprang up in the eighteenth century and which tended to see the common people in what Daniel Roche describes as 'the opposition between the healthy and the unhealthy'.[36] Similarly there should be an investigation of precisely what this social literature owes to the romantic movement, to what Balzac referred to as 'that school of disenchantment'; he was referring to material published in 1830 which combined a pessimistic view of reality with a mystique of the 'proletariat' identified as 'the suffering Christ' – who became 'the son of the workman of Nazareth'.

Other working-class figures

The uses to which Villermé's survey has been put for a century and a half illustrate the power of the 'proletarian myth' down the ages, and its effect as an obstacle to scientific understanding of the nineteenth-century working world. Only the most extreme and the most depressing descriptions have been retained from this minutely detailed study, to illustrate 'the tragedy of working-class circumstances'. This image of the proletariat, via the hazards of quotations requoted, has become the incontrovertible proof which is offered in all textbooks.

A straightforward careful reading of Villermé's work is sufficient, however, to reconstruct the working-class world of the mid-nineteenth century in all its complex detail, and simultaneously to underline the unique nature of French industrial development.

35. Quoted by Hatzfeld (1971), p. 11.
36. Roche (1981), p. 52.

The first requirement, as shown in recent studies of 'proto-industrialisation',[37] is to distinguish carefully between industrialisation and urbanisation. French economic development in the nineteenth century actually favoured the dispersal of industrial work into rural areas, thus reinforcing production methods and a type of working class first seen under the *ancien régime*. Statistics on workers belonging to the 'factory' of a given town refer to an institution consisting of two elements, one including all the establishments within the town and the other covering all the workplaces scattered across the surrounding countryside. The Reims area, one of the principal centres of major nineteenth-century textile manufacturing, may be taken as an example. The 'works' gathered in an apparently impressive number of workers: 50,000 in 1850. But only a quarter of that number worked within the city; the remainder were scattered throughout the surrounding rural communities. The strength of the textile business in Mulhouse involved not only the spinning and fabric-printing, which in mid-nineteenth-century France were generally urban occupations, but also the 85 per cent of the weaving which took place in rural Alsace and the Vosges. Similarly the Roubaix 'factory' covered several hundred kilometres, providing work for thousands of worker-peasants living in villages as far away as Normandy and Picardy. In Calvados, another important textile *département* of the period, 90 per cent of the spinning work-force were country dwellers. The factory at Cholet employed 50,000 workers, but they were spread out through 120 communities and the town had only two important spinning-mills within its walls at the beginning of the Second Empire. Even the Lyon silk industry, generally associated with the *canuts* (Lyon silk workers) of the Croix-Rousse quarter, employed more than 300,000 people in the 1860s living in an area of 150–200 kilometres radius around Lyon. The proof that this was not simply a relic of the past lies in the fact that while in 1830 rural work occupied fewer than 25 per cent of the total silk industry work-force, in 1848 the figure was more than 50 per cent.[38] Although this

37. For the various definitions and a discussion of this expression, see up-to-date comment in 'Industrialisation et désindustrialisation' (1984), which devotes some space to proto-industrialisation; also 'Aux Origines de la Révolution . . .' (1979).

38. See Fohlen (1956), p. 162 *et seq*; Lequin (1974), vol. 1, p. 29 *et seq*; and 'La France sous le Premier Empire' (1970). Marx himself stresses the importance of this phenomenon in France, contrasting it with the British experience. See in particular Marx (1971).

phenomenon is particularly noticeable in the textile industry, heavy metal-work – like mining – depended on a work-force largely made up of rural workers. One example is steel manufacturing, where the typical *ancien régime* distinction between 'internal' and 'external' workers was still a fundamental element, although it tended to die out in the largest establishments during the course of the century. Craft workers living close at hand, often in what were known as 'barracks', constituted the permanent sector of the work-force, even though they represented only a small fraction of the work-force when compared with the worker-peasants of the surrounding villages; these were generally employed on a temporary basis in transport, extraction of surface iron ore, and the various handling operations necessary to such 'heavy' industry. Even in Burgundy, home of the 'large factory' of Le Creusot, as Pierre Léveque has noted, 'heavy industry remained rural or semi-rural' until the middle of the nineteenth century, and the most obvious signs of industrial concentration are to be found in the traditional artisan sectors of towns such as Dijon.

The reasons for the survival, and even the expansion, of rural industrialisation will be covered in the next chapter. It is sufficient to note here that, as E. P. Thompson has shown with reference to Great Britain, the concentration of industry following increased mechanisation of work is far from being a linear process. It is undoubtedly true that Arkwright's spinning jenny destroyed rural home spinning; yet in the short term this invention also provoked a very great increase in the number of home weavers, transforming the vast quantity of spun fabrics which suddenly appeared on the market as a result of the improved productivity of spinning mills. Herein lay the origins of a unique category of workers which in France retained its vitality until the end of the nineteenth century.

The same analysis could be applied to improved methods of transport. Although in the end they brought ruin to small independent country manufacturers, in the short term they also frequently assisted the spread of industrial activity into village areas. In the Montbéliard area near the Swiss border, for example, the development plan chosen by the Japy family for their clock business was to take work to the workers until the 1860s and not the other way round; the improvement in methods of communication and the greater accent on the division of work combined to favour the expansion of manufacturing into the local villages. Within this 'proto-industrial' pattern, urban and rural activities were closely complementary. The town concentrated on bringing together all management and sales activity; that was where the 'bosses' lived, meaning the dealer-manufacturers who distributed primary materials and collected the finished product. In Montbéliard and Beaucourt the worker-peasants put together their completed items in lots of 12,[39] while in other areas the manager sent an employee round the villages to collect the merchandise. As well as providing the site of the large mechanised undertakings which drew in concentrated masses of unskilled workers, the urban centres were also the focus of 'finishing' or embellishing work: assembling clock mechanisms, printing fabric, making up the finest silks. For this reason the great industrial cities gathered in the major proportion of skilled workers.

Alongside the expansion of industrial work into rural areas, the persistence of small urban industry of the 'craft' type is the other distinguishing feature of French nineteenth-century economic development. Establishments that were part of inner-city factories were by no means all to be defined as 'manufacturing'. Of 234 manufacturers in Reims at the end of the First Empire 200 owned only one loom. Yves Lequin considers that the manufacturing structure of the Lyon silk trade remained unaltered between 1830 and 1870. The hierarchy developed under the *ancien régime* maintained its supremacy with a small ruling group of dealer-manufacturers at its head, doing business with several thousands of 'workshop proprietors', owners of several looms, usually employing a small number of workers but themselves dependent on the merchant and taking a direct part in the manufacturing process. The base of the pyramid consisted of hundreds of thousands of craft workers, wage-earners, but also sometimes owners of a loom hoping to become proprietors in their turn. In spite of the many blows they suffered through the concentration of capital and technical development, the number of urban looms in Paris under the Second Empire was maintained by adapting to the new realities of the world of work.[40] Although mechanisation meant downgrading

39. Maillard (1953), pp. 128–9.

40. In J. Gaillard's opinion, Paris manufacturing managed to adapt to its own purposes the industrial innovations resulting from the spread of steam-powered machinery: 'Its success is evidence of the adaptability of a means of production which is well able to be of use outside major establishments, responding to urban circumstances as well as to the ingenuity of Paris workshops.' Gaillard (1977), p. 461.

those sectors of the textile industry that it affected, it brought tremendous expansion for a new category of skilled workers through the great increase in metal-working crafts. In Lille the construction of mechanical looms was one of the underlying reasons for the new 'workers' aristocracy', consisting of 8,000 iron-workers, moulders, smiths, and mechanics, who were the highest earners among the local workers; and Denis Poulot's description of the 'sublime' workmen in the Paris metal industry makes it clear that they were of quite a different race from the average man-in-the-street.

In rural areas the progressive division of labour explains the proliferation of an entire artisan world in small towns and villages, craftsmen who specialised in work previously done by the peasants themselves. Historical research shows that in Calvados, as in Burgundy, this artisan sector was extremely diverse. A single village might have as neighbours a weaver working for a dealer-manufacturer, an independent craftsman selling his own work in the nearest market, and a craftsman working 'to commission', weaving, bleaching, or forging metal, to the specifications of local 'consumers'. It is hardly surprising that, as Pierre Léveque notes, in the general opinion of nineteenth-century citizens the typical worker was still the same artisan or journeyman as in the days of the *ancien régime*.

Similarly, the blanket phrase 'urban proletariat' hides a very great diversity of circumstances. In his Mulhouse survey Villermé distinguished very clearly between locally born workers, generally weavers working at home (who were often landowners) or part of the élite work-force engaged in fabric printing (engravers, printers, draughtsmen) or the metal industry, and the true proletariat. It was from the latter that the mechanised spinning mills drew their work-force, although the latter consisted principally of destitute immigrant families from Switzerland or Germany; their ragged clothing contrasted sharply with the local working-class citizens displaying the finery of their Sunday clothes.

The fact that such testing conditions of daily life were generally shared by all sectors of the working class adds to the difficulties of the historian seeking to identify the proletariat within it. Where work was concerned, for example, Villermé demonstrates that those working at home were better off than those employed in the great factories. 'It should not be thought', he says specifically, 'that these distressing examples are taken only from factory workers. . . . The trades of masons, shoemakers or tailors are no healthier than work in making woollen goods, or above all cotton goods.' Weavers working at home suffered from the repetitive nature of the work, an aspect recognised since days of antiquity, such as the Nîmes taffeta weaver throwing his shuttle, weighing between 24 and 28 kilos, 23 times a minute.[41]

It is also relevant to the wearisome nature of factory work that it was at this time that measures were first introduced with the aim of limiting its drawbacks. Villermé cites the example of the workshops that posed the greatest health hazard, such as those where cotton was worked; employers frequently arranged for staff to work in rotation, so that no individual suffered excessive exposure. Similarly he describes mechanisms fitted to the looms making it possible to bring the machinery to a halt. For this reason, he asserts, 'there are frequent rest periods in all our factories, even for the spinners and piecers, whose work is considered the lightest'. It is also important not to exaggerate the confined nature of factory work compared with the freedom of the small workshop. Norbert Truquin, experienced in both types of work, emphasises that:

> despite all drawbacks, conditions for factory workers were much more bearable than those experienced by out-workers. Nothing is more brutalising than work in a constricted area, even if it appears freer. The worker who labours at home breathes in all day long the unhealthy vapours of coal and the foul-smelling oil used for heating, so that the whole family is half stifled in its own few square metres. In the factories, on the other hand, the workshops are heated, adequately ventilated, and well lit; all is order and cleanliness; the worker there is surrounded by his companions. Foremen then were less demanding, regarding both quantity and quality. . . . In the absence of the foreman the workers would tell stories or narrate theatrical performances; jokers would improvise a pulpit and pretend to preach; time passed happily.[42]

41. Quoted by Cosson (1978); concerning the workers in Mulhouse, and also artisan working conditions, see Villermé (1840), vol. 1 pp. 21–52. It is worth noting in passing that when J. Kuczynski included weavers living in the famous Lille cellars, exposed and criticised by Villermé, Hugo, and many others since, with the proletariat of heavy industry, he misunderstood the circumstances. The weavers constituted a true 'trade aristocracy', descended from ancient working-class families in Lille. They clung to their 'unhealthy' dwellings because they were well suited to the traditionally social nature of working-class districts, complete with ventilator shafts up to the streets above, and provided the humid atmosphere necessary for textile working. See Kuczysnki (1969), p. 95.

42. Truquin (1977) p. 51.

Regarding the conditions of daily life, Villermé's work also indicates that what was considered the specific concern of major undertakings was in fact a general problem for urban working classes. Crowding, straw mattresses crawling with vermin, cesspits – all this was already familiar in Sébastien Mercier's eighteenth-century Paris.

Although the great nineteenth-century surveys consistently ignore the rural world, it is important, in the light of recent work, to emphasise that conditions of hygiene and mortality were no better there than in the towns. In the *département* of the Nièvre, for example, one conscript in every four or five was declared unfit for service, due to 'small stature', 'weak constitution', 'infirmity', etc. One report of 1849 on a village in the area indicates that its houses were 'small, damp, badly ventilated. . . . Beds, furniture and families are piled up in the same room'. The dung heap by the door, the polluted air, growing immorality – all were cited to emphasise the point that 'country dwellers are not tall, nor is their constitution robust. Townsfolk are usually taller.'[43]

Likewise, before we lament the 'destitution' of the proletariat, each case should be studied with great care to establish the exact nature of working-class resources. Recent regional history theses indicate the great disparity of circumstances from one individual to another. Cash payments were frequently only one element of a wage; rural workers were still frequently paid wholly or partially in grain, or were provided with board and lodging. Similarly, most out-workers owned one or more looms, while factory workers frequently owned a small plot of land. As will be shown in a later chapter, factory proprietors encouraged this type of ownership, which meant that workers became more rooted.

These factors indicate the difficulties involved in using material circumstances to establish a clear division between the 'proletariat' and other sectors of the working class; further, members of the proletariat were generally regarded as being 'trapped in their own circumstances', without hope of escaping within several generations. This leads to what François Simiand called the 'enduring nature' of the working–class condition.[44] As will be shown in greater detail in the next chapter, however, it appears that until the

43. Thuillier (1966), p. 69 *et seq.*
44. See Simiand (1932), vol. 1, p. 180 *et seq.* It is known that genuine, as opposed to theoretical, class mobility was one of Schumpeter's favourite arguments against Marxists: see Schumpeter (1984).

end of the Second Empire most of the proletarian workers described in surveys were pictured as being caught at a passing
moment of their lives rather than in a permanent set of circumstances; for the characteristic element of the working class at this
time was its versatility in response to the vagaries of life. In such
circumstances, manufacturing work (at least in its less skilled
applications) was often no more than supplementary for the peasant
during the slack season, for a woman before marriage, for young
men waiting for their military service. Workers' mobility added to
this versatility; in fact a fair proportion of the work-force employed
in large establishments was supplied by temporary or seasonal
migration, and the importance of foreign workers in factories must
be seen in the light of these migratory cycles. It has been estimated
that, in 1847, 250,000 out of 340,000 immigrant workers in France
were present on a temporary basis.

The vocabulary used by contemporary writers gives further
proof of the difficulty of determining the pattern of the nineteenth-
century world of work. When, in his book on trade guilds, Agricol
Perdiguier mentions 'the working class', he is referring only to the
world of craftsmen. It is the same image as that indicated by urban
writer-workers when they refer to the 'proletariat ' in their newspapers or their songs, while on the other hand their political
adversaries focus on factory workers, particularly in their surveys
of the 1840s. Right up to the end of the century the monographs by
Le Play and others, published in the review *Ouvriers des Deux
Mondes*, reflect a very broad concept of the working class, dealing
under a single heading with the artisan worker, the worker in
large-scale establishments, the peasant, the teacher, and even the
republican guardsman.[45]

The social complexity of the working world thus remains an
unresolved problem for historical research, although it is generally
accepted that until the end of the Second Empire the working class
was polarised into town or countryside and that, even if not so
widely separated as sometimes claimed, it varied considerably in
style and collective values. Even apart from the differing political
attitudes to be considered in the next chapter, the divergence
between workers in small-scale urban industry and those in heavy
industry in rural areas can be demonstrated through their patterns
of food consumption and their literacy rates.

45. See Perdiguier (1982); and Le Play (1877–9; 1856–1913).

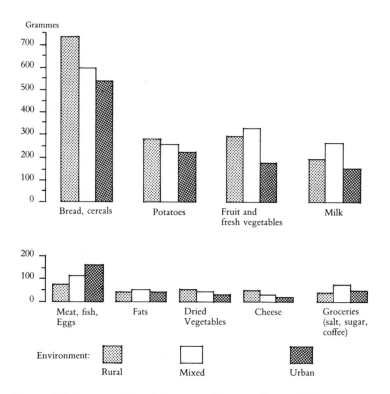

Figure 1.3 Patterns of Food Consumption according to Living Environment, per Adult per Day, in the Second Half of the Nineteenth Century

This diagram, based on Le Play's monographs on the working classes, shows that after the middle of the nineteenth century, patterns of food consumption were more varied in towns than in the country. Bread became less important, while meat and groceries were significant. Meanwhile, rural workers' food intake was very similar to that of the peasants.
Source: Noiriel 1985; and Dauphin and Pizerat 1975

From 1850 on, 80 per cent of the men in Lyon could read and write, as could half the skilled workers in Saint-Étienne, although only 10 per cent of the miners in the area were literate, and 67 per cent of the mining population in Nord-Pas-de-Calais were still illiterate in 1874. As this indicates, workers in heavy industry benefited the most from Jules Ferry's educational laws aimed at achieving universal literacy. Knowledge of arithmetic and writing was virtually essential for skilled workers such as silk-weavers, employed in small workshops or often self-employed. Rural workers, however, shared the peasant's distrust of city novelties which often appeared unnecessary and which might distract their children from the labour required for the satisfactory balancing of the domestic budget. In many areas industrialisation complicated the situation; as François Furet and Jacques Ozouf note, 'after the eighteenth century the districts that suffered a substantial and abrupt urban industrial expansion were those where literacy receded in subsequent decades'.[46]

46. See Furet and Ozouf (1977), vol. 1, p. 257 *et seq.*

2

The 'Enormous Paradox'

In his work on the industrial revolution in Europe Erik Hobsbawm suggests that France's slow capital development was the result of an 'enormous paradox'. France's political and legal transformation during both the 1789 Revolution and the Empire, and the widespread advances in scientific research and political economy, would seem designed to prepare the nation for capitalist expansion comparable with that seen in Great Britain.[1]

Until the 1880s, however, French expansion essentially remained rooted in the older-established sectors. Agriculture continued to be the vital element in the economic equilibrium; until the end of the Second Empire industry remained dependent on the craft sectors which had created its reputation under the *ancien régime*. Industry in France expanded along two different lines: a small, concentrated and dynamic sector which included mines, railways and heavy-metal industry, overshadowed by traditional occupations based on work in the home and the dispersion of industry in rural areas.

Several arguments have been offered in explanation of this paradox. On the one hand the revolutionary upheavals brought ruin and an abrupt halt to the expansion which first developed at the end of the eighteenth century; on the other, the two handicaps that restrained the development of major industry after the end of the *ancien régime* were the existence of a substantial body of small landowning peasants resisting the growth of an urban market large enough to stimulate demand for manufactured products, and the

1. Hobsbawm (1962), p. 177.

persistent influence of powerful trade guilds directing production towards craftsmen engaged in luxury export-orientated trades.

This chapter attempts to show that the paradox reflects the existence of a balance of forces between the chief social groups within French society, illustrating the working classes' powers of resistance when faced with upheavals in heavy industry.

While Chapter 1 was based on a specifically French tradition of historiography, this section concentrates more on a style of research developed in the Anglo-Saxon world. According to P. Thompson, doyen of this 'new social history', the working class should in effect be assessed in the light of prevailing social circumstances. In addition to economic criteria, a definition of the working class requires recognition of the collective values accepted within the class itself, including all the conflicts which resulted in its existence as an identifiable unit; hence the stress here on historical anthropology, an area still little explored in France.[2]

I. Causes for Workers' Attachment to Traditional Forms of Employment

The need for flexibility of employment

It is reasonable to suppose that between the Restoration and the Second Empire workers' wages increased in line with the national average,[3] yet during the whole of this period the working classes remained subject to the constraints of a subsistence economy. The primary concern of daily life was still the struggle against insecurity and unpredictable income; there was no legal guarantee of 'minimum income', so that workers and peasants were unremittingly subjected to fluctuations in economic or climatic circumstances. In the cities, for example, the fact that many looms were devoted to the manufacture of luxury goods for export meant that the volume of work available depended on the whims of a prosperous clientele with tastes as changeable as fashion itself. Similarly, events that were apparently far removed from the life of the French worker, such as the American Civil War, had serious consequences because of the resulting loss of jobs, and seasonal unemployment was

2. See Thompson (1975).
3. On the question of wages, compare the discussion in *Le Mouvement Social* between Lhomme (1968) and Rougerie (1968).

therefore a constant factor even in the absence of major crises. In mid-nineteenth-century Paris, for example, the slack season for tailors lasted from 15 June to 15 September, and again from 15 February to 1 April; and it has been estimated that at the same period silk taffeta workers in Nîmes worked for between 70 and 100 days in a normal year.[4] Outside the towns rural industry was still very dependent on the vagaries of climate: work in any iron-works, mines, or textile-manufacturing establishments that used water as their driving force might be reduced or even brought to a complete standstill by frost in winter or drought in summer.

Unemployment was only one source of insecurity. For most members of the working class there was no form of sickness benefit, no family allowance, no retirement pension. The work-man's value in the labour market was directly related to his physical strength, and 'old age' came early; the puddler in the ironworks, for example, had to think of changing to another form of work when he reached the age of 40, and from the age of 45 tailors and weavers, people who worked with their needle, would suffer from failing eyesight and need to look to other ways of earning their living.[5]

Since the inviolable principle of liberal political economy holds that wages reward the 'value of the work', the bachelor generally lived very much better than the married man. Many surveys have confirmed that the most difficult time for the latter was the earliest period of his married life, with young children preventing his wife from working: one wage alone was inadequate to support the whole family and contributions from all members of the family unit were therefore a vital necessity.

An appreciation of the full range of material constraints affecting daily working-class life brings understanding of the systematic logic of its attitudes and the reasons for its attachment to traditional forms of production. The advantage of 'proto-industrialisation'[6] in the workers' eyes was that it encouraged versatility of employment while still sustaining independent skills. The close observation of daily working-class life required to illustrate this is provided in the minutely detailed monographs prepared by Le Play's colleagues,

4. Cosson (1985).

5. Le Play (1856–1913), monographs no. 7, 'Tisseur en châles de Paris', 1857, and no. 13, 'Tailleur d'habits de Paris', 1856.

6. The expression is used here in its broadest sense, without any implications as to the various definitions suggested.

truly mines of information regarding nineteenth-century working life.

They provide the following description of a shawl-weaving family. The proprietor of the workshop is one of 172 weavers working their own looms in Paris. The son of a Nantes master-carpenter who suffered a reverse in his fortunes and worked as a carpenter's mate in Paris, he was reluctant to follow his father's trade because his physical constitution was not strong. He went to school until he was 15, was then apprenticed to a shawl weaver, and after several years of employment managed to set up in business on his own account. At the time of the survey he was the owner of four Jacquard looms, with a total value of some 4,000 francs.[7]

The most striking feature of this description is the importance of family solidarity. Although in this case the son did not pursue the same trade as his father, the importance of professional self per-petuation must be emphasised; two of the head of the family's three sisters married carpenters, and the third married a shawl weaver. He himself married the daughter of a shawl-weaving workshop proprietor, and his wife's two sisters were married to weavers. The survey also indicates that the workman received financial help from his father to enable him to set up his own business. This indepen-dence, however, did not reduce the evils of unemployment, for on average shawl makers worked only between 180 and 200 days per year. In times of hardship the couple were materially helped by the father-in-law; but the most important factor was that because he and his two sons were all shawl makers, the head of the family observed in the monograph could be sure of approximately six weeks' work every year within the family circle, during his time of unemployment. On these occasions he worked simply as a fellow workman. The importance of kinship is also apparent in the choice of godparents, who were chosen 'according to ancient custom', as the survey observes, from among close relatives. Here again necessity governed the choice. The head of the family, father of four children between four and ten years of age, was able at a difficult moment to hand over his eldest son to his mother-in-law (the child's maternal grandmother) who was also the boy's god-mother. She brought him up from the age of four, to the extent that the child was no longer considered his parent's responsibility.

---

7. Le Play (1856–1913), monograph no. 7, 'Tisseur en châles de Paris', 1857.

The complementary nature of husband and wife's work should also be emphasised. Among self-employed workers it was generally the wife who was responsible for managing the business side and this was one of the reasons for the early marriages of the Lyon silk workers – it was impossible for the proprietor to exercise all the workshop responsibilities as well as working his own loom, and in Belleville a wife's inability to manage the books or her refusal to continue doing so (in cases of divorce, for example) was one of the commonest causes of failure among self-employed workmen.[8] In the case observed the wife's illiteracy was a severe handicap, for the husband was compelled to waste precious working hours on managing the business himself; a further drawback affected their domestic arrangements, for the weaver's wife is described as 'unskilled at needlework'. This meant bringing in a skilled woman once a week, and the expenditure of one franc, to make or repair their clothing. This in no way prevented the weaver's wife from making a substantial contribution to the small family business; for she learnt how to work the loom herself so that it could be kept working when her husband was away from it. In addition the family chose to live in a house at Gentilly and not – like the majority of Paris shawl weavers – in the Faubourg Saint-Marcel; this enabled her to cultivate a large garden and sell most of the produce in the market.

Notwithstanding such energetic devotion to the support of his family, this particular workshop proprietor was no more successful than any other at avoiding poverty in times of crisis. Though by no means destitute – for apart from his looms he owned a superior quality signboard and some books, including a copy of Gaudeau's *Histoire Générale de Tous les Peuples*, paid for in instalments – he was not immune from unfavourable conditions, and in 1848 his family only survived through public assistance and private charity.

8. Jacquemet (1984), p. 311. The high incidence of cohabitation in the nineteenth-century working class should also be seen as a way of dealing with the demands of daily life. As A. Cottereau notes in his introduction to D. Poulot's book, each facet of marriage represents a response to circumstances. The Lyon silk-workers tended to marry young because the wife's work replaced that of a paid assistant, but among machinery workers in Paris there were frequently two separate stages: a long period when a settled household was not considered or was impossible, then a stable union with or without marriage, to bring up children and make the best use of declining strength. 'A universal constraint controlled these stages: the fluctuation of earnings according to age and the degree of physical capacity for work', see Poulot (1981), p. 37 *et seq.*

The head of the household in this case might work as a basic assistant for part of the year, but always worked at the same trade; it was his wife who was required to undertake a variety of work. Frequently, however, and particularly in the case of an unskilled worker, survival depended on being able to undertake several trades in succession through the year. Another monograph describes a shoemaker in the Malakoff area of Paris who turned to market gardening during his periods of unemployment, and another shoemaker who was also a teacher; in the words of an inspector appointed by Guizot, 'concerning this double existence, it would be a clever man who could say which was his true occupation, and exactly what was his principal "condition"'.[9]

A further monograph by Augustin Cochin on the working life of an embroideress in the Vosges reveals that in rural industrial life too the struggle against insecurity required concerted family action and flexibility. This case concerns the world of small business proprietors, illustrating the very marked division between the types of work undertaken by the two sexes in labouring families. The women – mother and daughters – were responsible for agricultural work including a field, a garden, a cow and a pig, supplemented by a share in the village supply of winter firewood. This very modest contribution could not on its own sustain the family, who would be forced to move elsewhere; hence the value of complementary resources. For the mother and her daughters the income from their needlecraft, distributed through the local villages by trader-manufacturers, was a boon, for this was an occupation which did not interfere with farm work. The men's contribution came from their outdoor work: the father was employed as a day-labourer in a quarry owned by a relative, and the eldest son was a wire-drawer in a neighbouring business.[10] Cochin stresses that the complementary nature of their agricultural and industrial labour gradually enabled this particular family to pay off the debts due from the purchase of its small agricultural holding, and thus escape from poverty.

This demonstrates how industrial work diffused through the countryside was of great value for peasants anxious not to uproot themselves. That such work was often compatible with domestic life, and that it could be adjusted to individual capacity, explains the exceptionally high birthrate which many historians have noted in

9. Furet and Ozouf (1977), vol. 1, p. 128.
10. Le Play (1856–1913), monograph no. 20, 'Brodeuse des Vosges', 1859.

rural industrial areas; indeed, Charles Pouthas considers this complementarity of agricultural and industrial work to be one of the
main causes of the great increase in the French population up to the
middle of the nineteenth century.[11]

Much official documentation proves that such dual activity could
provide relatively effective protection against periods of crisis. In
1848, when the hosiery industry in the Aube placed it among
France's leading textile *départements*, its *préfet* estimated that 34,000
workers out of 40,000 were able 'during the terrible crisis . . . to
turn to resources which were not available in the towns. Out of
14,000 working people in the Troyes district only 6,000 received
assistance, of whom 1,500 were heads of families'.[12] The same
concern for security explains why in the Tarn, as Rolande Trempé
notes, 'the Carmaux worker preferred to earn less as a miner and
continue labouring in the field "his own or another's" which
supplied an appreciable proportion of his sustenance, and provided
some insurance against hunger in times of crisis, such as strikes,
unemployment, scarcity, or high prices, which were all too
familiar'.[13] This same logic lay behind the attitude of peasants who
demanded factories close at hand, to provide work during the
agricultural slack season. It was still true under the Second Empire,
in the Nord, that 'people everywhere demanded spinning factories
to provide the labourer with work in times of rain or snow'.[14]

Exact statistics on this attitude are lacking, but it seems probable
that until the beginning of the Third Republic the working classes
looked on industrial work primarily as one variety of rural
employment.[15]

This raises once more the whole question of the 'permanence' of
workers' employment, which was touched on in the previous
chapter. All sources bear witness to the importance of 'part-time'
employment in nineteenth-century French industry; Villermé observes that of 50,000 workers employed in the *fabrique* in Reims,
many worked there for no more than two-thirds of the year. In the
south-east, silk spinning was seasonal and the businesses, which
might employ more than 500 people, mostly women, were open
for only three or four months of the year, drawing on the local

11. Pouthas (1956), p. 207.
12. Riccomard (1934), pp. 53–4.
13. Trempé (1971), vol. 1, p. 224.
14. Fohlen (1856), p. 228.
15. See Y. Lamy's excellent thesis on Périgord iron-works (Lamy 1984).

rural work-force. Similarly, the oil-pressing mills around Aix-en-Provence did not open their doors until the end of the olive harvest. In Georges Duveau's view the workman was no more than an itinerant, and the oil-making season lasted for between 40 or 50 days and six or seven months. It was the same story in the Picardy sugar refineries, where the peasant-worker was engaged only during the winter, or in the Midi madder dye-works which were only active for the seven months following the harvest. Many more examples could be quoted, from the worker-peasant who was not employed outside his industrial work except during the summer harvest, to the peasant-worker who sought workshop employment to improve his daily fare during the dead winter season. Children too would alternate periods in mechanised workshops with a wide variety of other activities; in Calvados they did not on average work in manufacturing for more than 100 days each year.

When multiple employment was not possible at home it could be found through seasonal migration. This varied greatly, depending on region and period, and reflected a whole economic and cultural universe; there were, for example, the expert mole-killers and rat-catchers in the Falaise district of Normandy, who for six months of the year travelled the plains of upper Normandy as far as the Île de France and Picardy to flush out moles and rats. Each had his own clearly recognised territory, which was passed down from father to son or given as a daughter's dowry; and not to be despised, for it was work which might bring in as much as 400 francs in a season. There were therefore some 'working men' who lived reasonably comfortably.[16]

Stonemasons in the *département* of the Creuse offer another example of temporary migration, and here Martin Nalaud's autobiography provides remarkable ethnographic documentation.[17] Thousands of workers left the Massif Central each year, initially for several months and later for several years at a time, to find work in the Paris or Lyon building industry. Their front-line presence in the proletarian struggles of 1848 and 1871 should be seen in the light of longstanding motivation springing from the interests and cultural values of an essentially peasant culture; departure to the capital was frequently inspired by the need to buy out a younger member of the family renouncing his share of the family inheritance in favour

16. Désert (1975), p. 248.
17. Nadaud (1976).

of his elder brother. In other cases it was a question of working temporarily as a stonemason in order to pay off some local debt, or to acquire the little patch of land which would round out an existing holding. The migrant worker always knew that sooner or later he would return to the community of his birth, and its corporate influence maintained strict control over migrant members.

Throughout these examples we can perceive the extraordinary communal pressures applied by the popular classes in their efforts to preserve their traditional way of life. In rural areas these methods were fostered by the great diversity of resources which were the source of the French countryside's vitality at that time. Hemp and linen manufacture, important elements in the comforts of eighteenth-century rural life, were in slight decline, but other employment was already replacing them. As well as cotton manufacturing there was the whole of the silk industry; in the Alps the ruralisation of silk working was a true benison for the peasants. First there was the 'golden tree', the mulberry, which grew at heights of up to 700 metres above sea level and was often a modest source of peasant income; added to this might be the complementary resources derived from weaving as well as silk-thread throwing, or intermittent spinning employment. Elsewhere, other plants with industrial applications resulted in production cycles that were perfectly adapted to rural life; madder, woad, and olives in the south, and sugar-beet in the north and Picardy, resulting in innumerable small sugar-refineries scattered across the countryside and dependent on temporary workers. And then there were the vines: in addition to providing peasants in many areas of France with a direct supplementary income, wine production generated a whole range of related industries such as cooperage, glass-making, and so on. In addition, at least until the railways arrived, each area had its full complement of traditional industries, such as rural metal-working, quarrying, tile-making, and flour-milling. Even large mines and building sites were dependent on the peasant work-force.

In the cities, the adaptability of trained workers perfectly illustrates the 'imaginative ingenuity of the people' described by Daniel Roche with reference to the eighteenth-century Parisian populace. Contrary to what might be expected, the appearance of the steam-engine did not immediately lead to the concentration of production in large establishments. Indeed, according to Jeanne Gaillard, artisan workers effectively resisted competition from big business by a collective use of steam, sometimes in a residential building. They responded to changing circumstances with increased specialisation and the invention of new professions – so that in metal-welding, for example, there were no fewer than 26 different specialised techniques by 1870.[18]

Similarly, from the beginning of the July Monarchy the *Echo de la Fabrique*, the journal for workshop proprietors in the Lyon silk-working industry, provided its readers with advice on how to 'tame' their machines so as to render them suitable for work at home.[19]

Outside the family the worker's social group could be relied on to provide support and protection against the uncertainties of the morrow. Working-class society in traditional districts such as La Croix Rousse in Lyon, or the Faubourg Saint-Antoine in Paris, still appeared solidly united, for new urban planning projects had not yet begun to disturb the familiar surroundings and in most cases work still occupied the same premises as domestic life.

One of the functions of working-class social life is to reinforce bonds between its members. In the Nord most of the Lille workers belonged to a club based in a bar (the strategically essential place for all workers' collective efforts, hence philanthropists' passionate fury against them).

Sickness societies, descended from *ancien régime* brotherhoods, assured their members of mutual aid in times of misfortune. Under saintly patronage such societies – however limited their religious ardour – imposed a certain discipline on their members, with regular subscriptions, a monthly general meeting, and an annual banquet, which strengthened group ties. These popular organisations made no secret of their hostility to the official mutual-aid societies established by the ruling classes in their attempts to increase control over working-class society, whether in the Nord or in a Rhône textile town such as Tarare. There, as Villermé confirms, the workers preferred their own more effective forms of mutual aid. In a crisis 'many would watch in turn through the night by the sickbed and help with care beyond the capacity of members of the family'.[20]

18. Gaillard (1977), p. 438.
19. Quoted by Perrot (1985).
20. Villermé (1980), vol. 1, p. 197; on working-class social life, see Pierrard (1965), pp. 289–312.

Popular social life was also apparent in the very great number of leisure groups, with a wide variety of interests, as indicated in this list of clubs in Lille dating from 1862, noted by Pierre Pierrard:[21]

singing and drinking	63
playing cards	37
beigneau	13
archery	10
crossbows	18
coulonneux	3
boules	23
reading	3
bird-catching	2
fencing	1
	173

There was a very close link between these clubs and the many feast-days dotted across the calendar. Members of drinking clubs would meet regularly to compose carnival songs, to be printed and sold on the appropriate feast-day. Apart from the *mardi gras* carnival, Lille was enlivened by five great festive occasions: the fair, the jumble sale, Saint Anne's day, the community feast (where local important people distributed meat and clothing to the poor), and the *broquelet*, originally the lace-makers' feast but now extended to include all the textile-industry workers. Even though this last began to fall into abeyance – like the majority of traditional festive occasions – at the end of the Second Empire, it was for many years the most popular fête in the Nord; it was celebrated in the spring, on 9 May, and lasted for three days. Philanthropists' contemporary

21. Pierrard (1965), p. 302. *Coulonneux* are pigeon-breeders, and the *beigneau* is an ancient game of skill in the Lille area. The importance of these group activities should not hide the fact that they were often used by the ruling classes to strengthen their control. The distribution of meat and clothing to the poor at the Lille fête enabled important people to demonstrate publicly their goodness towards the ordinary people. Similarly, the popular passion for music is worthy of attention. Music as a means of calming excitement was discovered in the eighteenth century and came to be used during the Second Empire as a political strategy to 'overcome class differences', deliberately encouraged by the *préfets* as a popular pastime. The new repertoire played by the band of the National Guard – polkas, mazurkas, etc. – came to replace the revolutionary songs of the July Monarchy. A 'neutral' genre, seen as 'authentic' and genuinely 'of the people', was thus created to displace the political song; on this point, see Lantz (1983).

descriptions indicate their bafflement at the logic underlying popular behaviour; one commented that workers would begin to save up three months ahead; 'economising not only on what was necessary, but even on what was indispensable, without considering what was superfluous', even going so far as to ask their employers for an advance, so that in one evening they would spend six months' income.[22]

An understanding of traditional working-class conditions is essential for a grasp of the social import of such attitudes; this includes the individual's substantial dependence on the network of relationships which he managed to establish. Someone who was well integrated in local society would often be able to find work again more easily when misfortune struck, as in the case of the shawl weaver quoted above, and mutual-aid societies offer a further example. In a social structure of this type, popular feast-days represented to some extent a test of the individual's importance in relation to his neighbours; this was apparent in the 'unselfish' commitment required from everyone involved in preparing and running the fête, and also in the 'casual' expenditure expected from everyone on such occasions, out of friendship for others – expenditure observed and assessed by the whole community without any need for the philanthropists' accusing finger.

Working-class expenditure is not a simple topic, for it forms part of the unwritten group code. In another context Martin Nadaud explains fully how 'knowing how to contribute' is governed by a whole series of rules which are none the less strict for being unwritten. The worker who does not from time to time make the ritual offer to stand his round of drinks in the bar on the corner is considered tight-fisted, and in a world where a word in the ear speaks volumes, such a reputation spreads rapidly through the community. Conversely, someone who is too ostentatious with his money, without regard to the code, is seen as a spendthrift. He is suspected not only of wanting to stand out from the group, but even of questioning the principle behind their exodus to the city, that money must be saved to send back to the family left behind in the village.

Although, as Paul Bois notes with reference to weavers in the Sarthe, those peasants who became skilled in industrial work eventually came to form a separate group, distinguished as much

22. Le Play (1856–1913), monograph no. 24, 'Lingère de Lille', 1858.

because of their mental attitude as through political choice, workers in the rural world were still most likely to be subject to the code of the rural community. They had to comply with the constraints of the commune, particularly in areas of open field cultivation, even if they owned only a small patch of ground. The agricultural calendar still governed men's hours, with harvest marking the high point of the year. Elsewhere within the framework of a subsistence economy systematic pilfering, which always involved the community, was often necessary to sustain life, either by poaching in the woods or by the theft of basic materials. Within the rural textile industry the importance of 'wastage' has often been noted. This could operate to the benefit of the whole community through the endeavours of a large-scale conspiratorial network. The study of the family of a tool-stripper working in Peugeot establishments in the middle of the nineteenth century indicates that workers living in the village of Valentigney were involved in local organisations. The worker in question was active in a sort of 'mutual-aid' arrangement, described as 'resourcefulness' and set up by the young men in the village in order to evade conscription.[23]

Autonomous skills

Professional autonomy was guarded particularly jealously within traditional industrial forms of production because the majority of proprietors were nearer to being traders than true business managers. The trader's 'craft' was therefore his most precious possession, rendering him less dependent on multiple employment; indeed, the more he exercised his trade the more skilled he became. Such proficient workmen formed two distinct groups: the 'skilled craftsman' in the tradition of the urban artisan, and the specialist within heavy industry (miners, slate-quarry workers, glass workers, blacksmiths, etc.) who were generally close to the rural world.[24]

23. Ibid., monograph no. 15, 'Décapeur d'outils d'Hérimoncourt (Doubs)', 1858. On stonemasons in the Creuse, see Corbin (1975). Examples of village solidarity in illicit trade in primary textile materials appear in Clause (1970).

24. The two groups are also divided by their differing technical qualifications. Specialists employed in heavy industry had above all concrete practical knowledge, while urban artisan workers frequently combined practical ability with a more theoretical understanding of their craft. For all, and particularly for those connected with the construction industry, 'drawing' – design – was of great importance. For many, technical drawing was the most attractive element in the evening classes set

The professional knowledge of these craft workmen could be compared with the skills of the artisan. It depended on 'tricks of the trade', a knack made up of a sequence of diverse memorised operations. At the beginning of the nineteenth century, for example, the skills of the blacksmith lay in a combination of 'coordinated actions and proportions achieved not through figures but through experience. This sort of physical application is learnt without being described in words'.[25] Practical skills of this sort made simultaneous demands on physical strength, endurance, and an intimate knowledge of the matter in hand which could only be acquired by experience. The skilled craft worker's independence can also be seen in the organisation of work in those sectors that he supervised, and each trade usually possessed its own characteristic and rigid internal hierarchy. Slate-quarry work was organised in teams of about 20 men, with a leader acting as spokesman, dealing with the managers, and sharing out profits every six months according to days worked. A long apprenticeship was necessary before it was possible to claim 'skilled' worker status, time spent acquiring the techniques of 'splitting', 'trimming' and 'smoothing off' the slates. According to skill of eye and hand, daily wages might vary from the basic rate to double this amount.[26]

The skilled craftsman's professional identity was emphasised by his highly specialised work clothes, such as the blacksmith's leather apron and broad-brimmed hat, and by rituals such as mnemonic chants or gestures or rites of passage designed to impress the novice with the social importance of his acceptance into the community. This body of symbolism reached its ultimate development in the trade guilds, as shown in Agricol Perdiguier's work;[27] but it was present in all trade associations, with varying degrees of institutionalisation. When the lowly slate-working apprentice was to be taken into a team, for example, he had to undergo the famous initiation ceremony of 'gaitering' in front of all the quarry workers; pieces of felt were tied on to the novice's legs with string, and the payment of 15 francs was required to provide celebratory drinks all round.

---

up in the big cities at the instigation of the École Chrétienne order, or of the Société d'Encouragement pour l'Industrie Nationale, etc., which provided the basis for all trade education available at this time.

25. The quotations referring to iron-works are taken from Woronoff (1984), p. 590 *et seq.*.

26. Turgan (1866), vol. 6, 'Ardoisières d'Angers'.

27. Perdiguier (1982).

Professional independence was seen most clearly in the mastery of teaching the skills of the trade. This body of knowledge could not be spelled out; it was communicated not by schoolmasterly dissertations, but by example, imitation and repetition. As has been shown by the anthropologist Jack Goody concerning cultures without written communication, the modern observer indoctrinated with the expectations of 'written truth' finds it hard to understand how an essentially oral culture can be transmitted.[28] 'The way to acquire such a body of knowledge effectively depends on full-time liaison between a master who knows how and an apprentice who learns how'.[29] This was one of the reasons – in addition to economic necessity, as mentioned above – for children's early introduction to such industrial work. Indeed, given the inefficiency of learning through imitation, long years of apprenticeship were unavoidable; further, the trades concerned were often extremely arduous. According to a forge master in Haute-Marne, 'experience of great heat from childhood onwards and the practice of violent activity while working for the master craftsmen was necessary in order to acquire such demanding and restricted patterns of work, before maturity brought greater strength.' It was for this reason that the apprentice, first as 'furnace assistant' (stoker) or at the forge as a junior lad, had to undergo four years of apprenticeship 'at the fire' before becoming 'junior caster' or assistant, then wait several more years before becoming a fully-fledged metal caster.

The legendary skill of Le Puy lace-makers was also a consequence of this youthful apprenticeship. Instead of a doll, the little peasant girl would be given 'a little square cushion with a pin and three threads hanging from the centre, which she would start plaiting as she played; as she grew she would be given a more complicated frame and soon she would begin to produce work, certainly very simple pieces, but which could be sold'.[30]

There is no doubt that in the domestic setting this familiarisation with the work was highly effective in terms both of technique and of the discipline which it demanded; hence the very strong professional homogeneity characteristic of such industrial categories. At the end of his meticulous investigation into marriage registers in the Lyon area, Yves Lequin concluded that 'almost seven out of ten

28. Goody (1977).
29. Deforges (1981), quoted in Jacoby (1983), p. 75.
30. Turgan (1866), vol. 2, 'Dentelle du Puy'.

workers were born the son of a glass worker, a glass-blower or cutter, . . . and almost half of them will marry the daughter of the man he works with at the furnaces'.

Such professional heredity formed the basis for the control of the labour market which these trades sought to impose on employers. Perdiguier's work provides many illustrations of the effectiveness – at a time when, it must be stressed, the labour market was still highly compartmentalised – of trade-guild practices in imposing 'work-rates' on a recalcitrant employer, controlling hirings from one town to another, or putting a workshop under interdict where necessary for months or even years when the workers' codes were ignored. By means of another method perhaps less spectacular but none the less effective, forge workers at the beginning of the nineteenth century benefited from age-old recruiting methods allowing them to extend their 'network of mutual acquaintance', and were able to 'prevent the creation of a true labor market; the system which took its place, based on inheritance and transfers, guaranteed a continuing hold on places once acquired'.[31]

Power lay in the possession of this professional autonomy – for example, within marriage: although women's position compared to men was one of greater inferiority than today, lace-making gave them a hold over their husbands, for 'within the family and the household it was the women who represented cash in hand; the men's work was almost entirely devoted to agricultural labour which, far from providing ready money, barely covered more than basic household materials'. Indeed, women preferred to pay someone to help their husbands with the summer harvest rather than put aside their own work.[32] Such independence, counterbalanced of course by their dependence on the trader-manufacturer, is also apparent in the fact that 'every Saturday the lace-makers sell their work in the shops', thus escaping the 'domestic imprisonment' familiar to all working-class women, particularly in mountain regions. Such circumstances explain the women's devotion to their

31. See Lequin (1974), vol. 1, p. 226; also Woronoff (1984), p. 590.
32. The women's great pride in their working tools is seen in the charming decorations applied to them, of cardboard or brightly coloured waxed fabric or decorative paper with shiny sequins or flowers. Some were even covered in silk. The lace-maker's 'pillow' was also 'the recipient of confidences and secrets, for the small silk-covered box at the centre would often hold letters and little mementoes from absent friends as well as the wooden strip used for rolling the finished piece of lace' (Le Play 1856–1913).

tools, a reflection perhaps of a specifically feminine work ethic:

> The women of the Velay feel very strongly about their lace pillow: it is the child's toy, the adult's source of income, the older woman's indispensable pastime. As the infirmities of age force her to revert to simple narrow lace patterns, the old woman works for as long as her eyes can see and her fingers can move, and when the bobbins are silent in the house it means that the old woman is dying.

While the mobility of workers was essentially linked to the multiple forms of employment reflected in most seasonal migrations, the mobility of craft-workers responding to scarcity on the labour market remains a constant factor of the period. Glass-makers, for example, were permanently on the move throughout France for additional technical reasons too, such as the need to repair furnaces regularly. This led to a substantial network of professional friendships, enabling news to circulate of work, hirings, or technical developments, reinforcing communal cohesion over long distances compared to the narrow territorial base of weavers working at home. Throughout the nineteenth century employers complained of these 'birds of passage', spreading unrest by their dissipated behaviour which clashed with that of the rural manufacturing population, but whose expertise was often necessary to get businesses going. In the Vosges these nomadic workers were often known derisively as the '28-day men' because of the four weeks' notice which they were required to give before leaving their employment. 'They often had no family ties at all in the area where they lived. Their furniture was reduced to the simplest needs: one or two folding beds, a kitchen stove, a table, a few chairs, their thread spools, a kitchen rack, mattresses, blankets, clothes packed into a trunk, and a few iron tools. They would abandon their jobs for no good reason: a reprimand from the manager or overseer, a sudden whim, a dispute with a neighbour or a domestic quarrel. The decision once made, all possessions would be loaded up onto the two-wheeled cart used every summer Sunday to fetch firewood from the forest, then they would take to the road with wife and children following behind.'[33]

33. Poull (1982), p. 423.

Working-class customs strengthened by the French Revolution

It requires only a reading of Karl Polanyi's work on the 'great capitalist transformation' of the nineteenth century to realise that the working–class world described above was hardly suited to the demands of the industrial revolution. Liberal doctrines meant for him the need to set up a 'self-regulating market' in which land and labour in particular would become pure commodities subject to the law of supply and demand; hence the need to expel millions of peasants from their land and turn them into a rootless proletariat in the great industrial cities. For Marx too, the freeing of peasant muscle-power was the essential precondition for the original accumulation of capital.[34]

In pre-Second Empire France, however, the tendency seems to have been almost the opposite, with a marked increase in working-class attachment to its roots. The image of the French Revolution as a complete break with the *ancien régime*, favouring the emergence of the modern type of working class required by heavy industry, should be disregarded as an explanation for such conditions;[35] in fact the fundamental steps taken during this period constitute genuine concessions to the peasant world.

Arthur Young, accustomed to the English countryside where small landowners were already very rare, travelled in France on the eve of the Revolution in 1789 and was shocked at the great number of peasant holdings which were frequently extremely small. The subsequent sale of national assets further exacerbated the phenomenon. Although in general such lands were bought by the nobility and the *grande bourgeoisie*, the peasantry of both lower and middle rank, and even the rural proletariat of day-labourers, bought some of these holdings. Often minuscule in comparison with the great estates, they none the less frequently offered the bare minimum needed for the poorest folk to sustain the subsistence economy described above, given maximum effort, and so avoid the rural exodus. To this economic obstacle barring the way of capitalism must be added the entire nature of group attitudes. In fact, as Max Weber has shown, the success of an industrial society requires a total transformation of the system of values prevailing in traditional society, and a substantial proportion of its members must develop

---

34. Polanyi (1944); and Marx (1975), book 1.
35. On this point, see Furet (1978).

'profit-seeking' attitudes.[36] As already indicated, the working class-es' preference for working at home and for multiple employment was based not only on the demands of daily life but also on the identification of this way of life as a complete popular culture with very strong ties for all its members. Seen in this light, the sale of national assets further reinforced traditional ways; it operated for several decades as a stimulus in the competition to acquire land, further accentuating the strong dislike of factory work. The re-quirement of the French civil code of laws that all offspring should share equally in any inheritance added further, at least until the Second Empire, to the rural land hunger evoked by Michelet.

Rural industry was thus a blessing, for it supplied the means to buy small portions of land in a world where the rule of self-sufficiency rendered actual money a rarity. Wool was woven in even the smallest hamlets attached to the Troyes hosiery industry; as the *préfet* commented:

> the weaver/agricultural labourer almost always owed his field to the loom, and by cultivating the land he improved his family's standard of living. Rarely left fallow, it was worked by father, mother, son, even the young daughter, and if any of them left, it was to go into agricultural work or other employment which would be of advantage to all.

Everywhere small amounts saved from rural industry were immediately invested in buying land. In 1859 the Caen public prosecutor noted that improvements in the local textiles industry had enabled most of the workers to become landowners, and at the same period landowners in Reims bought national assets in small lots in order to build houses which they then rented to immigrants. Even without savings, peasants with modest paid employment borrowed money to acquire land, their industrial labour serving to repay what Philippe Vigier[37] describes as 'debts of betterment', already noted among the embroideresses in the Vosges and the stonemasons in the Creuse. Such preoccupations with landowner-ship further underlined the extreme frugality of peasant consump-tion; even in times of relative abundance, comfort must yield to saving for land.

36. Notably Weber (1969a).
37. On all of this, see Duveau (1947), p. 407; Duharcourt et al. (1977), p. 68; and Vigier (1975).

In certain respects the same analysis is equally applicable to urban work. Intellectuals as preoccupied with questions of work as the encyclopaedists considered that industry was above all 'a quantitative extension of artisan production'. Advancement demanded practical education above all, based mainly on technical drawing and such thinking lay behind the foundation of the Conservatoire National des Arts et Métiers at the time of the French Revolution.[38] Scientific research was thus not immediately seen as aiding industrial production, and this served for some time to come to maintain the independence of workers' skills.

It has frequently been noted that capitalist expansion was considerably encouraged by the banning of the guilds: the suppression of the multifarious codes restricting production stimulated freedom of enterprise, favouring a concentration of establishments and the accumulation of capital. Although – as will be shown in a later chapter – guild traditions survived in the working-class world despite the legislation aimed at suppressing them, the removal of the *ancien régime* shackles, which weighed down the craft world, added to the social upheavals following the Revolution and Napoleonic wars, and also encouraged individual competition within this sphere for access to ownership of the 'means of production'. It must be remembered that as far back as the eighteenth century many assistants could no longer become master craftsmen, as had been the rule in previous centuries. They were condemned to remain workmen all their lives, while their masters tended to move towards a system of inheritance. The new atmosphere prevailing at the beginning of the nineteenth century seemed to indicate that success in industry was now dependent on nothing more than individual talent, energy invested, or 'luck'. And yet differences in wealth were initially an insurmountable obstacle for the less prosperous in early nineteenth-century France, and success in business was not well thought of. As Louis Bergeron has shown, the prosperous bourgeoisie preferred to invest in the ownership of land made available by the Revolution. Georges Duveau commented on the attitudes of such great figures of the pre-Second Empire industrial world as Cail or Rambourg de Commentry, who 'all the time they were building new factories were full of rural nostalgia'.[39]

There was therefore genuine scope for craft workmen to look

38. From Shinn (1978), pp. 39–71.
39. Duveau (1947), p. 11; Bergeron (1978), p. 36 *et seq.*

forward (though with considerable risk of subsequent disillusionment) to setting up in business one day on their own account. Such
powerful motivation was legitimately based on revolutionary principles of liberty and equality but scarcely conformed to the aims of
modern capitalism.

Studies of the French bourgeoisie indicate that until the middle of
the nineteenth century the world of the employers was still a
relatively open one, and one where there was no lack of examples
of workers' success.[40] The frontiers between employer and worker
do not appear to have become entirely rigid; hence the instability of
the urban craft-workers' world, reflected in contemporary documents. Monographs of the Le Play school, for example, show
many of the workmen in small-scale industry moving to and fro,
from one state to the other, for much of their working lives,
undiscouraged by commercial failure which sometimes involved
them in years of paying off debts. In the workers' eyes the wish to
be one's own master, which underlay the socialist-inspired
cooperative movement, strengthened the importance of family
solidarity, as in the case of the Paris shawl weaver. Elsewhere it is
illustrated by Michelet's own biography: son of a failed printer, he
became a professor at the Collège de France through the sacrifices
of his family.

In these circumstances French employers generally preferred to
build up their own businesses through the network of existing
factors rather than by an abrupt British-style imposition of change.

Two more factors helped to foster this approach. First, the
enduring substantial and largely self-sufficient peasant population
prevented the genuine development of an internal market; hence
the continuing uncertainty and instability of industrial production
and the need to export. In such conditions a labour market consisting mainly of migrant or peasant workers offered the great advantage of being extremely flexible. At the slightest economic reverse
the rural work-force returned to the fields, and it was only necessary for hiring to cease for itinerant workers to disappear. Similarly,
in those industries where seasonal unemployment often lasted
for several months, out-working made it possible to save on
depreciation costs on fixed capital during the slack season. The fact
that many employers were from social backgrounds without great
initial wealth lent added support to the pattern of working at home.

40. Daumard (1963).

This economic reasoning meant that in effect the worker supplied his own work-place and his own tools; further, in rural industry the status of 'landowner' was exploited by the trader-manufacturer to keep wage rates very low, in addition to the political advantages of dispersing work. This pattern helped the employer to evade legislation which, since 1841, restricted children's work in establishments with more than ten employees. But above all, the dispersal of production was the ultimate means of controlling over-assertive workmen. It was no coincidence that silk working was ruthlessly decentralised on a much broader scale across the Lyon countryside after the riots of 1831 and 1834.

In heavy mining and metal-working industries, generally established in rural areas, employers supported the system of independent workers in order to avoid confrontation with the work-force. Methods of managing the labour force will be covered in a later section, but as an example it may be noted that of the 567 workmen (representing 364 families) working for the Peugeot company at Valentigney in the middle of the century, 151 owned land. Frequently the employer himself was no more than the largest local landowner, as in the Périgord metal industry, where most of the ironmasters were part of the rural bourgeoisie. Business management was no more than one element in a much greater ensemble developed from the complementary nature of the various types of work. Work in the iron foundry really began when work in the fields ended, allowing labourers to alternate between the two occupations and providing employment throughout the year.[41]

During this period of 'proto-industrialisation' it was the old methods of controlling the work-force that remained dominant rather than 'factory discipline',[42]; powerful 'external' pressures provided an important element. In considering work at home Marx had already emphasised the system's 'invisible network' connecting worker and employer, without in any way affecting the latter's ultimate domination. The trader-manufacturer often profited from the rural industrial worker's fierce resolve to avoid the rural exo-

41. Lamy (1984), p. 510 *et seq.*

42. Analyses referring to 'disciplinary powers', which had much success in France after 1968, based sometimes inaccurately on the work of Michel Foucault, are in many ways regressive in relation to the Weber concept of 'domination' because they only look at one side of the power relationship. For Max Weber, on the other hand, discipline can only be effective when it affects those who are ready to comply 'by virtue of an acquired tendency': see Weber (1969), p. 56.

dus; weavers worked even longer days than manufacturing workers, for lower wages, and their exploitation increased as competition from the great factories destroyed the 'domestic system'. Although free from their employer's supervising gaze, outworkers endured a closely constrained life. As Augustin Cochin remarked of embroideresses in the Vosges:

> the division of labour gives the trader a greater hold over them: the women do not carry out the work in its entirety. He has a hold on them by making difficulties in accepting work: he can refuse to accept it on the pretext that it is badly done, he can reduce the wage or leave the work with the embroideress and claim back the cost of the fabric. . . . Finally, the trader can victimise his women workers by appointing unscrupulous overseers, women who fraudulently reduce the remuneration or refuse to accept the work.

In factories, as with work carried out in the home, employers profited from those forms of social dominance that existed in traditional society, and particularly in domestic circles; they took advantage of the submissiveness of women and children to force them to accept the least congenial tasks, which were also the worst paid.

At the heart of rural heavy industry, control of the work-force and the employer's authority were reinforced by the 'patronage' system. In a population where a certain degree of comfort depended entirely on industrial work complementing agriculture, he who provided the work was unconditionally regarded as a true benefactor, an attitude encouraged by the employer's prominence – a consequence of his wealth – at the centre of the charity and good works which relieved working-class poverty in times of crisis. The watchmaker Japy, for example, owned a mill; when food was scarce he distributed grain and bread, and found work for the older men. Frequently holding elected posts, like Jules Chagot, mayor of the industrial town of Montceau-les-Mines from 1856 to 1878, such local notables also turned the municipal charity office to their advantage. Even in the great cities public feasts enabled them to display their generosity through the distribution of clothing and meat to the destitute. Religion fostered harmony between employer and employees by encouraging charitable works, and close relationships between the two sides were possible because businesses were still modest in scale.

Somewhat similar to the paternalism in E. P. Thompson's description of the seventeenth-century gentry,[43] employer status had two aspects. Any element relating to the employer's true function, such as exploitation of the work-force, was carefully concealed, while his good works were widely and publicly displayed in a dramatic ritual in which wives played the leading role. The other face of the employer was concerned with extreme severity towards any who dared to show the slightest sign of dissent. External forces required the employer to accept autonomous working methods, but the ultimate boundaries were clearly and publicly expressed. In England the exercise of justice by the gentry allowed them, most obviously through the ritual of public execution, to demonstrate their overwhelming powers in similarly theatrical ways so as to discourage any challenge. In the setting of rural heavy industry this strategy was particularly applied through rigorous discipline made manifest in company regulations, with a whole hierarchy of sanctions ranging from fines to banishment, rendering any organised dissent virtually impossible.

The same principles of external controlling elements can be seen at a national level. The state rarely concerned itself with the people's affairs unless it was required to maintain order. There too, as Michel Foucault has shown, power was demonstrated ,through the public exercise of terror designed to stir the imagination and dissuade anyone from challenging the state.[44] Otherwise, techniques of social management remained very elementary; until the establishment of the railway network in the 1860s the primary preoccupation was always to avoid hunger riots, hence the hoarding of cereals and regulation of bread prices which was the chief concern of the French civil service.

II. The Impossibility of Creating a True 'Working Class' in Heavy Industry

This system of the 'invisible network' continued to sustain domination over the work-force for a small number of employers until the end of the nineteenth century, but the most innovative very quickly realised the contradictions inherent in such a system.

43. Thompson (1974), pp. 382–405.
44. Foucault (1974).

The inadequacy of the rural exodus resulted in a permanent shortage of workers in the most demanding work sectors, particularly coal-mining. As mine shafts sank deeper into the ground and the demands of the French economy increased, so the employers intensified their lamentations; Rolande Trempé, who has made an extremely detailed study of this problem, notes that in Carmaux a good harvest in the 1870s could still bring recruitment to a complete halt. In the Nivernais area the economic prosperity of the late 1850s led to 'disturbing signs of emigration' among the miners of Aubois, while in Le Creusot the mining companies stole workers from each other to such an extent that complaints were brought before the courts. Towards the middle of the century the mine at Blanzy was due to supply between 40,000 and 50,000 hectolitres of coal per month to fill orders, but the shortage of manpower was such that production was only some 30,000 hectolitres.[45] From the 1860s onwards this became the chief problem for managers, as can be seen from the annual Carmaux work reports. An added problem concerned the excessively 'peasant' nature of the work-force, and the managing director of the Carmaux company railed against the 'inveterate habits' of the worker-peasants, 'one of the greatest obstacles to coal extraction'. The miners did not work hard; in Blanzy they needed chivvying and the pit overseer himself did not show great zeal. In many such companies it was recorded that the workers were always tired; which is understandable since the combination of industrial and rural activity often resulted in working days of up to 19 hours. Elsewhere the scale of manpower turnover, which in the Toulon arsenal affected more than a tenth of the daily work-force, made it impossible for engineers to give reliable forecasts of the output to be expected from their establishments. In his discussion of the period leading up to the Second Empire Louis Reybaud notes that the factory was a 'temporary stopping place'; 'there was a *Tour de France*, or urgent harvesting, sometimes a local outbreak of saints' feast-days. Workshops continued to be the victims of the unexpected, alternately overburdened and bare.'[46] Recent research has shown that even in such an old-established textile-working area as Caen, it was rare before 1890 for workers to remain in a factory for more than five years, a

45. Trempé (1971), vol. 1, p. 151 *et seq*; Thuillier (1966), p. 309; and Peyronnard (1981), vol. 1, p. 144.
46. Reybaud (1977), p. 109.

third spending less than 12 months with the same company; this is without taking temporary workers into account.[47]

Quite apart from problems of business management, such circumstances made it impossible for employers to develop a trained work-force in the modern sense of the term. As Arthur Dunham confirms, the French employer paid dearly for planning based on the low wages of a rural work-force; this proved to be a fundamental obstacle, inhibiting apprenticeship to the new specialised crafts in heavy industry such as mining or metal-working. Not until the days of the Second Empire, particularly after the Great Exhibition in London, did the Saint-Simonian philosophical economists such as Michel Chevalier manage to convince a substantial number of employers of the fundamental importance of this problem. He considered that one of the principal reasons for the superiority of British industry was that 'the old steady workers who are the backbone of English manufacturing do not exist in France'.[48]

Voices were increasingly raised in complaint at the ineffectiveness of the traditional economic system. The textile industry, representing more than half the total French industrial work-force, was particularly dependent on peasant resources because of the modest scale of the home market. A series of poor harvests meant that what Michelet called 'this remarkable consumer, the people', was incapable of buying any clothing whatsoever, thus creating unemployment. The chain reaction of supply melted away, and the whole body of the working class was affected.

From 1860 onwards such structural weaknesses were aggravated by free-trade agreements with Great Britain, further exacerbating problems of rural industry and initiating a decline which continued into the following era.

French industry also suffered from inadequate levels of mechanisation which made its products uncompetitive. Until the arrival of the railways these disadvantages were offset by the compartmentalisation of local markets, but from the 1860s onwards this no longer applied.

Complete independence of production was increasingly suggested as one of the causes for what was beginning to be known as the 'archaism' of the French economy. In iron and steel making, for

47. See Hurpin (1975).
48. M. Chevalier quoted by Duveau (1947), p. 134; and Dunham (1953), p. 158; also Stearns (1978).

example, from the end of the eighteenth century 'the animosity of enlightened ironmasters, managers, and other experts, was focused on the workman's abilities. All deplored . . . the fact that he was so stubborn and irrational, and yet at the same time so indispensable.'[49] Such complaints expanded into other sectors of employment, while contemporary surveys began to indicate ways in which out-workers could stand up to the trader-manufacturer. Augustin Cochin has shown that the Vosges lace-makers could take revenge on their employers by passing on the designs from which they worked – often the secret of one particular business. They could lose or reduce the fabric, or undertake several pieces of work at once and delay the delivery. Since this was a trade entirely dependent on fashion, and since by the nineteenth century fashion changed swiftly, any delay could seriously jeopardise the profitability of the goods.

Small firms were particularly at risk from such work-force 'blackmail'. Slipper manufacturers in Fougères and tanneries in Mazamet were equally susceptible to the dangers of work remaining unfinished at the time specified. Since stocks were minimal and cash reserves very limited employers were in no position to be patient for long.

Finally, the hold over the market exercised well into the nineteenth century by metal-foundry workers, glass-makers or members of the close-knit building crafts guild, became less and less acceptable. In Émile Coornaert's view this was the point on which employers and employees increasingly divided into two hostile camps, particularly in the towns, even if in general they remained on reasonably good terms.[50]

All regions of France, however, can offer examples of effective popular resistance to measures designed to accelerate the rural exodus and thus supply heavy industry with the muscle-power it needed. In Burgundy the *sous-préfet* of Autun considered that 'any law ordering the sale of common land for the benefit of the commune would cause a virtual revolution'; similarly with reference to the suppression of common rights: 'I would seriously fear physical attacks on common-land wardens and mayors.' In many places managers simply gave up trying to direct their businesses through pressures on factory workers. In 1838 an industrial

49. Woronoff (1984), p. 558.
50. On Mazamet, see Cazals (1978); Coornaert (n.d.), p. 275 *et seq.*

employer in Alençon asserted that 'any attempt to bring these peasants into a factory would set off a revolution'; and indeed, out of the 45,000 workers he employed at that time, only 3,000 lived in the town.

Similarly, efforts to intensify work came up against the worker-peasant's discontent. For some decades employers in Carmaux tried to modify working hours so that their workers would not go on to their agricultural labour, but partial strikes forced them to drop these proposals. The miners in the Allier responded in the same way to a suggested longer working day which would have kept them away from the land.[51]

The scale of resistance in response to employers' attempts to mechanise work before the middle of the mid-nineteenth century has been shown by Michelle Perrot. Weavers and sheep-shearers feared a downgrading of their skills, a devaluation in the labour market, which must be prevented. Worker-peasants, on the other hand, feared above all that new machinery would make their accustomed work too complicated, and would only serve to increase profits.[52] The system of complementary industrial and rural labour exposed employers to opposition from the united rural working-class community.

An inquiry at Allevard in the Isère, for example, showed that increased ironworks' production was prevented by the opposition of all rural sectors: peasants, foresters, the municipal council. The latter refused to allow the extension of tree felling or the construction of new dams which would make the river overflow, and so on. Very often workmen's strikes – which were numerous though illegal – assumed the aspect of genuine peasant revolts, bringing the village community into conflict with the employer and frequently with the forces of law and order. The longest strike of the whole July Monarchy took place in the Lodéve from February to May 1845. According to the *préfet* the stubbornness of the workers' resistance was due to the fact that once they had left their looms the weavers 'immediately went off to work in the fields'. Similarly, in the great 1846 miners' strike in Anzin in the Nord, 1,200 miners lived out of doors for several weeks, sleeping in the fields and fed by their families.[53]

51. On Burgundy, see Lévêque (1983), vol. 1, p. 154; on Alençon, Dunham (1953), pp. 172–3; on Carmaux, Trempé (1971), vol. 1, pp. 190–210.
52. Perrot (1978).
53. Aguet (1954), pp. 344–5.

This collective ability to resist innovation was also very noticeable in urban industry. Many regions give the impression of a kind of permanent guerrilla warfare between employers and employees; the out-workers in Roubaix, for example, were known for their unreliability, working for several traders at a time so as to extend their independence, given to late delivery of their work, creating considerable problems for their employers. For their part the business managers applied themselves to reducing factory rest-times by forcing their workers, in Lille, to eat in the workshops or, in Paris, by restricting their metal casters from going out more than three times a day, so as to reduce the time spent drinking in the local bars during working hours. In Amiens wages were nibbled down by holding back money for oil used during night shifts. Combined resistance was commonplace; the Paris metal casters quoted above responded to the employers' decision with an immediate all-out strike, and one reluctant striker was subjected to a tremendous and noisy row.[54] Mechanisation and attempts to increase the size of manufacturing businesses were hampered by lack of cooperation on the part of the workers. The Paris shawl weavers, for example, opposed the introduction of Jacquard looms because they were more expensive than the plain looms and more complex to operate, two factors which encouraged businesses to integrate. In the early days of the restoration of the monarchy the richer employers attempted to set up 'factories' by bringing together some dozens of workers who were paid by the piece-rates or by the day. The workers, however, 'lacking the stimulus of self-interest in the establishment, failed to take care of their looms, and maintenance and repair costs became a heavy burden for the manufacturer'; indeed some went bankrupt, and in 1832 there was a revival of small concerns with their advantage of returning machine maintenance to the worker's responsibility.[55]

Attempts to decentralise production from the towns to the countryside met with numerous revolts, as in Nîmes, where taffeta silk workers went on strike in 1834. They gathered at the gates of the city, intending to intercept and destroy goods made by peasants in the surrounding areas, but were prevented from doing so by the police. Similarly, as the American historian Robert J. Bezucha has shown, the Lyon silk workers' riots, which impressed the whole of

54. Ibid., p. 27.
55. Le Play (1856–1913), monograph no. 7, 'Tisseur en châles de Paris', 1857.

Europe, particularly in 1834, were a response to the trader-manufacturers' attempts to destroy the traditional working community through mechanisation and by dispersing work into the country and new town districts, introducing deadly competition for the genuine silk-weavers known as *canuts*.[56]

At the time of really serious crises, as in 1848, these everyday disturbances spilled over into extremely violent explosions of anger demonstrating to the full the combined strength of traditional working-class communities. Taking such activity in the Var region as a typical example, Maurice Agulhon has described the pattern of behaviour in rural industry. The workers in the village of La Garde-Freinet formed a group which included artisans, journeymen and agricultural wage-earners, all closely involved in village life. Consequently, when the cork-cutters increasingly distanced themselves from their employers they were supported by other elements of rural society. In 1848 the cooperative system of production which they founded met with added favour among the peasants because it provided them with the means of supplementing their income, a vital factor in times of crisis. It was for this reason that when in 1851 the authorities decided to close down the cooperative system the whole community united and rose up against the decision. This example from the Var shows clearly that inherited traditions of conflict, an integral aspect of the rural world, were put to good use by worker-peasant groups to demonstrate their resistance. In 1850 at Vidauban the subversive power of the carnival was used against the public authorities: despite the mayor's interdict, a farandole (the popular traditional dance of Provence) was organised and a dummy dressed in white was presented for judgement by a 'tribunal of the people' and then decapitated with an axe. The conservative newspapers called it 'a justification of the Terror through imitation of a revolutionary execution'. Other reports indicate that such practices were not unique to the Var; in 1848, from Saint-Étienne to Rives-de-Gier, the miners in the Loire basin rallied and demonstrated, marching in carnival-type processions with dummies representing their works' managers.[57]

Written forms of protest also give evidence of the world of agrarian revolt. Once again E. P. Thompson has taken the lead, showing that the impossibility of any 'democratic' expression of claims – the

56. Bezucha (1974).
57. Agulhon (1979), pp. 407–17.

consequence of the 'absolute' concept of power – forced anonymity on workers who sought to make demands. Between 1848 and 1850 the Creusot director received many anonymous letters: 'I warn you', ran one such letter in February 1849, 'that if you continue to resist the workers . . . all the company-owned houses will be burnt'. A strike broke out in April 1850, following the announcement of a cut in wages, and an illspelt handwritten notice was fixed to the entrance of the Saint-Éloy mine shaft: 'We the mining citizens of Le Creusot are today in deepest despair, and you see how we are treated. . . . There is only one thing for us to do. Yet all we want is our wages as they used to be, otherwise we will not work unless there is an agreement made by the citizens of the Republican government.' The notice was signed: 'The Miners of Le Creusot. Liberty, Equality, Brotherhood. Kyrie Eleison.'[58] Although lacking in coherence, the document indicated the workers' confidence in the new republican government as well as the continuing influence of religion on this section of the working class.[59]

The greatest threat to local authorities, however, arose from revolts within urban industry. It was indeed one of the most distinctive features of the French social and economic system that the city containing all the essential workings of central power, that other inheritance of Jacobinism, was also the city with the greatest concentration of working-class citizens in the whole of France, hence the vulnerability of the state throughout the nineteenth century. The many studies devoted to the revolutions of that period have emphasised the central importance of the workers during such conflicts. One example, described by Charles Tilly, is the central role played in the 1848 Revolution by stonemasons, carpenters, and mechanics. Furniture making, metal-working and building construction supplied the 'classic insurgent types' of the revolt, with its central objective of guaranteed work and new labour relations which could well be described by the anachronistic term 'contractual'. Similarly, although during the 1871 Commune the social composition of the insurrection reflected more the

---

58. The French text reads: 'Nous citoyens Mineur de Creusot nous sommes aujourd'hui au dernier désespoir et vous voyez comme l'ong nous condui. . . . Nous n'avons qu'une chose à faire. Mais cependant nous ne demandons que notre salaire comme aux premier abord ou sinon nous ne Travaillons pas ou en cas qu'un arrangement fait par des citoyens du gouvernement républicain. . . . Les Mineurs du Creusot. Liberté, Égalité, Fraternité. Quirrier Eleison.'

59. Lévêque (1983), vol. 2, p. 168.

concept of 'the people' than that of the Marxist 'proletariat', Gérard Jacquement stresses that in Belleville, the heart of the revolt, workers made up 84 per cent of the insurgents, mostly skilled men. Elsewhere in France, studies of Limoges and Marseille provide a more precise composite picture of the typical revolutionary. William Sewell and Alain Corbin also affirm that the number of revolutionaries was greatest among the 'open' skilled trades, in other words those most threatened by competition from the employers' mass recruitment of new workers. Correspondingly, there was very much less involvement of trades that could be called 'restricted', where there was some form of closed shop.[60]

Working-class districts had been left very much to themselves since the Revolution, and this factor contributed substantially to the strong collective identity and traditions of struggle among those who had lived there for several generations; nineteenth-century urban revolts can rightly be seen as the continuation of the 1789 Revolution's sansculotte conflicts. The 1831 and 1834 riots in Lyon occurred in the same quarters as the uprising known as the *deux-sous* episode of 1786, and the involvement of the Faubourg Saint-Antoine in Paris from the taking of the Bastille to the 1871 Commune is well known. Collective memory plays an important part in the repetition of the revolutionary process. Bloodthirsty repression of demonstrations made a powerful impression on mass awareness; as in Lyon in 1853, where the public prosecutor considered that the city's workmen saw their employers as relentless enemies partly because they could not forget the uprisings and repressions of 1831, 1834, and 1848.[61]

So in spite of the suppression of trade guilds and the apparently radical measures designed to wipe out even the memory of the *ancien régime*, as William Sewell has shown, craft workers turned to

60. See Sewell (1971), and Tilly and Lees (1974); Rougerie (1965); Corbin (1975); and Jacquemet (1982). In seeking an explanation for such revolutionary events the other chief element of the Paris working-class world of the period must not be forgotten: workers who had arrived recently or temporarily from their place of origin, generally crammed into furnished rooms, quick to act for reasons and in ways more peasant-orientated than 'proletarian'.

61. Quoted in Lequin (1974), vol. 2, pp. 158–9. Despite 'Haussmanisation' districts such as Belleville retained their working-class homogeneity to an impressive degree. Gérard Jacquemet's study of official marriage registers shows a consistently recurring axis of the rue du Temple–Faubourg du Temple–Belleville, for both spouses and their witnesses. In 1865, 53.2 per cent of marriages were between men and women living in the same street (see Jacquemet 1982).

pre-revolutionary collective tradition in their search for ways to take action, gradually adapting practice and terminology to the changed circumstances.[62]

This working-class independence proved fertile ground for nurturing the concept of a distinct class identity, explicitly resisting spokesmen from other social groupings. The news-sheet *L'Atelier* (The Workshop) undoubtedly offers the finest example of this direct expression of working-class speech. Its editorial team, consisting almost entirely of craftsmen from the élite of artisan skills (jewellers, mechanics, and above all typesetters, who made up more than a third of the publication' s manpower), reflected communal interests. The most frequently recurring themes were principles of fellowship, of workers' cooperation, maintaining dignity and honour among ordinary working people, and resistance to any kind of state intervention in production.[63]

The purposefully 'working-class' style generally adopted by craftsmen of this period should not, however, be accepted unquestioningly. Many of them – and here several of those involved in *L'Atelier* were very successful – wished for nothing more than to escape their own origins. The importance of reduced social status as part of the process of working-class revolt may indeed be open to question. The sociological upheavals of the revolutionary period were genuine dramas for numerous families, precipitating individuals from more highly esteemed social milieux into the proletariat. There are several such examples in Le Play's monographs, and no lack of working-class writers who suffered such an experience. Michelet has also shown that a reversal in fortune was felt as a major catastrophe in those families of modest origin who sacrificed some members so that a talented son might rise in social status. 'The aspiring artist' turned workman cursed his fate, conceived a hatred for his workshop and his craft. 'Oh Liberty! Oh Light! Do not abandon me for ever.'[64]

62. Sewell (1980, p. 256 *et seq.*) speaks of the 'flexible idiom of corporatism'.

63. Cuvillier (1914).

64. Michelet (1974), p. 110. No doubt because it deals with a time when 'socioprofessional categories' were not yet clearly defined in either social or personal terms, Michelet's work is an important sociological document on social mobility; he shows how the individual's past continues to affect his present circumstances. In his clarity, no doubt derived from his own unusual background, he proves himself a better historian than many of his successors, demolishing in advance the arguments of all those who claim to see revolutions as nothing but the results of 'a chance combination of circumstances'.

It must also be remembered that the revolutionary process which began in 1789 did not reach its conclusion until the Third Republic. The entire period covered in this chapter is marked by a political instability sustained on the right by nostalgia for the *ancien régime* and on the left by spokesmen from the middle class who were unable to achieve the status to which they aspired. As was shown in the preceding section, the 1840s' passion for the 'proletariat' cannot be understood without reference to the specific problems of contemporary France's various social groupings, each one seeing an alliance with the working class as a means of satisfying its own aspirations. If popular militancy explains the multiplicity of studies of the proletariat, it is also not without relevance to the emergence of a new kind of intellectual drawn to a fine career: the theoretician well-nourished on political economy and social science.[65]

III. The 'Neo-Liberal' Compromise

This section illustrates the problems faced by supporters of wholehearted liberalism in imposing necessary reforms on the nation. It could reasonably be argued that such sociological resistance gave rise to a distinct version of the theory of capital which for at least half a century met with a large measure of agreement in France. The principal lines of French 'neo-liberalism' were elaborated round Adolphe Blanqui and the *Journal des Économistes* from the time of the July Monarchy.[66]

Great Britain was seen as the antithesis of the ideal. The way to avoid the excesses of the 'untamed capitalism' seen on the other side of the Channel would be through complementarity of economic activity. Heavy industry was acceptable provided it did not challenge the central role of traditional small businesses; this was the only way to avoid massive proletarianisation on the British model, and defuse social tensions.

It must be emphasised that the 'neo-liberal solution' did not give heavy industry complete freedom of choice of location. Very much the reverse: it was to be kept away from the cities, forming a sort of island among the fields, in order to avoid any contact between the two main elements of the French working class. Frédéric Le Play

---

65. On this point, see Ansart (1970).
66. This topic is well covered in Gaillard (1981a), pp. 146–50.

undoubtedly offered the best theory of the need for non-urban industrial development: he considered that cities meant uprooted workers who would fall into the hands of youthful intellectuals with ambition and no scruples. In rural areas the worker benefited from the benevolent paternalism of the company manager, while complementary agricultural-labour demands supplied work for women and children, as well as for the head of the family in times of crisis. The Polytechnique graduate Émile Martin, who was director of the Fourchambault ironworks, also consistently pressed the argument in favour of working-class landownership. Apart from considering it the best way of augmenting the family income, he saw in the possession of a piece of land the central element of 'rationalisation of behaviour' by means of which the work-force could be educated. It would, he said, provide an excellent means of approach to moral persuasion for the ordinary unskilled workman to become an agricultural producer on a modest scale. And, above all, landownership appeared to offer the best means of combatting the workers' chronic instability, encouraging them to settle and gradually become skilled workers. These considerations, which were shared by the majority of French employers, explain the steady increase in the number of landowning workers in heavy industry up to the end of the nineteenth century. At the beginning of the Third Republic 200 hectares were sold over a period of 20 years at Fourchambault, and similarly at Pont-à-Mousson, where one observer noted with satisfaction that the blast-furnace workers 'were like the Lorraine agricultural workers who were their fore-bears, very thrifty, regular in their ways, generally owning their modest homes, and very different in character from the workers in the great cities'.[67]

In contrast to the beginning of the century, the notion of land-ownership had become an integral part of an overall strategy designed to enhance managerial control, so avoiding the disadvantages of the independence already discussed; such an overall strategy might be called paternalism. Closer consideration reveals that beyond the debate on land, the theme of ownership turned towards the house with its garden round it, even a small field. In earlier days working-class landownership was generally independent of industrial enterprise; henceforward it was the latter which granted it and therefore controlled it in one way or another. At Le

67. Quoted by Perrot (1974), vol. 1, pp. 212–13.

Creusot, for example, it has been noted that after the strikes of 1848 which developed in the 'barracks', the accommodation blocks, this type of construction was completely abandoned in favour of a policy of 'access to land'. Émile Cheysson, for many years director of Le Creusot and theoretician of paternalism, explained that the worker's better moral condition depended on his house and no longer on his land: 'his house soon possesses him, it improves his moral standards, settles him and transforms him'.[68] But in their wish for ownership many of the workers borrowed money from the company which thus became the focus of the loan system – a means of control to which was added the paternal stranglehold on collectively-owned equipment and methods of communication.

Furthermore, the land granted by the company was usually very near the factory and apart from the village, making it possible to draw workers away from rural influences. Detachment from peasant life at the La Machine mine could also be seen after 1860 in the fact that the housing provided was built of stone and no longer of beaten earth. Higher wages, another form of 'industrial-worker control', turned miners into 'consumers', which attracted various forms of trade (grocery, haberdashery, bakery); there would be a weekly market in the community; habitual patterns of food consumption began to develop. After 1870 workers even had several changes of clothing. 'Parallel with this transformation, which detached the miner from the agricultural worker's way of life, the company took a stronger hold on working-class life', noted Guy Thuillier. The same pattern was appearing at Carmaux. Beginning with housing, the employers' ascendancy could be seen in the system of 'social work' which at the end of the Second Empire developed substantially in large industrial establishments throughout France. In the Lyon area the 1872 inquiry shows that the system was already widespread, particularly in businesses with several hundred wage-earners who chose deliberately, according to Yves Lequin, to settle themselves well away from cities, and in particular well away from Lyon. In 1866 company-controlled 'social housing' was to involve 38 establishments and 65,000 workers. In 1871, 37 per cent of miners in the Nord-Pas-de-Calais were already housed by the company, the number of house-owning workers being already then in decline. Where the company system had become more highly developed, as with the Montgolfier paper factory,

68. See Cheysson (1911).

there was a company shop, a crèche, a school – on leaving which the child would automatically find work in the factory – and a music society. There was almost always a relief fund, also retirement funds, and insurance against industrial injury. Seniority gradually became the basic qualification for such benefits; for example 25 years of uninterrupted work were required in order to qualify for a pension.[69]

At the same time, and always with a view to encouraging the work-force to put down roots and provide the succeeding generations of skilled workers which were in such short supply, large businesses attempted to give credence to the idea of the worker's 'career'. Buret had already observed that 'the industrial army offers no promotion' and added: 'I would like them to tell me what future there is for the workers in our factories, what encouragement to stimulate them and to relieve their fatigue?'[70] Answers to this question were sought from the 1860s onwards, with the additional aim of detaching workers from the land.

In the Carmaux mines the hitherto vague structure of basic crafts was clarified and new categories were created, to extend the hierarchy; to encourage competition the job of the worker hewing out the coal, considered a 'simple dust-swallower', was transformed into a 'skilled' occupation. As a departure from the traditional hierarchy of furnace-workers' crafts, metal-working teams were developed to create rungs of social advancement (the blast-furnace, for example, was served by the decoker, the second caster, the leading caster, and so on). At Hayange, Wendel even set up a system of workers' ranking, dependent on seniority and the nature of the work.[71]

Generally speaking, however, such evolution was only in its initial phase. In all areas of heavy industry the traditional worker-peasants were still very numerous; and the boom conditions of the 1860s brought shortages of labour resulting in great working-class mobility which prevented genuinely coherent management of the work-force.

Without going into great detail at this point, it can be stressed that during this period the French government also attempted to

---

69. On developing paternalism, see in particular Thuillier (1966), p. 342 *et seq*; Lequin (1974), vol. 2, p. 114 *et seq*; and Guerrand (1967), pp. 126–40.

70. Buret (1840), vol. 2, pp. 141–2.

71. Cited by Reybaud (1977), p. 229 *et seq*.

improve the means of controlling the working classes. After 1848 the reduction of crowding in working-class districts was the order of the day, legitimised by the concern (certainly sincere, but that is another subject) of hygiene experts. The reward for clearing the cellars of Lille was also the disintegration of revolutionary working-class identity. Baron Haussman's policy, put into effect simultaneously in many French cities, forced artisan workers to leave the central districts, their ancestral living quarters, for outlying suburbs. Jeanne Gaillard has described the same principle in relation to the development of charitable work; after 1848 Paris had no wish for poverty-stricken hordes to crowd in to the public hospital from all sides – hence the decision to set up a workhouse in each administrative district, so that public assistance as well as potential revolution could be decentralised. Here too reappears the wish to stabilise the floating population, to individualise the worker's world. Instead of the mob in the central public hospital there grew up the system of free medical treatment at home, which was inaugurated in the most crowded Paris *arrondissement*, the tenth. In the same way the multiplication of charitable institutions in residential areas helped to develop the constraining network.[72]

There remained still the genuinely political question. Since at least the time of Guizot, the enlightened representatives of the ruling class had been haunted by the problem of establishing a 'political market' capable of resolving the 'problem of the masses', so as to avoid any repetition of the traumatic events of the Terror during the French Revolution. Universal suffrage, not even sought until the 1840s, was finally achieved in the euphoric revolutionary days of 1848. The era of political representation would not really begin until the end of the Second Empire, but, as Albert Hirschman stresses, by granting universal suffrage the ruling class embarked on a strategy, whether consciously or otherwise, which defused the insurrectional notions of the Parisian working class; its violence would appear even more unwarranted now that 'democratic' means of political expression were available to the whole French nation. This innovation, however, was a double-edged weapon, as will be shown in the next chapter.[73]

The elections from 1848 to 1852 illustrated the sound basis of a strategy designed to foster separation between the worlds of the

72. Gaillard (1977), p. 310 *et seq.*
73. Hirschman (1982).

urban artisan and of heavy rural industry. In the craftsman's world support for the 'reds' and the 'democratic socialists' prefigured the social commitment of the following decades. Among rural workers, whether in Burgundy (particularly at Le Creusot) or in the Limoges area, the hopes of 1848 quickly gave way to disillusionment, and finally Napoleon III reaped a full harvest of votes. In 1848 the Peugeot workers 'spontaneously offered to work on credit, deferring receipt of their wages until after the crisis. In 1848, 1851 and 1852 they voted for the party of order. They were in any case entirely unaccustomed to political debate, very rarely read newspapers and were incapable, as their conduct proved so nobly in 1848, of letting themselves be drawn into the turbulence of any unrest whatsoever'.[74] Admirably expressed!

74. Corbin (1975), vol. 2, pp. 787–90; Lévêque (1983), vol. 2, p. 454; and Le Play (1856–1913), monograph no. 15, 'Décapeur d'outils d'Hérimoncourt (Doubs)', 1858.

3

Fin de Siècle
Neurosis

The precarious equilibrium established in French society during the earlier phase of the nineteenth century was profoundly shaken by the great depression which seriously affected the whole nation during the 1880s. It was a decisive period in working-class history, for it resulted in the definitive retreat of a working world based on multiple employment and mobility, yielding to the characteristic twentieth-century 'proletariat'. The most important aspect of this period, however, more significant than social changes which would not come fully to the fore until subsequent years, was the emergence of the modern worker movement and the system of collective representation which it successfully introduced. The two decades running from 1890 to 1910 saw more intense working-class militancy than any other period in recent French history, contributing to profound disarray among the governing classes of the day. The '*fin de siècle* neurosis' (Jean-Marie Mayeur's phrase) was apparent in what Émile Durkheim called the 'collective melancholy' and which he considered the outward expression of any society's most significant contradictions.[1]

1. Durkheim (1983), pp. 422–4; Mayeur (1973), p. 193.

I. The Great Depression

The economic crisis

Historians acknowledge the intensity and duration of the crisis which shook the late nineteenth-century French economy, setting off a Kondratieff cycle of regularly lowered prices from 1873 until 1896.[2] The main element of this crisis was the extent of the agricultural depression, seen in a definite slowing down of growth of production together with lowered prices; hence the reduction in peasant buying power. Among the underlying causes of the crisis relevant to this book must be included those concerning the establishment of a genuine nationwide market and the introduction of free trade. The 1880s crisis was largely the result of changes achieved under the Second Empire; the railway network started at that time was all but complete and coordinated during the 1890s. As François Caron observes, 'it was only then that the railways became a determining factor in the development of a genuine national market, as seen in the growing multiplicity of connections between different lines'.[3] It would be impossible to exaggerate the importance of this 'homogenisation' of France, and not only for economic reasons. The needy peasant, already dependent for survival on the availability of supplementary industrial employment – which also turned him into a 'worker', as has been shown – suffered a severe blow through competition from foreign goods, or goods from regions where productivity was more advanced; he was inexorably driven to abandon his subsistence economy and conform to market forces which required him to commercialise his output. This coincided with the arrival from England and the 'new countries' of cheaply produced grain, the product of mechanised and much more profitable large-scale cultivation; perhaps even more serious, the various supplementary resources traditionally available to the French peasant since the eighteenth century all became less reliable. Natural disasters added to the burdens; the phylloxera blight completely halted vine cultivation in many areas, while sweet chestnut and mulberry trees were both in turn victims of disease which in many cases devastated the system of plurality of occupations described in the previous chapter. It was, however, the

2. Lévy-Leboyer (1971), pp. 485–507.
3. Caron (1973), p. 242.

overall range of rural industry which proved unable to cope with the 1860 free-trade treaties with Great Britain. Claude Fohlen notes that the rural weaving industry, in slow decline from 1850/60 onwards, collapsed without hope of recovery after 1870; 41 hand-weaving establishments went out of business in Reims between 1876 and the end of the century. The 300 weavers in the Saint-Rémi district who, like the thread makers in Lille, symbolised a whole chapter of French industry, were forced to retrain; it was the beginning of an irretrievable decline in the region's textile industry. Three-quarters of the non-mechanical hosiery looms in Troyes were put out of work. According to Yves Lequin, the Lyon silk works collapsed. Traditional glove-making in Grenoble crumbled away in the face of foreign competition. The textile sector was not alone in its problems; the Saint-Étienne arms manufacturing out-working system could not compete (despite its flexibility) with the Belgian gun which cost 85 francs, against 130 francs for the Saint-Étienne product. Traditional metal-working, based on alternating rural and industrial employment, was equally impotent in the face of technological change. The discovery of the Briey basin iron-ore deposits meant ruin for hundreds of small local mines which were an important factor in the lives of the worker-peasants. Similarly, the success of the great metal-works in the north and the east of France was a mortal blow for small traditional ironworks. This period marks the end of metal-working in many French regions, such as the Dordogne. As with textiles, the terminal decline of rural industrial work went hand in hand with regional specialisation, the new geographical distribution of work being aided by improved means of communication. This moment above all marked the inception of southern France's retreat from industrialisation, apparent in the Ardèche as well as in Languedoc or the south-west. The rhythm of traditional industrial expansion faltered everywhere in France between 1875 and 1895; to quote Yves Lequin again, 'these years were the pivot of industrial destiny in the Lyon area, and perhaps even more for the whole of France'.[4]

The crisis in the peasant world was thus inescapably that of a type of working class born under the *ancien régime*, but fading in the early nineteenth century with the development of rural industry, while many artisans were overwhelmed by competition from the factory-made goods flooding the countryside. Henceforward artisan

---

4. Lequin (1974), vol. 1, p. 52.

production appeared dearer and frequently of lesser quality than factory products.

The great depression, however, was also a severe blow for urban artisan workers. In Jeanne Gaillard's opinion the crisis in weaving which was latent under the Second Empire only became fully ripe with the general economic recession. While France maintained free trade wholly or in part until the 1880s, many other nations closed their frontiers to French products. What had been luxury production tended, from the enlargement of the market dating from the Second Empire, to slide towards mass consumption; this led to lowered standards of quality and finish, damaging the interests of the highly skilled craftsmen who were so numerous in Paris. Since peasants still made up the nation's largest social grouping the home market not only remained modest, but tended to diminish where everyday consumer goods were concerned because of the reduced standard of living in rural areas. The crisis in trading outlets therefore coincided with an offensive on the part of big business into areas traditionally the preserve of the artisan class, thereby hastening its disappearance. As has been noted in the final report of an international inquiry into small business enterprises, it seems that the 'economic crisis of the 1880s must in the final analysis be judged a structural crisis at the expense of small business'.[5]

Heavy industry did not entirely escape the slump. The problems of making capital work profitably, encountered in the 1880s by the first big metal-working public companies in Lorraine, have been indicated elsewhere.[6] Investment everywhere was reduced to the barest minimum: production of coal, iron and steel stagnated. Not only did recruitment cease, but managers made maximum use of work-force mobility, typical of the 'flexible' system of worker management, to reduce the numbers employed, often drastically. Women, children and migrant workers were the first to go, further undermining the system of complementary industrial and agricultural work. One of the most distinctive aspects of French expansion, the nourishment of the labour market through a mobile work-force following traditional patterns of migration as circumstances demanded – locally, nationally, or even internationally – was thus assailed. Heavy industry, hitherto always hungry for manpower, found itself for the first time with a surplus of workers.

5. Gaillard (1981a).
6. Noiriel (1984), p. 40.

In the Loire basin, for example, a quarter of the miners were dismissed between 1883 and 1887, as well as a fifth of the men working in the heavy-metal industry.[7] By filtering out the less settled workers and at the same time strengthening the attachment of the most stable section, as will be shown, management in French heavy industry played a determining role in the processes leading to the rigidity of labour at the cost of flexibility, which has resulted in so many complaints from their latter-day successors. The working population, thus deprived of its complementary resources, was in effect forced into irreversible decisions, in particular that of exile to the cities.

Census counts between 1866 and 1906 indicate a net increase in urban populations, from 30.5 per cent to 42.1 per cent of the total population of France. During the same period the number of people making their living from agriculture was only a little more than 40 per cent of the population by the beginning of the twentieth century compared with 51 per cent in 1866. This reduction in rural work-force numbers is particularly applicable to agricultural labourers – those in maximum need of multiple employment – whose numbers dropped by 500,000 over half a century, or just under 20 per cent. These figures do not, however, give a clear indication of the qualitative difference in mobility compared to the preceding period. In the Lyon area moving house from one place to another henceforward took precedence over occupational migration, illustrating the break with the pattern of previous occupational migrations. In Lyon, as well as in Normandy or the Nantes region, moves generally involved shorter distances than formerly, but were more rural; henceforward the surrounding countryside would supply the towns with workers who increasingly resembled the modern proletariat. The Paris region offers perhaps the best example of such changes: beginning with the 1880s the traditional pattern of migration towards the capital became less clear-cut, with stonemasons from the Creuse settling in greater numbers and new arrivals, particularly from Brittany, representing permanent migration, even if they still sent the greater part of their wages back to their home villages. This migration was oriented not so much towards specific crafts based on specialisation in the home territory as towards the unskilled labour market of the large factories. Significantly, the majority settled not in Paris itself but in the suburbs, notably

---

7. Lequin (1974), vol. 1, p. 140.

Saint-Denis and Aubervilliers, which from the late nineteenth century onwards saw a great increase in large metal-working and chemical factories. As Louis Chevalier notes at the end of his study on 'the development of the Paris population', the burgeoning suburbs introduced new sociological principles and a new population structure.[8] It was also at this time that Lyon lost its working-class aspect, with the crisis in the silk industry, the consequent disappearance of the silk workers, and the corresponding increase in new social categories such as service employees and workers. The true proletariat was henceforward to be found in neighbouring communities which gradually grew into veritable 'suburbs' such as Vénissieux, Villeurbanne, or Saint-Fons, with new factories representing the 'second industrial revolution'. In many respects recent historical surveys confirm Philippe Ariès's assertion of 35 years ago: that it was in the years leading up to 1900 that France, three-quarters of a century behind Great Britain, began to develop a genuine industrial proletariat.[9]

The new inflexibility of the labour market had a bearing on the exceptional rate of unemployment in the 1880s. As Jacques Néré has shown, between 1882 and 1886 there were almost 200,000 unemployed workers in the Paris region alone. At a national level, in so far as it is possible to calculate for a period when the very concept of 'the unemployed' was far from being precisely defined, some 10 per cent of the industrial work-force was affected. But the chief characteristic – in contrast to 1848, for example – was that on the one hand the crisis in employment continued almost throughout the 1880s, and on the other hand it tended to be concentrated in heavily industrialised regions, making it even more prominent.[10]

Heavy industry's adaptability

Although the depression of the 1880s in France was one of the most serious 'that ever marked the history of an industrial nation',[11] it did not represent a crisis in all sectors, and in effect it allowed major employers to work out a coherent management strategy. Since the economic slump meant less demand for new workers, industrial managers were able to rationalise the method of controlling the

8. Chevalier (1950).
9. Ariès (1971). See also Lequin (ed.) (1983).
10. Néré (1959).
11. R. Cameron, quoted by Mayeur (1973), p. 61.

work-force known as 'paternalism', while lack of employment encouraged workers to look more favourably on changes that had previously been unacceptable. Rolande Trempé observes that it was only during this period that the mining world of Carmaux became genuinely worker-oriented; she suggests that the transformation was complete by 1890. The mining corporation was established so that when recruitment picked up again with expansion towards the end of the century, it did not disrupt the social group which had developed in preceding years; Philippe Ariès makes the same comment of the 'Pays Noir'. It was only as recruitment slowed down that mining society developed stability and form,[12] and it was only at this time (which also saw the publication of Zola's *Germinal*) that the notion of 'the mining son of a mining father' became a sociological fact. The very high birthrate in the mining families of Bully-les-Mines meant that when trade expanded again in the 1890s and 1900s they were largely able to supply the companies' recruitment needs. During the 1880s there was no longer a labour-force problem in Blanzy; the mine, with 2,000 miners in 1893, henceforward saw its miners' children flooding in, and this development was even more noticeable where recruitment difficulties had hitherto been less pressing. In the Nord textile industry, for example, Belgian immigration ceased after 1880. There too, mobility was much reduced, and identical shifts in the pattern were observed at Le Creusot where the factory remained only partly detached from the rural world, still subject to rural rhythms, until the end of the Second Empire.

It was at this time that company control was extended to cover local life in general. The social institutions mentioned in the last chapter were found everywhere, to the extent that the image of the worker cared for by the business 'from the cradle to the grave' began to become a reality, strengthening stability and the self-perpetuating work-force – the result specifically of the teaching system, from the crèche to the apprentice school attached to the factory, and policies which favoured the family. The crisis in agriculture was also turned to good advantage by moves to cut the worker-peasant off from his rural environment. At Carmaux, those who had been reluctant to come and live in housing blocks near the mine shafts finally gave in; and similarly, in the Nord, many gave up their long journeys on foot from village to factory to settle in

12. Ariès (1971), p. 85.

modest individual houses which the company built to replace the old miners' quarters, giving the miner an appearance of privilege compared with his peasant neighbour. The price of this evolution, however, was a restructuring of domestic life. Compared to the earlier way of life it was a step up the social scale in that the workman gave up all rural employment, although the lessons of the ironmasters such as Émile Martin were not forgotten. If the husband had to devote himself entirely to his industrial labour his wife – and to a lesser degree their children, who had no paid work in these single-industry regions – had to supplement the household resources by cultivating the garden which went with the house. At Denain around 1900, for example, 'more than half the families fatten[ed] up one or two pigs a year'; a third of the miners still made their own bread; and the family's only source of fruit and vegetables was their own garden. These resources were turned to such good account that they have been calculated as the equivalent of perhaps 40 per cent of the miner's annual wage.[13] Even if the worker thought of himself as the 'owner' of his house, since he lived there until he died and it was often a son, another miner, who 'inherited' it, at this stage it was in fact the companies that had direct control over housing and landownership. Through company shops they also had total control over the pattern of workers' consumption, particularly through the fortnightly credit system whereby the cost of purchases would often be deducted direct from the wage on the fifteenth or thirtieth day of the month. In such circumstances, although it was the husband who submitted to work allocation, it was the wife who submitted to the stranglehold over consumption or the reproduction of the work-force. She was transformed from her peasant status, while maintaining some control over what grew in her garden, into a workman's wife. In the Nord, when her husband was on the morning shift, she would get up at 3.30 a.m. to prepare his meal (his snack, or *briquet* in the local dialect). She then did all the household work, interrupted by getting the children ready for school, and prepared both the mid-day meal and her husband's meal on his return from the mine, a pattern possibly further complicated when other members of the

13. The working-class housing still seen today in Lorraine and the Nord is part of 'industrial archaeology'. In the Denain area, 'the house usually consisted of, on the ground floor, a kitchen-living room with an alcove for the parents' bed or a separate bedroom. Upstairs there were one or two attic rooms for the children. There was a cellar for the beer-barrel, the potatoes, and the coal' (see Dauby 1977).

family were also working in the mine but not necessarily on the same shift. There was the garden to cultivate, and frequently the added labour of a field which was also rented from the company and which took up the children's 'playtime'out of school, or the spare time of elderly relatives when they were no longer employed at the mine.

Economic dependence was finally complete through the linked social network of numerous recreational clubs for activities such as music, physical fitness, or drama; in 1900 in Denain, in the Nord, there were over 800 such clubs. Even though many were not directly set up by industrial companies, and sometimes reflected an ancient tradition of popular camaraderie, the large metal-working and mining companies tended here too to take the place of older social structures. In the Pays Noir, the French 'black country', 'all such societies, whatever their purpose, received the approval and the aid of the company and the factories, for they kept miners and metal-workers away from involvement in unions or politics; foremen and overseers were asked by the employers to act as club chairmen or treasurers'. By such methods was management control established over the 52,000 people dependent on the Compagnie d'Anzin in 1884, or the 10,000 Le Creusot workers, of whom 6,000 now lived no more than two kilometres from the factory.[14]

This period also saw the establishment of the principal policies for the integration of railway staff, rules which remained in force right up to the 1960s. In this troubled transport sector there was regular state supervision even in the days of the private companies, providing the work-force with a status and guarantees which continued and increased into the twentieth century. The prime concern being the safety of passengers at all costs, the railway companies built up a vast system of staff dependence. Workmen were recruited young and trained by the company, and there were also attempts to provide a career structure. In order to channel railway workers' future expectations along lines that conformed to the network, the rail companies developed very strong compartmentalisation of skills and the working milieu. By definition this could not be achieved by geographical isolation, as in the case of heavy industry, and it was for this reason that technical and clerical demarcation was so important in the railways. Three major development services were set up, each with many vertical channels and

14. On Le Creusot at the beginning of the twentieth century, see Parize (1981).

each channel possessing ranks and scales which a whole working life could not encompass when started from the lowest level. To this was added the regional demarcation which corresponded to the territory covered by each railway company.

Together with this working structure staff received company benefits at an early stage. Although wages were low the workers generally enjoyed security of employment, free medical services, and a retirement pension fund, all combining to explain why from the beginning of the twentieth century onwards a large proportion of the work-force came from 'railway' families; employers encouraged professional heredity as being a guarantee of company loyalty.[15]

The 'great depression' also brought about fundamental changes in the structure of French capitalism. The arguments of Le Play or Adolphe Blanqui were challenged by an openly liberal tide which found popular support, with Leroy-Beaulieu its most visible proponent. This was also a time of remarkable scientific and technological progress, the birth of the 'second industrial revolution': electricity, the internal combustion engine, the Solvay process, and many other discoveries, overturned traditional forms of occupation and initiated new branches of employment. Mechanisation made enormous strides, stimulating heavy industry which also benefited from the discovery of the Lorraine iron deposits.

The amount of energy used by French industry increased by 1,400 per cent between 1864 and 1913. Power-driven looms, which in 1873 represented only 5 per cent of the total in the Lyon silk industry, made up a third of it in 1900 and four-fifths in 1913. Mechanised glass-blowing revolutionised the glass industry, which had remained almost unchanged since the days of the *ancien régime*.

The work processes of heavy industry were thoroughly reorganised at this time, aided by the greatly increased number of engineers available and the flexibility offered by technological innovation. Amalgamation of business enterprises increased greatly. According to Émile Levasseur there were 57 companies in France employing more than 2,000 workers in 1901.[16] On almost all sides the family factory system was in terminal decline, and with it the complementary pattern of agricultural and industrial work. At the Japy factory, for example, work was no longer brought to the worker, the worker must now go to his employment; this was the

15. From Ribeill (1984), pp. 26–30.
16. Levasseur (1907), p. 274.

origin of the vast Beaucourt workshops assembling together the work-force hitherto scattered across the countryside. In the same way the Peugeot brothers put their conversion from ironmongery to bicycles and cars to good use by enlarging their factories. The popular classes' improved standard of living also favoured the setting up of large establishments whose proprietors, confident of more stable demand, did not hesitate to make the necessary investments. Following the substantial crisis of 1877, the reconstruction of the Lyon silk works indicated a fundamental break with the former system, with the manufacture of fine fabrics destined for a luxury clientèle and for export giving way to assorted machine-made fabrics for the more plebeian customer.[17] Employers in sectors of light industry with irregular patterns of employment wished to preserve the advantages of out-working, but on a reorganised basis. Production in the Paris hat trade provides an example of systematised decentralisation, begun in preceding decades. After the opening of the railway line the upper Aude valley, with numerous peasant workers and an ancient tradition of craft work, was chosen as the new centre of production; within a few years it had become the leading French felt-hat-making region. Those final decades of the century also saw the Paris clothing industry move from its Sentier quarter in the city in a mass emigration to Blois or Orléans in order to benefit from the female rural work-force in the Berry region. In such ways the capital became increasingly a commercial centre.[18] Businesses that remained in Paris made ample use of home-based female labour; at the beginning of the twentieth century such women constituted more than 85 per cent of Parisian out-workers. With universal availability of the sewing machine the 'sweat-shop system' reached its peak, as shown in a Labour Office survey which describes young women as earning no more than 15 centimes an hour by sewing.

Commerce showed the same process of concentration. The appearance of the first 'supermarkets', introduced to Paris by Félix Potin, meant the ruin of many small retail shops, and a definitive break developed between 'commercial' and 'artisan' activity, hitherto frequently interchangeable.

Large-scale establishments were also reorganised in ways designed to break the work-force's former autonomy. Apart from

17. Lequin (1974), vol. 1, p. 83.
18. Example quoted by Bachelard (1978), p. 295.

more restrictive workshop regulations, the most important innovations concerned methods of payment. According to the Labour
Office, in 1893, 34 per cent of provincial workers, and 28 per cent
of their Parisian counterparts, were paid according to their output;
increasingly, however, employers were turning to bonus payments, making it possible to reward assiduity, output, outstanding
work or, conversely, to penalise the half-hearted.[19]

Crisis in working-class values

The upheavals at the end of the century provoked a fundamental
crisis of identity at the heart of the working class; the substitution
of machinery and scientific knowledge for traditional forms of
expertise was very deeply felt by trained workers. Joan Scott has
shown that the introduction of mechanical glass-blowing annihil-
ated a proud and self-confident community centred on the exercise
of a very arduous skill even more dangerous than that of the
miners, which was its sole *raison d'être*.[20] Many others faced a
similar challenge: on the Vendée coast the welders who made tins
for preserved foods, 'jealous of their knowledge and their technique, acquired in the course of an extensive apprenticeship' and
which they had developed into a 'true art, a mysterious alchemy',
were relegated within a few years to the ranks of machine minders
when their work was mechanised.[21] Even among the skilled workers
of the 'first industrialisation', laboriously trained by their employers over earlier decades, many were overtaken by fresh technological changes. In metal manufacturing the puddlers, for example,
were of no further use after the invention of the Bessemer converter.
The spinners of Roubaix were faced with the spread of automatic
self-propelling looms, leaving them with nothing to do but watch the
machines.

Apart from these genuinely technical causes, the working-class
crisis was precipitated by breaks in traditional community links.
Haussmann's urbanisation, mentioned above, was applied progres-
sively throughout France's great cities, dispersing workers from
the town centres; to this was added the acceleration of the rural
exodus whose major function, according to Maurice Halbwachs,

19. Office du Travail (1893).
20. Scott (1982).
21. Régourd (1981), pp. 39–42.

was to break 'man's identification with his local group, by individ-
ualising him'. Improved standards of working-class life also contributed to the break-up of traditional relationships; working-class
purchasing power appears to have grown substantially between the
days of the Second Empire and the beginning of the twentieth
century (by as much as 40 or 45 per cent in certain cases, according
to experts). Elsewhere the extension of the mass market resulted in
workers receiving wages more regularly, since crises and seasonal
unemployment were less frequent. This period can therefore be
seen as the first distinct phase of popular consumption's greater
importance. The final third of the nineteenth century saw, for the
first time in French history, the disappearance of the spectre of food
scarcity even in bad times. As Maurice Halbwachs states, there was
certainly considerable variation between the different sectors of the
working class; the more prosperous now spent more money on
meat than on bread, but for the great majority the reverse still held
true. Apart from more regular and better-balanced nutrition, this
progress in consumerism is seen in the first purchases indicating a
modest expansion beyond sheer need: a watch, a newspaper, Sunday
clothes. In the villages, and above all in Paris, the early years of the
twentieth century saw passionate working-class enthusiasm for
sport; the extraordinary success of the four leading newspapers
which achieved circulation figures never equalled since, and the
first 'leisure activities' of what was beginning to be called *le
weekend*, together indicated a genuine break with the immediate
past.[22] Even in more isolated areas such as the Nivernais, in these
late nineteenth-century years 'new ways of life sprang up, men did
military service and learned about city ways. Many women
worked as children's nurses in Paris or elsewhere. Others worked
as domestic servants between the ages of 12 and 20'.[23] The spread
of compulsory education brought awareness of other circumstances, offered new patterns of living.

22. See Halbwachs (1970). This was the period when the owners of the big daily
newspapers systematically gained control of the popular market. Newspapers cost
five centimes, equivalent to 12.5 per cent of a kilo of bread (compared with 53 per
cent in 1980), 17 per cent of a litre of milk (88 per cent in 1980). 'Buying a newspaper
showed that the household conformed to the new pattern of consumption fostered
by urbanisation and industrialisation', according to A.-M. Thiesse. The daily serial,
such as *La Porteuse de Pain*, introduced in 1884 – its heroine a widow working as a
factory caretaker, whose husband had died in an industrial accident – was one of the
chief reasons for the success of this type of journalism. (See Thiesse 1984.)

23. Thuillier (1966), p. 57.

This, however, was a development with more than one facet. Levasseur observes that the Anzin miner spent 70 francs on his clothes in the decade 1820–30, and 230 francs between 1880 and 1887 but was still not satisfied because 'habit reduces the feeling of pleasure'.[24] Without necessarily adopting a favourable attitude in order to legitimise the established order, there are many indications that, at the same time as the working class took to consumerism, it became aware of the 'deception' which, as Albert Hirschman suggests, has been a constant factor in western society since the time of Rousseau's 'trinkets' – but one which workers had not been able to appreciate fully until then.[25]

It is also important to note the extent to which the substantial expansion of cash transactions at this time emphasised the individual's feeling of isolation. The spread of the banking system, seen in the growing number of deposit banks, together with growing basic wages, meant that cash payment became the norm in everyday dealings. Ready money has a powerful effect in reducing individuality in personal relationships and interaction, tending to make such dealings more abstract and less direct. Georg Simmel saw this as a factor that encouraged working-class emancipation from domestic types of dominance, but saw also that the widespread use of liquid cash led to new techniques of control over others, compartmentalising the individual, and rendering the exercise of power much more impersonal.

The spread of literacy increased this tendency, splitting up basic groupings, as has been shown recently, making individuals part of much larger basic units and above all linking them to the national community.[26]

At the end of the century the combination of such factors, which call for closer study, provoked a crisis in local structures and the hierarchy of local district and village community values. The physical strength and endurance at the furnace, which were the glory of the puddler in his local setting of the traditional ironworks, no longer offered a model for succeeding generations. The mechanisation of work meant a devaluation of muscular strength, and stressed the division of labour. These objective factors of working-class 'devaluation' multiplied repetitive tasks, adding still more to

24. Levasseur (1907), p. 105.
25. Hirschman (1982).
26. See Simmel (1920); Furet and Ozouf (1977).

the crisis in traditional labour. Many young workers questioned the continuing merit in sacrificing the years of their youth to the laborious and painful acquisition of skills which were no longer admired and were increasingly ill-paid.

This weakening of autonomy in transmitting skills was one of the underlying causes of the 'apprentice crisis' so frequently deplored at the end of the nineteenth century, to which may be added the decline in traditional master–apprentice relationships. At this time only 10 per cent of apprentices enjoyed the security of a written contract, and two-thirds failed to complete their apprenticeship. The problem was exacerbated by the lack of genuine professional training for workmen. Even though the late nineteenth century saw the beginnings of true technical instruction, in reality this was confined to an élite, often of *petit-bourgeois* background, and consisted almost overwhelmingly of foremen and technicians. Around the year 1910, 3.5 per cent of the under-18 age-group received some kind of vocational training at school; 8.5 per cent were trained through courses of vocational instruction. Almost 90 per cent of workers, therefore, had no technical training whatsoever outside their own workshop.[27]

The abandonment of the multiple employment system accentuated the crisis in labouring work. In fact in rural industry the unskilled worker (in many sectors the most numerically significant element) carried on with such work as one element in the pattern of rural employment. Compartmentalisation of employment added considerably to the 'professionalisation' of unskilled work, relegated to the bottom of the ladder of what were soon to be called working qualifications.

Loss of rooted stability and the crisis in traditional values – as well as the improved average standard of working-class life – were essential factors in the great increase in working-class alcoholism at the end of the century which alarmed philanthropists as well as trade unionists such as Pelloutier. After tuberculosis and syphilis, alcoholism was the third plague that affected the working-class world of Belleville. The problem increased markedly after 1890, notably in the abuse of absinthe, by far the most harmful drink, with consumption rising from 8,000 hectolitres in 1874 to more than 200,000 hectolitres in 1905. 'Among the Parisian working class, and particularly in Belleville, the excessive consumption of

27. See Charlot and Figeat (1985), pp. 139–62.

alcoholic drink was considered entirely normal', notes Gérard Jacquemet. 'It was practically a permanent side-show of the Belleville streets to see assorted individuals calling the police such names as "pigs", "donkeys", or "lazy-bones", quite apart from other less elegant epithets. Offensive behaviour was relatively common, and almost always attributable to drunkenness.' The increase in alcoholism is also cited by Gabriel Désert as a possible cause of the increase in violence throughout the nineteenth century. 'From a proportion of 26 per cent of total crimes at the end of the Restoration, crimes against the person reached 36 per cent of the total during the first decade of the Second Empire, and more than 44 per cent at the beginning of the twentieth century'.[28]

II. Strikes and Unions: Two New Factors of Everyday Working Life

The period stretching from the 1880s to the eve of the First World War saw an intensive collective working-class militancy, undoubtedly the peak of such activity in the history of the French working-class movement. 'Like an irresistible tide, strikes swept through the land and all occupations', notes Michelle Perrot.[29] The distinctive aspect of the working class's readiness to fight was primarily that it affected all categories of worker. Although the skilled craftsmen, with their longer experience, continued to lead the movement, textile workers and above all the miners and metal-workers from the great establishments – whose calmness Louis Reybaud was still praising at the beginning of the Third Republic – became increasingly active. Between 1895 and 1899, for example, 35 per cent of strikers were in heavy industry. Even the rural proletariat, almost entirely quiet since the Second Empire, entered the fray. The Cher

28. Jacquemet (1982), p. 258 *et seq*; Désert (1981), p. 260. The increase in violence over a long period is difficult to assess because of the methodological problem of evolving social attitudes; social definitions of violence are liable to change and invalidate comparisons. The difficulty in establishing a realistic assessment of working-class alcoholism lies in the fact that alcoholism was one of the favourite 'class-racist' themes which became commonplace, starting with Zola's *L'Assommoir*, showing the middle-classes' bafflement at certain aspects of working-class behaviour. Alcohol and a certain amount of violence were prime elements of working-class identity, part of their self-image of virility and strength.

29. Perrot (1974), vol. 1, p. 59; on strikes at this time, see also Andréani (1965).

woodcutters' great strikes in 1891/2 and the general uprising of the Languedoc winegrowers in 1907 represented high points in a permanently unsettled atmosphere.

The strikers' determination is evident in the increasing average length of each dispute, growing from seven days in 1875 to 21 days in 1902. Certain strikes, such as that of the Rives-de-Gier metal-workers in 1894 or the Fougères shoemakers in 1906, lasted for nearly a year. Similarly, observers were impressed by the sol-idarity, even the unanimity, of work stoppages. The general miners' strike of 1902 was observed by 108,000 workers from 77 companies in the Nord, peaking on 1 May 1906: 'One striker for every 16 industrial workers', noted Madeleine Rebérioux, 'the century has begun with striking as part of the proletariat's normal way of life'.

The strength of commitment to the fight can often be explained by its foundation in long-established collective practices of the communities now struggling for survival. Older forms of action were still often preferred in the cities, such as the 'blacklisting' applied for six weeks by Grenoble glove-makers in 1894, to bring pressure to bear on manufacturers who did not respect agreed charges.[30]

It was also among trained workers that traditional forms of solidarity were to be found. In the Faubourg Saint-Antoine in Paris, strikers managed to find other employment without too much difficulty during their dispute, through the goodwill of small employers and finishers who were also suffering from mergers and mechanisation. Such group solidarity was apparent in the financial support from all sides and it helped to prolong the strike.

Where heavy industry was not yet completely cut off from rural life, strikes often represented an entire district's combined resist-ance to the invasion of large-scale manufacturing and its intention to disrupt the customs of past generations. Michelle Perrot states that many late nineteenth-century strikes were still in harmony with the rhythms of rural life, 'evidence', she remarks, 'of a still half-rural working class, a semi-developed region. . . . There is something of the peasant in this avid looking forward to spring'.[31] Rural influences can also be seen in the form of resistance adopted; taking advantage of the First of May carnival in 1890, the miners of Anzin disguised themselves and roamed the streets armed with

30. Barral (1967). See Rebérioux (1974), p. 88.
31. Perrot (1974), vol. 1, p. 113.

cudgels, preventing others from working.[32] There too the solidarity of support from other groups of workers meant that strikes could endure for longer periods. Traders in Le Creusot in 1899 and Longwy in 1905, resentful of employers' stranglehold over workers' spending outlets, gave credit or supplied food without charge to the 'communist soup-kitchens' which were highly successful at that time. Support for the peasants is even better documented; as at Rosières, where the metal-workers on strike for five months in 1906 were only able to hold out for so long because they could find labouring work on local farms; or at Revin, where the whole Ardennes hinterland gave solid support to the foundrymen. In addition, better wages and increased consumption had not yet modified to any great extent the frugal ways of the popular classes. 'Brought up to penury, poor societies have an unsuspected capacity for endurance when they have hope to sustain them.'[33]

In large industry one of the strongest incentives for the workers' struggle was their disenchantment with paternalism, already evident in the growth of a virulent anti-clericalism. Despite all its efforts – the Society of Saint-Vincent-de-Paul had 913,000 members in 1869 – social catholicism never managed to develop deep roots in the working class. The anti-clerical propaganda of Guesde's followers, which met with a growing response among the miners, contributed to the strength of popular positivism in urban artisan circles from the 1880s onwards. The practice of secular burial, which became part of bourgeois custom at the end of the Second Empire, was adopted by the working class in subsequent decades: out of just over 3,000 ninth category (free) burials in the strongly working-class Paris district of Ménilmontant in 1883, more than half took place with no religious ceremony. At Saint-Denis on the northern edge of Paris the rate of secular funerals in 1911 was about 50 per cent; the figure in the mining community of Hénin-Liétard (Pas-de-Calais) was 40 per cent, and in Carmaux 21.5 per cent.[34]

Industrial paternalism was not discredited solely by religious factors; it was in effect the victim of a combination of changes in French society accelerating the breakdown of direct personal relationships. The social distancing stemming from the spread of cash wages, and the raised standard of consumption which rendered commonplace what had hitherto appeared dependent on charitable

32. Ibid., vol. 2, p. 555.
33. Ibid., vol. 2, p. 725. On the Revin strike, see Auffray et al. (1978).
34. From Pierrard (1984), p. 468.

activity, encouraged the growth of a sudden critical awareness among the workers. Elsewhere, stability among the work-force fostered by economic uncertainty and the employers' efforts, increased workers' concern over what was happening inside their factories. All this is apparent in the aims of the struggle proclaimed during disputes. Steel workers at Le Creusot began to demand payment for maintenance work carried out on Sundays. However much the managers might point out that this was an old 'tradition' (reflecting, moreover, the independence of workers paid on piecework rates), the strikers were unyielding; proof both of disillusionment regarding their employers (no more working 'for him' or for 'the big factory family', it was for money now) and of their internalisation of the new attitude to working hours (time spent at the factory should be paid time). After 1883 strikers at Carmaux no longer demanded the abolition of piecework, as in 1869; now it was the denial of promotion and the managers' refusal to take on children at the mine which provoked the fiercest confrontations. As the century drew to a close retirement pensions became a primary demand'– further evidence of the break with the rural economy.

Strike activity at the end of the century reflected a working world at a crossroads. On the one hand, as shown above, miners and metal-workers in the large establishments already appeared to be integrated into the factory world, accepting its rules and advantages; on the other, numerous other disputes offer evidence of the scale of resistance to innovation.

Wage-related problems were pushed to the back of the stage; the arguments most frequently advanced concerned resistance to piecework, new regulations or machinery, opposition to overseers who were considered too authoritarian, or the wish to achieve implementation of rates of pay already agreed by the management.

The workers' struggle frequently developed into demands for 'worker control'. Almost everywhere in the mines there was an expressed wish for independent management of aid funds, and in the south-west and the Loire basin movements also sprang up which claimed 'the mine for the miners'. The workers' solution to the strike in many cases was to set up a 'cooperative' unit; this was what brought to an end the Carmaux glass-workers' bitter fight against mechanisation, the Albi workers' glass factory set up by strikers having long been the leading light of the movement.

It was, however, in modest urban industry that the cooperative movement reached its peak, the related end-of-century strikes constituting in many areas the culmination of several years of conflict. In the Lyon area this period even constituted 'the apogee of corporate management'. The battle over work-rates begun (and lost) by the Lyon silk workers in 1830 was renewed 50 years later, but this time the silk workers managed to impose the new rates on their employers. Many other corporate bodies were affected by similar activity. In the Roanne area the 1889 strike which began in the town spread through rural communities engaged in silk and cotton work, indicating a unity between the long-time rival factions in textiles. For four years the Lyon glassworks had a worker-elected council, a genuine parallel power to which the employers submitted and which allowed the workers to exercise a genuine monopoly over recruitment. 'Among the tannery workers and glove makers the practice degenerated into a totally enclosed trade entirely dependent on inheritance.' Annonay in the Ardèche saw the resurrection of past corporate customs such as the 'introductory premium', the substantial fee to be paid by the new entrant unless he was himself the son of a tannery worker. Yves Lequin suggests that this was surely 'an attempt at British style trade-unionism which eventually faded out for other reasons?'[35]

A further element of the worker movement added to the strike as part of workers' everyday life was the trade union. From 1884, when the unions were legalised, membership increased substantially until 1914. Union strength was never so great as at the same time in Great Britain or Germany, particularly because of changing membership, but in urban trades, miners, and railwaymen, the greater part of the work-force was unionised. The Lyon silk-weavers' victory can only be understood in the light of the action of their 10,000-strong combined union committee, and in Roanne 11,000 weavers were unionised. Closed-shop practices were only achieved through union activity, as described above, and worker organisations influenced many more than their paid-up members. In many rural or semi-rural areas it was a strike that first inspired union activity: following its 'spontaneous' beginnings it was subsequently channelled, stabilised, and sustained by the organisation offering solidarity (particularly in material matters) with fellow workers in other French regions, demonstrating in practical terms to strikers the existence of a body of national, even international, proportions.

35. Lequin (1974), vol. 2, p. 275.

The organisation's unifying role was paramount. Isolation, the bulwark of the dominant classes in preventing 'contamination' of the heavy-industry proletariat by the revolutionary ideology of the urban élite, was demolished. The railway-based unified transport system meant that leaders in Paris could reach any confrontation promptly and contribute the experience of worker groups with the longest traditions of militancy, and developments in the press aided militants who were kept regularly informed of all disputes anywhere in France. This breakdown of isolation was often at the root of confrontation, hence the employers' belligerent reaction to 'leaders from outside'. At Le Creusot, for example, workers realised that an unskilled labourer earned more in Paris than a skilled Schneider employee; this was one of the causes quoted for the 1899 strike. General strikes, usually organised for 1 May, were another eloquent demonstration of the stimulating effect of unity within the movement.

The creation of the CGT (General Confederation of Workers) in 1895 is a vital date in this context; the most distinctive feature of the period, however, is the combination of activity coordinated on a national level with activity very deeply rooted in the 'grassroots' or the local district, supported by local *bourses du travail* labour exchanges. These were initiated in the 1880s and were highly successful, increasing in number until the war.[36] Their manifold activities (finding jobs for workers seeking employment, worker education, surveys investigating industrial health in collaboration with doctors, providing solidarity of support in all disputes) contributed greatly to the development of the worker movement's strong roots in everyday working-class life. It was certainly the most effective way of recruiting skilled urban workers, and workers in heavy industry. When the metal-workers of Rosières took action in 1906 the support of the Bourges labour exchange was a decisive element in their success; in 1892 their first strike had benefited from the experience of the Vierzon deputy, a former porcelain worker and ex-communard. Such examples demonstrate how widely the French working movement was able to extend its fighting traditions;[37] the political network was the final element which completed the overall picture.

36. A *bourse de travail*: a labour exchange run by trade unions for educational, social and trade-union activities. For the first full study of the *bourses de travail*, see Schöttler (1985).
37. Pigenet (1982).

With the introduction of universal suffrage the working class, initially almost unrepresented on the political scene, became of prime importance. After 1880 the parties claiming the proletariat for their own began to establish themselves by taking over increasing numbers of municipal authorities, and during the 1890s Parliament began to fill up with the workers' elected representatives. The first applications of worker management were tried out in cities won by the socialists, based on policies of social aid, support in disputes, and attacks on government – growing evidence of a new political style which generally won the loyalty of the working-class electorate. 'Representatives of the people', such as the miner-deputies from the Nord, became securely established; the socialist tradition which they created in their own regions would thereafter prove almost unassailable.

A whole series of symbols was developed elsewhere during this period of intense struggle, providing the working class with elements of its collective identity. After the Paris Commune of 1871 the red flag became the badge of highest honour; it became the late nineteenth century's rallying emblem for workers and their struggle everywhere, to the detriment of the tricolour flag symbolising the Republic which had proved such a disappointment to the workers. Similarly, the *Marseillaise* was abandoned in favour of the *Carmagnole* and, increasingly, the *Internationale*. The workers' separatist intent was further developed by the decision to label 1 May 'Labour Day', a day specially marked out for strikes and large-scale demonstrations which were often repressed – further adding to their revolutionary value.

The strong impact of this period of intense militancy on the working world's collective memory is clearly apparent in the oral history of recent years taken from older workers, and in popular literature such as the works of Navel or Guéhenno. It also provides the origin of the 'worker Messianism' so characteristic of the late nineteenth century, which perfectly symbolises the passion for the 'general strike'. The ideology, or myth, that production workers are deeply affected by the groundswell of a changing work structure, grew from the notion that if all workers simultaneously decided to down tools, capitalism would 'fall like a ripe fruit'. This conviction was shared by most sectors of the working world, particularly during the 1890s, and indeed far beyond it. When the Paris floor layers were asked why they joined in the building strike of 1891 they offered no specific reason; they were simply on strike because they were absolutely determined not to miss what they described as 'one of the greatest demonstrations in the world'.[38] And when one militant admitted in his memoirs that, at that moment, 'caught up in the atmosphere, I saw the Revolution close at hand',[39] he was merely reflecting a widely shared attitude.

III. At the Crossroads

Belief in the 'end of an epoch'

During these closing years of the century the broad extent of the strikes resembled 'repeated blows with a battering ram which crack the building and prove it vulnerable. They help to nourish the governing classes' pessimism, their belief in the "end of an epoch", in contrast to the revolutionary hopes of the workers'.[40]

Yet it requires more than the development of a powerful worker movement to explain the *'fin de siècle* neurosis'. Other classes were also affected by the social crisis, particularly the intellectuals who were affected by restructuring in the university world, the victory of market forces in art and literature. The new generation of the 1890s challenged traditional authority; even at the heart of the religious hierarchy the crisis of positivism and of republican values added to the general disarray. None of this was exclusive to France: the greater *malaise* there than in other nations was the consequence of simultaneous backwardness and precocity.

The backwardness was the result of a society which until about 1880 sustained the economy and values of a rural economy and was suddenly confronted with abrupt change; hence the violence of the rejection of industrialisation, which was felt as an onslaught undermining the age-old collective identity. The precocity lay in democratic rights, particularly concerning freedom of expression; first recognised politically at the time of the Revolution, such rights lay at the heart of republican planning as introduced from Gambetta's time. Freedom of the press, for example, was a decisive element in the dissemination of the concept of strikes and of the proletariat. For Michelle Perrot it was the social disturbances of 1880 in the Nord which marked the beginning of the worker movement's

38. Quoted by Levasseur (1907), p. 662.
39. Quoted by Lefranc (1975), p. 318.
40. Perrot (1974), p. 717.

popularisation. Statistics for engravings referring to strikes in *L'Il-lustration* show an increase from 23 between 1870 and 1879 to 57 between 1889 and 1899, increasing further to 111 in the first decade of the twentieth century. In 1880 the journal *L'Événement* bore the heading: 'We must not be blind. We must see clearly: we must prevent society from being overwhelmed in the flood.' Such dramatisation, coinciding with the corresponding specific interests of certain journalists who were already building their success on the spectacular news item and current-affairs paragraph, was particularly noticeable during major confrontations; these were covered on a day-to-day basis by reporters who never missed an opportunity to keep their readers waiting spellbound by playing up the slightest encounter. The strike was thus the determining factor whereby 'the worker appeared in shadow-theatre silhouette, then in full view, in uninformed representations'.[41]

France's democratic precocity also explains why the worker movement and the parliamentary political system came into being at virtually the same moment. Universal suffrage, the determining element in republican identity (as seen by Gambetta, for one) was intended, as recent work has rightly emphasised,[42] to settle the matter of revolutions once and for all; this 'French speciality', based on mass uprisings of the urban – and principally Parisian – populace, had brought down the current regime from 1789 to the Commune of 1871, by way of 1830 and 1848. Gambetta proclaimed that universal suffrage rendered revolution impossible: fine optimism on the part of the founders of the Third Republic which found little support 20 years later. Not only was the spectre of revolution not dispelled: what had been no more than a custom of the Paris élite of skilled workers seemed thereafter set to become the communal right of the entire working class. We know now that on this point at least Gambetta's comment was accurate. What mattered was the belief, widely shared at the time, in the imminence of danger and the mechanisms from which it developed. Apart from the press, the parliamentary system's own reasoning must be recognised. Workers' interests being henceforward protected – that is, they were represented within the National Assembly by people whose advantage lay in giving credence to the strength of the class they represented – the force of polemical

41. Ibid., p. 32.
42. Rosanvallon (1985).

eloquence, flowing speeches, etc., was highly effective in convincing the whole political sector of the danger. An example may be quoted, the political impact of the first 'massacre' of workers by the Third Republic on 1 May 1881 at Fourmies in the Nord, where the army killed 10 and wounded 80; a few days later Clemenceau let fly on the rostrum of the National Assembly: 'Paving stones in Fourmies bear the stain of innocent blood which must at all costs be effaced. . . . Take care! The dead are great persuaders; we must pay attention to the dead.' And, referring to this 1 May which had been highly successful both in France and abroad, he added:

> So much so that the blindest eyes could not fail to see that workers were aroused throughout the world, that something entirely new was impending, that a new and awesome force had arisen which henceforward politicians must acknowledge. What is it? We must have the courage to name it, and in the very form adopted by the movement's promoters: this is the Fourth Estate which is arising, and which is near to taking power.[43]

It was at this moment that the dominant image of the worker throughout the entire first part of the nineteenth century, as the élite of urban craftsmen, began to give way to the image more familiar to the twentieth-century observer, of the miner, the proletariat of the large textile factory, and soon of the metal-worker. The Ruskinian disdain for anything that might recall industry in art was challenged. With artists such as Constantin Meunier worker iconography took shape in the form of 'the powerful image of the male worker brandishing hammer or pickaxe, and always with his torso stripped bare'.[44] In the political arena the 'proletariat' came to play an essential role, due above all to the followers of Guesde who introduced Marxist thinking into France.[45]

Renewed shortage of manpower

The strength of industrial recovery during the final years of the nineteenth century poses once again the burning question of work-force recruitment. The large steel and car factories established at that time were a powerful attraction for skilled workers,

---

43. Quoted Dommanget (1953), p. 150.
44. Hobsbawm (1978).
45. On the Guesde movement, see in particular Willard (1965).

who took advantage of their favoured position in the labour market to revert to old patterns of mobility. At Décazeville on average 65 per cent of the workers left the factory within a year of being taken on. In the period 1880–1902 it had been necessary to take on two men to retain one; in the first years of the twentieth century it became necessary to find five in order to have one who was content to stay. Other French regions suffered similarly. At the well-established Cail steelworks in the Nord, turnover reached 75 per cent. After the 1910 strike the railways suffered an 'intolerable degree' of manpower shortage; but it was in the mines that the recruiting crisis reached its peak, a factor deserving detailed consideration in view of the myth of 'miner father and miner son' which is still so persistent today. Discussing the situation in the Monthieux mine in 1890, one observer noted: 'People often talk of the miner's devotion to his calling, it is compared to the sea-fever which seizes the mariner's son. At least as far as the Loire basin is concerned, this attitude appears to me to be entirely romantic.' This understates the case, for turnover at the time ran 101 per cent and 'not only was it difficult to recruit workers, it was becoming more and more difficult to keep them'. In the Nord the miners' professional permanence was, according to Odette Hardy-Hemery, 'the most unrealistic stereotype'. The Anzin Company saw its rate of turnover rise from 8 per cent in 1896 to 14.6 per cent in 1906, and to 33.8 per cent in 1911–13, without taking internal moves into account. Marriage records in Valenciennes show a substantial reduction in professional heredity. By 1913 almost one miner in two was giving up his trade to work in a mechanical engineering company, and there were virtually no apprentices joining the mining companies. Even in Carmaux the mine managers' patient efforts over half a century seemed all at once to have been in vain. 'To add one more worker to the payroll it was necessary to take on two or three in 1889, one or two between 1890 and 1892, four or five in 1900/1, six or seven in 1911/12, 16 or 17 in 1913, and as many as 29 in 1909.' Rolande Trempé adds: 'Dislike of underground work, which had been noted earlier, turned to genuine repugnance.' In 1907 all coal-mining areas were short of hands, and the Central Coalmining Committee estimated that 15,000 workers – equivalent to 10 per cent of the current total – should be taken on immediately in order to maintain production.[46]

46. On the Nord, see Hardy-Hemery (1984), particularly p. 32; on the railways,

The much more reliable census counts from the end of the nineteenth century supply useful pointers illustrating the stagnation in the working-class labour market, with this period providing evidence of a substantial increase in the numbers belonging to the 'middle classes'. Wage-earners in public service approximately doubled in number between 1866 and 1906, the same pattern was apparent in banking and insurance, and qualified members of the liberal professions increased by a third. Shopkeepers (particularly café proprietors) increased by a third between these dates, despite competition from large establishments. Furthermore those who figure in statistics as 'independent' (self-employed workers without employees of their own, finishers, etc.) grew from two million in 1866 to 3.4 million in 1896 and 3.9 million in 1906. Further proof of the survival of small-scale business is that 50 per cent of workers were employed in establishments of between one and five people in 1906, against only 10 per cent working in factories with more than 500 employees. Numbers of industrial employees showed the smallest growth; between 1891 and 1906 there was no increase at all in the work-force, at a time when so many businesses were short-handed.

The renewed turnover seen almost everywhere at this time was therefore partly due to the opportunities to climb the social ladder, which were a consequence of structural changes in French society. It also provided a personal solution for workers affected by industrial reorganisation or repression of strikes, or feelings of disillusionment towards paternalism. Although most of them probably did not rise very high up the social hierarchy, in the *département* of the Manche the sons of workers and employees entering the teacher-training school at Saint-Lo, 3.4 per cent of the total between 1880 and 1884, constituted 34.5 per cent between 1910 and 1914, while in the Nord in 1896, 26 per cent of teachers were of working-class origin.[47] Above all, however, it was the internal mobility of the working class that was numerically significant; this was particularly true of miners who sought professional training

Caron (1973), p. 564; on the Loire mines, Le Play (1856–1913), monograph no. 89, 'Piqueur sociétaire de la mine aux mineurs de Monthieux', 1895; on Carmaux, Trempé (1971), vol. 1, p. 159; none of this prevented the growth and spread of the legend of the 'miner's love for his work', as in the journal *Le Temps* in 1892: 'He loves it as the winegrower loves his vines', quoted by Lequin (1974), p. 536.

47. Based on Muel's (1977) sample.

for their sons so that they could enter the new professional trades so highly valued by the workers, such as engineering. In many cases such aspi:ations towards social betterment replaced the preceding generation's hope of landownership. An observer at Blanzy noted that only the offspring of very large families were sent down the mines, from financial necessity; many limited the size of their families and through self-denial managed to give them an academic or professional education qualifying them for a different career from that of their fathers.[48] By these means the older generation's legacy of thrift enabled them to use the modest savings put aside from increased wages to plan their escape from their original class.

This pattern demonstrates how the demographic crises affecting the whole of France during the second half of the nineteenth century can to some extent be seen as a form of popular resistance to proletarianisation. The net rate of reproduction in the French population decreased steadily from 1871–80 onwards, and dipped below replacement level in 1891. In many working-class areas this Malthusian approach was a new factor which tended to intensify at the beginning of the twentieth century. Given the strength of the popular response and the political power derived from universal suffrage, successive republican governments had no means of forcing an increase in the size of the work-force; indeed, their policies had the opposite effect. Thus, stating that the Jules Ferry primary school made it possible for the son of a peasant or an artisan to become a civil servant, Jean-Marie Mayeur considered that it was 'the good fortune of the Republic, and one reason for its rooted stability, that it could thus offer plenty of jobs to a social class which sought to better itself'.[49] Such a state of affairs was naturally unpopular with factory managers.

Contradictory solutions suggested for releasing the labour market

Everything proceeded as though the main mechanisms of late nineteenth-century French society had seized up, and almost all observers have been struck by the speed of recession in French strength during these decades. Over a period of 20 years the nation lapsed from second to fourth world ranking in terms of industrial production; its population was at a standstill; in all the new econ-

48. Quoted by Peyronnard (1981), p. 251.
49. Mayeur (1973).

omic sectors France was challenged and then overtaken by Germany. And yet no one was prepared to pay the price of adaptation to this new world, and there seemed to be no power capable of imposing it.

The managerial sector was keenly aware of this contradiction, which was surely not unconnected to the fact that contemporary France was a veritable powerhouse of ideas, both political and social, a laboratory of theories and experiments which would in many cases find acceptance in the twentieth century but which then still reflected the uncertainties and hesitations of a society in the full flow of change.

Business proprietors did not yet appear confident of how best to solve problems of labour shortage or the crisis of authority shown up by strikes.

Managers turned first to traditional methods to supply the labour market, drawing on reservoirs of female labour to a greater extent than ever before; the proportion of women workers rose from 31 to 37 per cent of the total working population between 1866 and 1906. By the end of the century women constituted 51 per cent of textile workers and 30 per cent in the chemical industry; this stirred up the hostility of the bourgeoise belonging to the 'populationist' trend which fought for a return of 'women at home' – hence the recourse to another traditional solution, that of worker-peasants, in spite of the disadvantages of seasonal absenteeism and the minimal personal identification of such workers with company interests. Increasing numbers of workers' trains enabled the mining companies in the Nord to draw in thousands of workers from as far away as the remote villages of Picardy, and this new method of travel also brought thousands of workers across the Belgian frontier every day to work in the textile factories of the Nord or the Longwy metal-works.[50] The use of immigrant labour, which also increased at the beginning of the twentieth century, was nothing new for France. However, where previously traditional migratory patterns had regulated the availability of work within the framework of seasonal migration, recruitment of foreign workers now became more systematic, and after 1889 mining companies in the Nord introduced organised recruitment of Belgian workers. In Reims,

50. In 1897, 74 per cent of the Denain factory work-force lived within five kilometres of the factory; by 1912 the workers' trains meant that this applied to only 47.7 per cent; see Hardy-Hemery (1983).

experienced touts were commissioned to seek out Belgian workers who could be employed in the town's big carding factories, while 'large foreign contingents were sought for the first time' in the Lyon area as work picked up at the end of the century. Ironmasters wishing to exploit the Lorraine iron-ore deposits sent their recruiting agents to Italy.

The diversity of response to the reforms needed to restore calm in the working world gives some indication of employers' disarray in the face of powerful strike movements which often caught them unawares. Those areas where the working class was most effectively organised and where the conflicts were most significant provided the first outlines of a contractual policy, of which the miners' signing of the Arras Convention in 1891 offers the clearest example. Social catholicism expanded, particularly under the pressure of Léon Harmel, the supporter of the organised expression of workers' interests who recommended the creation of a large Christian party capable of opposing the French Labour Party (POF). Émile Cheysson, director of Le Creusot, criticised the traditional style of over-authoritarian paternalism. 'Employers' guardianship has had its day and now looks like an attack on freedom. Management is turning liberal on all sides under the influence of democratic progress; in its new form it subtracts nothing from the duties and sacrifices of employers, it simply offers a more appropriate expression of the nation's political and social circumstances.'[51] There were, however, numerous examples of employers' actions that flagrantly contradicted such fine words. Even at Le Creusot the 1899 strike was suppressed with ruthless ferocity; the union was destroyed. The policy of 'total control' was accentuated by reinforcing the company's hold over the whole of local activity, and by the proliferation of paternalistic-style associations. Although better standards of living had been encouraged during the preceding period with the intention of detaching workers from peasant values, henceforward there was an attempt to control workers' consumption in order to restrain incessant demands for wage rises. Schools of domestic arts were opened, where girls intended for domestic work could learn how to be content with what they had, and manage on it.[52]

51. Quoted by Peyronnard (1981), vol. 2, p. 23.
52. Three schools of household management were established at Le Creusot at this time, with François Coppée's maxim as their motto: 'Knowing how to be

Traditionally, the 'social question' was governed by force, demanding of those in power neither any great imagination nor any great need for knowledge of society, but which could sometimes bring about its downfall. The introduction of universal suffrage as a means of 'pacifying' the popular classes marks the birth of a system of integration requiring very different techniques of control.

Here too, at this opening period of the twentieth century, there is a crossroads. During these years when Clemenceau was Minister of the Interior, republican repression was seen on an unprecedented scale; hence his designation by the workers, who detested him, as 'France's head cop'.[53] The government's many efforts to conciliate the working class should, however, not be overlooked. The 'social question' took up a substantial proportion of the Third Republic's pre-1914 legislation and appreciable efforts were made to protect the work-force. Without covering this reasonably well-known ground, mention may be made of laws on industrial accidents (1898), relief funds in the mines (1894), reduction in length of the working day (1900), weekly rest-days (1906), and workers' and peasant's retirement pensions (1910). During the same period there were manifold attempts to encourage the development of genuine contractual relationships. The 1884 union law had the same purpose as universal suffrage: to drown the small extremist minority in the mass of 'peaceful' workers who were not concerned with power but simply wanted weapons capable of protecting them on purely corporate grounds; the same concern led to support for labour exchanges. At the end of the nineteenth century, notably under the influence of Millerand and the 'solidarist' tendency, this policy was strengthened. The very important law of 1892, which encouraged 'social partners' to seek arbitration from public bodies in regulating conflicts,[54] was extended by a whole series of regulations, at the head of which must be placed the Senior Labour Council, made up of a third each of employers' representatives, union officials, and civil servants.

One of the functions of this institution was to improve the flow of information between state and society. In fact, if a strategy of

---

content with modest means – therein lies wisdom and truth', quoted by Parize (1981), p. 157.

53. Julliard (1965).

54. According to E. Shorter and C. Tilly, 25 per cent of disputes between 1892 and 1904 were settled by arbitration: see Shorter and Tilly (1974).

power based on force can dispense with recognition of social realities, the strategy that boasts of universal suffrage and contractual relationships cannot afford such a luxury, and in this respect the contribution of intellectuals who favoured the Republic was highly significant. 'There have been profound changes, and over a very short period, in our social structures' stated Émile Durkheim, the founding father of university-level sociology which was then emerging in France. 'We are suffering not so much from ignorance of the theories on which previous practices were based as from the fundamental disturbance of certain aspects of these principles, leaving us with something new and unformed.'[55] Following this statement, Durkheim designates the development of new forms of social regulation as the ultimate sociological objective. The 'worker question' in France has, however, been primarily a political matter since the days of the July Monarchy, and therefore sociologists, anxious to enhance the reputation of a discipline still not entirely acceptable in the university world, prefer to take their stand on less controversial research. Although there are many surveys on the working world of this period they are for this reason generally the result of initiatives undertaken by national bodies (particularly the Ministry of Labour) and militant journalists.

It is worth noting that at the very moment when the revolutionary movement was insisting strongly on control of production, economists and sociologists intensified their investigation of matters concerning consumption. It was at this period that theorists defined norms of popular consumption, with the famous 'Engel's law' on the structure of workers' budgets, definitions which were laughed out of court by CGT militants. At the same time there was a proliferation of studies aimed at establishing ultimately reassuring correlations between economic circumstances and the number of strikes, although such a link is scarcely perceptible for the period under consideration.[56]

55. Durkheim (1967), p. 105.

56. The popular theatre, particularly in Pierre Hamp's play *L'Enquête*, satirised the sociological surveys carried out by economists and historians, contrasting working-class practices with the statistical working-class budget. None the less, following the strikes in 1910/11 against 'the high cost of living', the CGT took up the theme of 'domestic training'; see Flonneau (1970). Explanations for strikes based on economic circumstances appeared notably in articles published at the beginning of the century, in the *Revue d'Économie Politique* by Charles Rist and his team. On this point see also Bouvier (1964).

Amidst all such attempts to diagnose the malady should also be noted the development of the nationalist doctrine which found its most effective theoretical proponent in Maurice Barrès. Here was another possible solution to the problem of worker integration; Barrès responded to Marxist class principles with the principle of the nation which allowed the construction of a political consensus at the expense of the 'outsider'. The success of Boulangism in working-class circles during the economic crisis and the violence of the xenophobia then rife proved that this was no abstract notion: a fact which the twentieth century was to confirm in full measure.[57]

This was the context which saw protectionist laws voted in, due mainly to Jules Méline, as a concession to employers but also to the workers and above all to the peasant class, still numerically strong enough to be capable of making and unmaking governments at elections. The movement towards 'proletarianisation' therefore slackened as soon as it had begun, while at the same time expansion in heavy industry was held back for lack of labour.

The contemporary government's contradictory attitude can also be explained by the divergent interests of the various social groups which it sought to protect. The law on weekly rest-days, for example, was vigorously supported by the CGT union workers but violently attacked by small business employers who saw it adding to their expenses. Such social laws, together with the new militant style of speech consistently promoting the sole legitimacy of the factory worker at the expense of finishers and all intermediate categories, contributed to the decisive break which occurred at this time between the 'left' and the 'shop'. In Paris the 'democratic municipalism' of the descendants of the Commune veered to the right while the shopkeepers' movement fell under the thumb of the large employers and provincials.

All end-of-century legislative efforts thus tended to establish the individual in an increasingly rigid social hierarchy, and in this sense contributed to the modern definition of the working class. The backwardness of French social laws is too often evoked by quoting the 'egotism' of the managerial classes, but it should be emphasised that, as Henri Hatzfeld has shown, this paralysis was the result of differing concepts of bonus payments which were in conflict

57. Although restricted by the classic history of theories, the work of Zeev Sternhell provides many illustrations of the enduring themes of French nationalism; see in particular Sternhell (1983).

throughout the nineteenth century. From the time of the July Monarchy onwards Thiers was opposed to any law on the subject, not only in order to preserve this traditional domain from the interference of Christian philanthropy, but also because in his eyes the finest retirement pension any worker could have was the acquisition of a modest capital sum which would render him independent. In view of what has been shown in the preceding chapter about working-class behaviour it is understandable that such an attitude met with some response in French society. In present-day terms it might be said that the conservative opposition to social legislation urged by the republicans indicated resistance to any extension of 'the wage relationship' (to use Robert Boyer's expression), combining the legal guarantees of a statutory regulation and the generalised spread of cash bonuses, because this would result in lines of demarcation between social groupings: 'You must see, gentlemen', stated Thiers, 'what is wrong with your plan is that it divides the nation into two classes, separates them into two camps, wage-earners and employers. In reality the two camps are intermingled, the two classes blend together.' And he considered it a great drawback that the proposed law would exclude independent workers such as modest artisans and small employers, whose conditions were often worse than those of the wage-earners.[58]

The conclusion of this chapter turns to the worker movement's lack of decisiveness; it too was at a crossroads. Despite substantial popular militancy, those in power were never apparently in any real danger. Governmental concessions contributed to this state of affairs, and its strategies of integration or repression; but there were also internal reasons.

Beyond the proclaimed unanimity, the workers' collective identity was riven with numerous contradictions. Firstly, the new social pattern arising from universal suffrage was less than welcome to the inheritor of the French Revolution's 'sansculottes' with nearly a century's tradition of 'direct action'. Putting a voting-paper into a ballot box, entrusting his interests and ideas to a 'spokesman', all this made him one of the great dispossessed – which explains why these inheritors were critical of parliamen-

58. On this question, see Nord (1981); and, covering a longer period, Berstein (1980); on the stakes involved in social legislation, see Hatzfeld (1971), particularly pp. 83–8; the theory of 'wage differentials' is fully considered in Boyer (1985).

tarianism. Such criticism sharpened as the century drew to its end, as scandals tainted politicians, and also – especially – as strikes were repressed. But experience of the parliamentary game also reinforced, for elected representatives of working-class origins, the 'class instincts' of revolutionary socialists, in addition to their feeling that this kind of politics was 'not for them'. As has been shown in recent work, the elected worker was not slow to realise that Parliament is no neutral stage for equal debate. At a time when eloquence carried the day, working-class speech was sufficient to disqualify its user in the eyes of the greater number; for the elected representatives, even if 'on the side of the working class', were almost all from the bourgeois or lower middle-class backgrounds. This probably explains Jean-Baptiste Dumay's disappointment in parliamentary politics.[59] Those working-class representatives who accepted the new pattern generally underwent a gradual change, often becoming distinguished politicians – thus giving the advocates of direct action further proof of the system's evils.

This wish to continue to think and to act independently within the framework of small homogeneous groups, and above all separate from the intellectuals – whom these 'worker movement activists' held in distrust, which was also an instinct for self-preservation – explains their refusal to centralise and codify the worker movement, as advocated by, for example, the followers of Guesde who saw the proletariat as a disciplined army blindly obedient to commands from the 'leaders'. But by refusing to play the new political game they denied themselves the opportunities it offered for the collective representation of their interests as workers. This damaging result was intensified by the rejection of a vertical structure, depriving them of such useful tools as the POF or the industrial federations at union level.

The conflict between adherents of trade guilds and those who advocated federated industrial unions reached its peak in the first years of the new century. Weakened by the repression of the Commune (which claimed more victims than the revolutionary Terror) and by technological advances, organisations devoted to workers of a particular trade were still not defeated; evolution of the worker movement on American lines (based on trade corporatism) still appeared possible.

---

59. See Dumay (1976). See also analysis in Offerte (1984).

4

Factory, Suburb,
Housing Estate:
Here Comes
the Modern Worker!

It was not until the 1900–30 period that France experienced a true industrial surge forward into the leading group of developed nations. Between 1913 and 1929 the index of industrial production increased by 40 per cent which, according to Jean-Charles Asselain, 'placed France at the head of all the great industrialised nations (not excluding Germany or the United States) in terms of progress achieved between these two dates'.[1] The principal explanation for this dynamism was the vigorous development of new sectors of industry: in 1919 France ranked second in the world for aluminium production, and third for steel; in 1930 (which was, admittedly, an exceptional year) France actually led the whole world in iron-ore production.

The following pages indicate the extent of the transformation wrought in the working class by such advances, the factors which made it possible to get round the paralysis described above, and the subsequent birth of the world of work which is perhaps now in its final phase.[2]

---

1. Asselain (1984), p. 26.
2. Specifically political elements of this development appear in Chapter 5 on the Popular Front.

I. A Labour Market to be (Re)built

The expansion of the French economy began with the new century and picked up speed in the following decades, with the First World War playing an essential role in its development. The metal industry expanded considerably in the pre-war years through its links with armaments and this growth was further accelerated during the years of conflict. After 1918 the rebuilding of the nation provided the driving force for further expansion; the north and the east of the country, the vital centres of French heavy industry, had suffered particularly severe damage. In 1919:

> the devastated industrial zone extended over territory which in 1913 had provided 74 per cent of the nation's coal, 81 per cent of iron smelting, 63 per cent of steel, 55 per cent of forged iron, and 76 per cent of sugar – but only 25 per cent of engineering-construction businesses, which were generally established well away from the frontier.[3]

Apart from industrial capacity, there were whole towns to be rebuilt, including houses, schools, hospitals, and all other amenities.

The most dynamic expansion in such circumstances was seen, naturally enough, in sectors supplying capital plant and equipment, while consumer industries such as textiles remained stagnant.

Figure 4.1 illustrates how the work-force developed between 1906 and 1931 and reflects the imbalance in growth between the different sectors. As a total of those in work, the contrast with the preceding period is clear. In 25 years the number of workers in the active population grew from 7 million to 8.4 million. If agricultural workers are disregarded the growth is even more marked – from 4.3 to 6.3 million, a growth of two million workers; thus the proportion of the working class in the active population grew from 33.7 per cent to 38.8 per cent.

Examination of the work-force according to industrial sectors is highly instructive. Textiles, after employing 5 per cent of the working population throughout the nineteenth century, went through a net recession and were overtaken by metal-working; in 1930 each of these sectors employed 25 per cent of the total industrial work-force, heavily outnumbering all others. The metal

---

3. Caron (n.d.), p. 190.

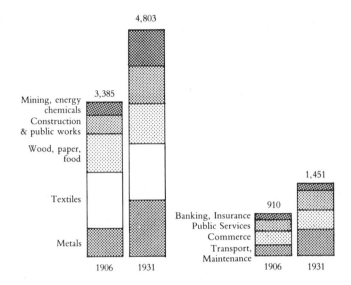

Figure 4.1 Changing Patterns of Distribution of Workers in Various Sectors of Employment between 1906 and 1931 (worker numbers in thousands)

Source: Toutain 1963.

industry gained most in numerical terms, expanding from approximately 600,000 workers in 1906 to 1.2 million in 1931. The detailed charts of the SGF's census counts show that although traditional sectors such as basic metal-processing were at a standstill, more modern areas were enjoying a dazzling expansion. The number of metal-working employees trebled, reaching 150,000 in 1931; motor vehicle manufacturing increased fivefold, to 100,000 workers in 1931, while electrical engineering multiplied 7.5 times, to 150,000 employees by the same date. Similar factors apply to the chemical industry, which doubled its numbers; match manufacturing was stagnant, but the labour-force in the general chemical industry – including such areas as acids and dyes – grew sevenfold, and by the end of the 1920s rubber manufacturing reached a total of 63,000 workers, representing an increase of 400 per cent. To these figures should be added the expansion in industries that were already substantial before the war, such as building and public works, with a manpower growth of 50 per cent, representing more than 800,000 workers in 1931, and above all in the mines, where numbers increased by 75 per cent between 1906 and 1931.

Expansion was equally substantial in the service sector, with an increase of more than 540,000 workers, notably in public services and transport. Employment on the railways reached its peak during the inter-war years, rising to 500,000.

This fresh expansion in various sectors of employment was matched by a corresponding shift in the ratio of businesses of differing sizes. During this period 41.5 per cent of new wage-earners were taken on by enterprises with more than 500 workers; in 1906, 60 per cent of wage-earners worked in establishments of fewer than 100 employees, but by 1931 the absolute majority were taken on by businesses with over 100 on their payroll, and 25 per cent worked in large factories of more than 500 people. At the same time the number of 'independent' workers fell to 12.7 per cent; 1.5 million had disappeared in 25 years, equal to 40 per cent of the 1906 working population.[4]

These figures illustrate the spectacular growth of big business. The enormous human concentration at Le Creusot, a notable exception in the late nineteenth century, was now typical of many French industrial regions. From 1913 onwards the Longwy steel works employed 6,500 workers; Citroën, with 4,500 workers in 1919, employed more than 31,000 in 1929. In 1898 Renault boasted six workers; in 1900 the figure was 110, by 1914 it was close to 4,400, rising to 14,600 in 1919 and more than 20,000 in 1930.[5] This was indeed the beginning of a new era in the history of the working class, further marked by substantial growth in urban populations; in 1931, for the first time more people lived in towns than in rural surroundings.

Finally, the economic expansion provoked a substantial realignment of the national industrial map. New vigorous sectors of employment came to join the old centres of work: steel in Lorraine, electrochemistry in the alpine valleys – many observers were struck by the abrupt change from a rural world to one of heavy industry, frequently referring to the 'Far West', or the 'French Texas'. But this was above all the time when all the great French cities gave birth to the suburbs which are so characteristic of the twentieth century. In this age of industrial maturity, factories were estab-

4. From Toutain (1963). Statistics on this period are much more reliable because of the strict comparability of census counts between 1896 and 1936.
5. Most of the facts on Renault and Citroën are taken from Depretto and Schweitzer (1984); Fridenson (1972); Schweitzer (1982); and Touraine (1955).

lished on the edges of large urban centres, creating residential areas and, in general terms, completely separate from town-centre inhabitants. The big factory and the suburb thus worked together to generate a world of work very different from that of the preceding era.

This was particularly apparent in the Paris area, where economic growth was very marked during this quarter-century, turning the capital into France's leading industrial area. Worker employment in mechanical engineering grew by 260 per cent, in electrical engineering by 500 per cent, in the dyeing industry by 220 per cent,[6] all leading to the development of large establishments on the edge of Paris, at Ivry, Saint-Denis, Aubervilliers, and Boulogne-Billancourt. The Lyon region was similarly affected, particularly at Vénissieux where rapid expansion in the chemical industry, and above all in metal-working, deeply disrupted the prevailing socio-economic balance: where in 1873 one-third of its inhabitants gained their living from agriculture, by 1931, 80 per cent of the commune's active population were employed as factory operatives.[7]

The preceding chapter gave some indication of how the labour market was disturbed by the new sectors of employment symbolising the 'second industrial revolution' – the source of many problems for employers. In the following decades the shortage of labour reached even greater proportions; in effect, two million more workers were needed over 25 years to satisfy the demands of a dynamic economy. Over the same period the number of actively employed workers, in approximate terms, also grew by 40 per cent, filling roughly one million more jobs; the civil service in particular grew by over 50 per cent, reaching a total figure of nearly 500,000 in 1931. Yet during this quarter century the active population increased by only 900,000; and in addition working-class Malthusianism, which had become apparent at the end of the century, grew and spread. Carefully detailed calculations have shown that, among couples who married between 1920 and 1934, the average number of children born during the first ten years of marriage was 1.8, taking all social categories together, and 1.85 for the working class taken separately. Even in France's Black Country, where the miners had previously proved their enthusiasm for family life, the birthrate fell noticeably during the inter-war years.[8]

6. From Ariès (1971), p. 161.
7. See Videlier (1984), p. 30.
8. See Ariès (1971), pp. 105–6.

To this were added new constraints. There was the eight-hour law which reduced each worker's daily productivity; but above all there were the dramatic consequences of the First World War, estimated to have deprived the nation of 3.3 million active individuals, either directly – by death in battle – or indirectly – through disablement or chronic incapacity. Consequently, when the call to work came in 1919 and France's need of workers was greater than ever before, there was a 10 per cent shortfall in the industrial labour-force.

For those workers who had escaped the massacre the state of the labour market was extremely favourable. In the *Revue d'Économie Politique* for 1928 William Oualid gave a factual account of the problem. Calculating that the total deficit resulting from the war was four million people, he stated that:

> The result is that the survivors, trained workers or senior employees, are mainly occupied in positions of management, supervision or responsibility, or in tasks requiring an advanced technical qualification, such as precision work or design. Elsewhere, the growth of new industries such as automótive engineering, electrical industry, transport, and the growth of new jobs, draws on the limited supply of men aged between 40 and 55 and also requires back-up from the younger groups. Thus there is a sort of promotion or advancement of national elements in the professional hierarchy.[9]

This is evidence of the main reasons for the scale of turnover during these years. The scale of reconstruction turned whole areas of northern and eastern France into a vast building site. The mass of small and medium-sized construction companies maintained a pool of skilled workers who were constantly on the move from one employer to another, taking advantage of better wages and also the ceaseless launching of new firms and closing down of others as buildings, houses and other amenities were completed. In the Valenciennes region Odette Hardy-Hemery refers to a veritable carousel of workers within the local labour market. It was even more difficult to find staff for a large undertaking such as the Denain steel factory; the war had caused a 12-year close-down and it had thus lost all advantages gained from the pre-war policy of worker stabilisation.[10] Similar problems sprang up everywhere in

9. Oualid (1928).
10. Hardy-Hemery (1983).

France; in the Sambre valley, a large centre of metal processing, 'recruitment has been difficult since the war. There is a shortage of trained men in the area . . ., a black cloud on the Maubeuge horizon which inevitably causes misgivings as to the future'. A general report quoted by Marthe Barbance on the naval shipyards of Saint-Nazaire emphasises the delays in production caused by the shortage of workers: 'Finding operatives was difficult. The whole of France lacked specialists in the new techniques, the riveters, turners, metal edgers and scarfers.'[11]

The destabilising effects of the war further exacerbated this lack of permanence. Apart from the millions of Frenchmen who were mobilised and sent to the front, there were many who were forced to move, principally from the north and the east, by the German occupation; and thousands of workers escaped active service only to be sent to factories carrying out war work. Many firms threatened by the war moved to other areas during the period of hostilities (mainly to the Paris region, but also to Nantes, Lyon and other cities) to become 'war factories'. Metal-works, chemical works and mines outside the occupied zones were, however, heavily utilised: 20,000 people were employed in the Schneider factories at Le Creusot in 1917, which was an increase of 38 per cent since 1914. Many workers were from the Paris area or the Nord, contributing to the spread of unfamiliar working-class values. The coal mines in the Gard were similarly affected; during the First World War the number on the payroll increased by 35 per cent, with 1,500 prisoners of war and 1,500 miners from the Nord arriving in the midst of a hitherto entirely local working population. There too the war 'aided contact and interaction, the inter-relation tending to lead to uniformity of worker behaviour and changes in traditional attitudes'.[12]

Practical confrontation of this type was helpful to the most modern sectors of employment, where qualifications and wages were highest, principally in mechanical engineering in the Paris area. Worker migration developed on a greater scale as firms set up veritable 'man-hunts' in the older employment zones where earlier paternalism had established a body of skilled labour. Renault sent recruiting teams from Billancourt, in Paris, to trawl through the Nord, Le Creusot, Hayange and Lorraine. Emissaries came to

11. On Maubeuge, see Matton (1927); on Saint-Nazaire, see Barbance (1948).
12. On Le Creusot, see Parize (1981); on the Gard, see Huard (1978).

Saint-Nazaire for some on-the-spot recruiting, with advertisements in the journal *Le Travailleur de l'Ouest*; the result was a veritable exodus during the 1921 recession to more active industrial zones such as Caen or the liberated zones. In the post-war years 18,000 miners moved from the Nord to employment in the Paris region, while the legendary stability of the work-force at Le Creusot was severely challenged, with 5,000 workers leaving between 1920 and 1923 – almost 30 per cent of the total work-force. One witness recalls that 'there were real Le Creusot colonies in some districts who came [to Paris] through the agency of well-organised networks, working mainly for Renault and encountering a different kind of working world with genuine unionisation'.[13]

II. Two Popular Solutions to the Poverty Problem: Work Rationalisation and Immigration

Mechanisation and Taylorism

Although French nineteenth-century employers were famous for their caution in the face of technological innovation, there were abrupt changes during the first decades of the twentieth century. According to Edmond Malinvaud France achieved a greater rate of industrial mechanisation between 1906 and 1931 than either the United States or Great Britain, putting it on a par with Germany. The total power of primary engines increased by 14 per cent per annum while in the outstanding decade following the war all records of productivity were broken by a growth rate of 2.8 per cent between 1924 and 1929.[14]

Coal mining in the Nord was typical, with mechanised production rising from 4 per cent in 1913 to 86 per cent in 1927, and the pattern was similar in motor manufacturing: Citroën had 3,450 machine tools in 1919 – and 12,260 ten years later.

Almost all branches of production could quote parallels, notably steel and the chemical industry. Significantly, this mechanisation was increasingly seen in combination with Taylorism, as developed by the American engineer Taylor at the beginning of the twentieth century. The first phase of the process, tried out in France in the

13. Quoted from the debate at Le Creusot in May 1976, of which the main points appeared as, 'Au Pays de Schneider', in *Le Mouvement Social*, no. 99 (1977).
14. Carré, Dubois and Malinvaud (n.d.), p. 70.

years leading up to the war and notably at Renault, consisted of timing physical labour in order to eliminate wasted time. In the Nord the Anzin company used the system to reduce the time taken by miners to reach their place of work; next they reorganised work by introducing 'extended face cutting' which replaced flexibility of occupation, and team activity by specialisation and individualis-ation of operations.[15]

Scientific management was introduced above all in construction engineering in the 1920s. The procedure has been fully described in relation to the naval shipyards of Saint-Nazaire, and can be sum-marised as follows: the first trials, in 1916, brought home to engineers the difficulty of maintaining control over a production process involving 55 different skilled trades, all completely inde-pendent of each other. For this reason their first concern was to replace the 'old machines which only the operatives could get to work satisfactorily' with modern equipment and standardised tools. Elsewhere they decided on a complete reconstruction of the stock of separate items. An industrial design department and a parts list service were set up for this purpose, to break down to its simplest elements the entire range of parts needed to construct a ship. In each case these services were required to supply an exact plan with directions for tooling which the operator must follow down to the smallest detail, and in addition the management set up a time section to break down into basic units. A list of instructions assigned to each operation the speed of execution, the nature of the item, and how to make it, with a summarising 'follower' sheet to go to the operative's central office, in order to calculate the bonus – paid to the worker who accomplished his task within a shorter time than that allotted – to be added to his fixed wage.

This system was a fundamental challenge to the independence of skilled workers and also of the foremen. 'Before the war', notes Marthe Barbance, 'in order to establish the workman's machining time, the foremen and senior workmen were consulted, who were considered to have the necessary experience to make all sorts of decisions on time and cost. Their reference documents were gener-ally simple notebooks tucked away at the back of a drawer and usually entirely lacking suitable allowances for relevant working conditions.'

15. Hardy-Hemery (1984); on Taylorism, see also de Montmollin and Pastré (eds) (1984); and Murard and Zylberman (1978).

From the management point of view the efficacy of the new system was undeniable: a repair time calculated by a foreman by the old method at 12,000 hours of work was reduced by the time section to 4,600 hours through a scientific analysis of operations.[16]

Rationalisation had enormous consequences for worker occupation as exercised in earlier days. The absence of overall professional statistics prevent any precise assessment of its effect on employment, but it was widely observed and noted that the system modified the demand for new workers for the greatly increased production. In construction, for example, 'in the Rhône as in the Seine, in the Nord and elsewhere, public works industry everywhere was profoundly affected by technical progress. The use of excavators, mechanical shovels, rollers and tar-spreaders, and other machines, reduced labouring jobs by an estimated 30 or 40 per cent'.[17] In the textile industry the new Northrop looms with automatic shuttle change enabled an operator who supervised six looms in 1920 to be in charge of 14 or 16 ten years later. In steel manufacturing, mechanised loading of blast furnaces or metal strip rolling meant large-scale redundancy in labouring employment. Jobs requiring traditional qualifications, the most difficult to fill in France, disappeared on an equally large scale, affecting metal forgers, textile doublers, boilermen in the steel industry, glass-blowers, and other similar craftsmen. Even the new skilled work for trained operatives, such as mechanics, adjusters or assemblers – the majority of employees in the Renault factory at the beginning of the century – represented no more than 70 per cent in 1914, and by the end of the 1920s skilled workers were no longer an absolute majority of employees in this particular company.[18] The change was particularly favourable to the machinists and those workers known in the automobile industry as 'comparable', who would after 1936 be known as 'unskilled', undertaking the most easily learnt jobs. They made up a third of the Renault labour force in 1913, and more than 53 per cent in 1925. In the Lorraine steel industry their numbers doubled in 20 years.

But technological advances also brought an increase in new skilled jobs. In the heavy-metal and chemical industries mechanisation demanded increasing numbers of maintenance workmen,

16. Barbance (1948), p. 416.
17. Letellier et al. (1938–1949), vol. 1.
18. Touraine (1955), p. 84.

almost unknown at the end of the nineteenth century, who constituted up to a third of employees by 1930. In the vehicle industry it
was the tool makers and adjusters who gained most from Taylorism changes. Further, the ever-increasing application of scientific
methods in industry led to a great increase in monthly-paid staff. In
1927 only two-thirds of the employees in the Citroën factories in
the Paris area were directly involved in manufacturing, the remainder being concerned with setting up the work or checking operations. The proportion of Renault's monthly-paid workers grew
from 6.5 per cent to 11.7 per cent of the total work-force between
1919 and 1927. Although in 1896 the Longwy steelworks had only
45 salaried staff, in the broad sense, against 2,800 'workers', their
numbers had grown to approximately 650 by 1930: from 2 per cent
of the total to nearly 12 per cent. Apart from those properly called
office staff there was the training staff, known at that time as
'colleagues' rather than managers, personnel working in the lab-
oratories set up by each large factory close to its workshops. On a
national scale, the total of these professions, known to the SGF as
'industrial salaried staff', grew from 220,000 in 1906 to 560,000 in
1931.

Large-scale immigration

Rationalisation of work patterns certainly reduced the dramatic
consequences of the shortage of manpower; mechanisation
superseded many operational tasks, and frequently simplified the
work of trained workmen. Such a solution could, however, never
be more than one strand of a much broader strategy for recruiting
fresh workers.

The first plentiful source of supply for industrial leaders was the
peasant world, where more than 8.8 million people were still
actively engaged in 1906. The upheavals of the war led to a
greatly accelerated rural exodus during the 1920s: over one million
people left their rural roots, particularly agricultural or self-
employed workers. Philippe Ariès's research on the Paris region
shows that a substantial proportion of the increased suburban
population came from a rural background. A province such as
Brittany contributed thousands of pairs of hands to the great
factories of Saint-Denis or Aubervilliers between the beginning of
the century and the 1930s, to other factories in the suburbs of
Nantes, and even to the Michelin works at Clermont-Ferrand; this

firm carried out mass recruitment of unskilled workers throughout western France. Ariès also shows, however, that during the 1920s it was no longer a matter of escaping genuine poverty, for the movement was relatively independent of economic circumstances. In many cases it was more of a deliberate choice following the broadening of horizons during the war years; for this reason, although some migrants swelled the numbers of the working class, many moved towards other professional spheres and in particular to public service. Pierre Bastié suggests that a substantial number of families moving from the occupied zones after losing their land or the head of the family, such as war widows or disabled ex-servicemen, came to settle in the Paris area to take advantage of the administrative jobs reserved for these categories.[19]

The solution of employing women, widely tried during the preceding period, seemed less and less appropriate. The working female population grew little in overall terms between 1906 and 1931; in industry numbers even diminished slightly, from 34.1 per cent to 28.4 per cent, while the number of women workers in the tertiary sector increased by 300,000 jobs. Although more numerous in metal-working, where numbers trebled in 25 years, there were 350,000 fewer women working in the textile industry even though this sector was still very much the leading area of female employment, with 75 per cent of the industrial total in 1931.

For all these reasons massive immigration became essential after the war. In the ten years between 1920 and 1931 more than a million foreign workers – representing two million people, with their families – were brought into France to make up three-quarters of the losses due directly to the war; by 1930 immigrants made up 15 per cent of the working class in France. It must be emphasised that these figures are only approximate since census methods of counting foreigners were still in their infancy, and in addition the recession already developing in 1931 encouraged some of the recently recruited foreign workers to return home. Finally, there was massive unofficial immigration, estimated by Georges Mauco as equal to a third of official immigrant numbers. Even if many such workers regularised their status once settled in France, it is obvious that anyone whose position was more or less illegal would do much to avoid census counts.[20]

19. Bastié (1964), p. 232.
20. This is why surveys based on company personnel registers generally show a greater proportion of foreign workers than those based on census figures.

The census figures should therefore be taken as a minimum; yet the scale of demand for immigrant workers in certain sectors of employment is remarkable. In the mines, for example, immigrants represented 6.5 per cent of the labour force in 1906 and 42 per cent in 1931. In heavy-metal industries the proportion rose from 18.4 to 38.2 per cent; in excavating and earth moving, from 11 to 29 per cent. Even in traditional industries based on women working at home, such as the clothing trade, immigrants henceforward played a large part, with 17 per cent of the total in 1931.

It is unfortunate that the statistics of this period cannot specify the proportion of foreign workers according to their qualifications. This would give a more substantial basis to the almost unanimous affirmations of contemporary observers, summarised by Philippe Ariès as follows: 'In France, after 1918, foreigners acquired a near-monopoly of wearisome or distasteful work, abandoned by the native Frenchman.' Referring to the Paris area he observes that 'these social elements are not absent; building and metallurgy recruit their operatives for heavy work among foreigners, Italians, Poles, North African Arabs'.[21] In the south-east an academic observer noted before the Second World War that the French were increasingly becoming a managerial élite; 'the popular masses are from another race, immigrant Italians'. In all sectors, the more unattractive the work the more numerous the foreigners. They provided almost all underground labour in the Lorraine iron-ore works; and in the Nord-Pas-de-Calais foreigners made up 17 per cent of surface workers compared with 46 per cent underground. Few in number in the car industry immediately after the war, they arrived *en masse* as rationalisation spread and took effect. At the Berliet works near Lyon, for example, the work-force was 70 per cent French in 1921; ten years later more than half the workers were immigrants. At Pont-à-Mousson in Meurthe-et-Moselle almost all the labour was French at the time of the great strikes in 1905; by 1930, when the skilled artisan work of the metal caster had given way to conveyor-belt production, more than 50 per cent of the work-force consisted of foreigners.[22]

The link shown earlier between immigration and the mobility of French workers must be appreciated in order to understand the social significance of this phenomenon, as noted by William Oualid

21. Ariès (1971), p. 186.
22. On Vénissieux, see Videlier and Bouhet (1983), pp. 204–5; on Pont-à-Mousson, see Baudant (1980).

in the article quoted above:

> This abandonment of disagreeable work, this rise up the professional ladder, left a gap at ground level which must be filled at all costs, by elements summoned from elsewhere. The consequence was a phenomenon similar to that long since noted in the United States: foreigners, and in particular the latest arrivals, were taken on to do any work that did not require specialised or trained skills or trade apprenticeships.

In stressing this factor it is reasonable to look at the contribution of massive immigration in the 1920s to the process of unlocking the labour market which was characteristic of the period. As already indicated, the combination of favourable circumstances had allowed the working classes to resist economic change in the nineteenth century; such changes were based on post-Revolutionary democratic rights and above all on universal suffrage, forcing successive governments into compromises which increased the labour market's inflexibility. The majority of these problems undoubtedly vanished with the arrival of the immigrant workers; moreover it is strikingly apparent that although much was granted to French citizens in terms of human rights, it was at the expense of those who did not belong to the nation. In the inter-war years not only were immigrants denied fundamental political rights, they were ineligible to take part in trade elections even where, as in the iron-ore fields, they made up the overwhelming majority of workers. France's immigration policy seems to have been very much less liberal than that of the United States at the beginning of the century and, despite official speeches on the freedom of labour, many foreign workers were held in a veritable legal straitjacket. After the First World War the state and large industry worked together to channel immigrants carefully into those sectors of the labour market that were most disliked by French workers. Recruiting agents travelled to countries of emigration to select manpower and direct foreigners towards the great concentrations of heavy industry, bound by contract and caught in a web of administrative decrees designed to keep them where they were most needed. Between 1890 and 1930 the foreign national was subject to a reversal of the universalist values of the French Revolution; as Georges Mauco notes, 'the exercise of each individual's right to dispose of his person and his destiny', considered an 'inalienable' right by jurists in the 1880s, yielded to close police surveillance. By 1930 the immigrant had lost 'a large part of his individual liberties. . . . He was subject to permanent supervision, and anything concerning his wages or the place and nature of his work was subject to French administrative directives. Without authorisation he could neither move house nor change his job.'[23]

This dependence on very large-scale immigration during the 1920s became one of the primary sociological factors underlying the boom in French industry during those years. Immigrant workers were, moreover, most numerous in the most dynamic sectors, with the greatest profits. Economists of the inter-war years were well aware of the advantages to the nation's industry of this type of manpower: 'It is undeniable', notes William Oualid, 'that the introduction of a fully-trained adult endows the nation with an immediately productive element, and his education has cost the community nothing (birth, maintenance, education, apprenticeship, etc.).'[24] Such workers were also highly adaptable to changing conditions, offering the labour market a flexibility which the French economy had not known for many years; and, as will be shown, large-scale immigration had a reductive effect on wages which is not without relevance to the scale of benefits gained.

III. New Divisions in the Labour Market

Staffing policies in heavy industry

It was in the mines, in steel, in the electrochemical and electrometallurgical establishments of the Alps and the Pyrenees, sectors absolutely essential to the development of a modern economy, that labour problems were most pressing. The first reason for this is technical: such undertakings were effectively forced to remain close to their primary materials or sources of energy and so were frequently in isolated or harsh settings. The Péchiney factories and power stations at Maurienne, in the Alps, for example, were described as 'cells superimposed on primitive terrain'.[25] Elsewhere, basic industry did not require large numbers of trained 'modern' workers, for, despite mechanisation, most jobs at this time were still for manual workers. Jobs for trained production workers always required practical experience gained through actual work by

23. Mauco (1932), p. 132.
24. Oualid (1928).
25. Rambaud and Vincienne (1964), p. 149.

means of a long apprenticeship, and were often physically demanding. The labour famine which developed at the end of the nineteenth century encouraged young French workers away from such harshly undervalued trades: hence the recruitment problems which were exacerbated by almost uninterrupted expansion in such sectors up to 1930.

Without embarking on a detailed analysis of the iron industry in Lorraine (which has been developed elsewhere)[26] it is valuable to look at the solutions adopted by its managers; they were to be of great significance in the development of the working class in this sector in subsequent decades.

The basis was the system of dividing up the work-force by intensive recourse to foreign workers. In the mines, for example, the departure of French workers demanded the immigration of a settler population, designed to secure a body of trained miners for the establishment; hence the Nord coal-mines' recruitment of whole families of trained Polish miners, imported from Rhine-Westphalia where the German employers had settled them before 1914. But immigration fulfilled even more satisfactorily the demand for manual workers, highly prized by managers for their strength and youth, and who therefore did not need to settle permanently in one place. In such circumstances the Nord mining companies recruited 'bachelor' peasants directly from Poland, and where there were sufficient numbers of French workers immigration policy was restricted to manpower of this type. Thus at the end of the 1920s foreigners supplied 20 per cent of the total work-force in Le Creusot, from widely diverse nationalities including Chinese, North African Arabs, and Ukrainians, living in 'bachelor' hutments. Michelin at Clermont-Ferrand had the same arrangement, with only 2,800 immigrant manual workers out of a total work-force of 17,500; numerous working-class housing estates surrounded the town and the overall 'Michelin system' was designed for families who had emigrated from Brittany or the Massif Central.

Heavy industry was more heavily dependent on worker-peasants. In the coal-mines they provided the majority of French nationality coal-face workers, and in the steelworks, with their longstanding local connections, they often supplied a large proportion of traditional skilled workers. Right up to the 1960s whole

26. Noiriel (1984), chapter IV.

sections at the Denain-Anzin factory drew on trained workers from the surrounding villages. Thus the foundry metal casters mostly came from the village of Douchy, the laminators from the Avesne-les-Aubert rolling-mills, and so on.[27] This form of worker management based on complementary blends of immigrants and rural workers was even encountered occasionally in processing industries; Peugeot specifically refused to settle in the Paris region in order to avoid repeated strikes. Benefiting from a long-established labour-force trained in cutlery and clockmaking, they chose to settle instead at Sochaux, near the Swiss border, and base their expansion on employing foreign operatives – a quarter of the total number in 1930 – supplemented by trained workers with rural roots. This is one of the reasons suggested for the 'social tranquillity' of the area before 1936.

All firms in this sector, however, maintained a greater or smaller core of French workers who were closely integrated into the factory, preferably living in the town or in the new 'garden housing estates' which had been built for them. They were primarily to be found doing the modern skilled jobs in the maintenance sector, as mechanics, adjusters, or electricians, where numbers had expanded with mechanisation. In the mines they made up a large proportion of surface workers. Their presence can also be explained by the fact that they, or members of their families, could rise easily to managerial positions (foreman, salaried staff, or even engineers for those who had done well in the company's own school) or to the *petite-bourgeoisie* of trade and local artisan crafts, which was also expanding with the growth of the population.

The segmentation of the local labour market helps to explain the revival of paternalism during the 1920s after being discredited in earlier years. The paradox, frequently mentioned as a cause of worker 'disenchantment' at the beginning of the century, between the need for direct relationships linking employer and employees, and the increasingly large size of firms which fostered anonymity, here found its solution. The system of task and bonus was henceforward reserved for a small number of employees, those whose continued presence was desirable because their skills were necessary; divisions developed on a basis of familial criteria and were apparent in differing styles of living. Manual operatives, treated as

27. On the recruitment of Polish miners, see Hardy-Hemery (1983), and Ponty (1985); on the worker-peasants at the Denain factory, see Veltz (1982), p. 89.

unmarried men, were gathered together in barrack-style housing or hastily built hostels, away from other people. At Le Creusot, for example, 'the only people excluded from settling in the town were foreign workers (Chinese, Italians, Polish) who lived in distant camps'.[28] The division was reinforced by a new pay policy, with workers' remuneration in future split in two: the wage proper was to 'recompense', according to the specialists, the workers' 'professional value', and the 'family allowance' indicated recognition of his 'social value'. The tendency during the 1920s was to reduce the former element in favour of the latter.[29]

The other great dividing factor in the work-force, which often accentuated the first, lay in the criterion of nationality. In heavy industry the employers' hegemony increased considerably during the inter-war years, following the disintegration of old communities which had earlier been united in their struggles against the company. The 'releasing' of the labour market favoured attempts to recreate a consensus because it operated in favour of French workers. Elsewhere the trauma of the war strongly reinforced the policy of national loyalty at the expense of foreigners. Further, as Max Weber has shown in respect to poor white American workers vis-à-vis black Americans, working-class xenophobia is explicable because the 'social honour' of the group most nearly corresponding to the dominant norms depends on disparaging newer arrivals, those who appear different.[30] It therefore only needed the managerial classes to emphasise such tendencies for the divisions in the working class world to deepen. The many 'company' celebrations, from honouring 11 November to the banquet for retired workers, via distributing the prizes at the apprentice school, were so many opportunities for the managing director to make his presence felt and demonstrate his benevolent deeds publicly to the small group of 'selected' workers. As John Condevaux has commented with reference to the Lens mines, all these occasions helped the worker to understand that his usually distant boss was a man like other men, simple, approachable, thoroughly good natured.[31]

28. Parize (1981), p. 89.
29. Villey (1927).
30. Weber (1969), p. 419.
31. J. Condevaux comments that at these informal feasts 'the miner would be surprised to find his boss a cheerful and friendly man, not what he had expected of someone important, and it is not unreasonable to say that he developed great enthusiasm for him' (Condevaux 1928, p. 47).

Policies of giving medals to workers, long-service awards, or prizes for the best gardens, were part of an overall effort designed to reinforce the skilled workers' interest in the business, and presupposed isolation from other centres of employment. For this reason the large factories preferred to avoid the cities, whose social diversity might present workers with other models. The mono-industry characteristic of such regions was therefore a fundamental consequence of the shortage of labour. Similarly, the rooted stability of the work-force, particularly in areas such as Lorraine or the Nord where there was intense competition between companies to lure workers away, could only develop with very strict demarcation of recruitment zones. Each establishment therefore had its own 'fiefdom', a territory where it had basic control over employment, where it performed its 'social works', and where it built its housing and its hospital.

This style of staff management proved extremely costly; hence the need to keep wages very low and to preserve non-monetary forms of bonus, so that it was virtually essential for each working family to have a garden or even a field to cultivate. Worker-peasants and mobile immigrant workers offered other means of limiting the expenses of training and maintaining the work-force.

Other forms of labour management

Problems of labour recruitment were much less pressing in other sectors of employment. By reason of their history and the demands of production three main types of labour market can be identified.

Companies in the new processing industries preferred to be based near the big cities, and in particular near Paris, so as to draw on their immense reservoir of workers. This sector demanded many workers with skills in line with new scientific and technological advances, preferably with the added attraction of a professional training. In mechanical engineering the workers' artisan knowledge of nineteenth-century small-scale metal-work was still of considerable value, and from this worker élite, mostly to be found in the great cities, came the highly qualified work-force of the great factories at Boulogne-Billancourt, Saint-Denis, or Ivry. This élite was, however, present to an even greater degree in the vast mass of subcontracting businesses which gravitated round the giants, and which provided a kind of refuge for the descendants of the older skilled artisans, providing shelter from some of the effects of industrial restructuring. It has been estimated that the metal-working industry in the Paris area in 1925 included more than 11,000 firms with fewer than 20 wage-earners.[32]

The urban labour market could also accommodate 'the large numbers of unskilled manual workers. The principle known as 'Ravenstein's Law' showed that since the end of the nineteenth century migrants, when given the choice, tended to seek the nearest large conurbation with its wider range of employment opportunities. The majority of those leaving their rural homes in Brittany, the Massif Central, or elsewhere, headed for the Paris area, as did many foreign workers. The fact that immigration was organised by and for heavy industry did not prevent a large number of foreigners avoiding it. Many came in by their own means, legitimate or otherwise, from the countries bordering France, others, after brief experience of the paternalist fiefdom, broke their work contract. Such workers were drawn to the cities in their hundreds of thousands like moths to the light, and provided manufacturers with cheap and abundant labour. The city of Marseille, with a population which was already 20 per cent Italian in 1914 and which became increasingly cosmopolitan during the 1920s, can be compared in this respect with the great American cities where the 'law of the jungle' governed the interaction of supply and demand.

A third advantage for this branch of manufacturing of reserves of diversified labour in the great urban centres was that demand was insufficient to ensure regular production throughout the year. In the motor-manufacturing industry, for example, employment remained seasonal because the clientèle was still restricted to the prosperous classes and to the rural world;[33] this led to widespread redundancy after the Motor Show and renewed demands for staff in the spring.

Despite the shortage of skilled workers, as everywhere in France during the 1920s, the more attractive type of work and the higher wages combined with the size and variety of population available so that the worker needs of the great urban manufacturers were satisfied without the need for great efforts to recruit or retain manpower. In the Marseille region, for example, the large companies had no strategy for stabilising the immigrant population; organis-

32. Lojkine and Viet-Depaule (1983), p. 60 *et seq.*
33. Similarly in the naval construction world; when a ship was completed, 40 per cent of the workers were discharged. See Bleitrach and Cornu (1979).

ations that were independent of management, client-based or company-orientated concerned themselves with new arrivals, particularly in the docks. Even at Port-de-Bouc, where the naval shipyards were the big employers, the management did not seek a monopoly hold over the labour market, investing in neither urban amenities nor local political activities;[34] nor did Renault have any real policy of worker housing at this time. The work-force being greater than in heavy industry, there was even an attempt, alongside work rationalisation, at a modern Taylorian type of policy of 'scientific selection' of staff based on psycho-technological tests and recruitment registers.

In those industrial sectors that had already seen substantial development before the war, old forms of manpower management generally changed little. The ending of seasonal migration in the construction industry opened up many prospects for immigrants, notably Italians, who in some areas held a quasi-monopoly of jobs. This was a sector where the still very numerous small companies offered a refuge for the old 'guild' workers such as joiners, carpenters and stonemasons.

The world of the textile industry already appeared stable. The size of establishments, their locale, their degree of mechanisation, would not vary greatly from the beginning of the century until the 1950s, apart from the hosiery sector where worker numbers doubled between 1906 and 1931 and which became increasingly concentrated in the Aube *département*, and the artificial-silk industry which employed 34,000 people at the end of the 1920s compared with 9,000 25 years earlier.

This stability strengthened workers' traditions in the textile industry. When Belgian immigration in the Nord ceased at the end of the nineteenth century the urban growth which had been spectacular since the July Monarchy stopped too; the population was settled, and paternalism in textiles took root too. The size of Roubaix companies, which had impressed the observers of the preceding period, now seemed modest, suited to the 'family' style of the establishments where employers and workers had known each other for many years. The pattern in the Vosges or in Normandy was similar: the isolation of factories in rural surroundings encouraged rooted stability and paternalism. Generally in light industry the major factor may have been the reorganisation of some

34. Bonnault-Cornu (1981).

sectors to the advantage of certain large establishments. Shoe manufacturing in the Paris area, for example, developed large mechanised workshops with enormous capital sums invested in advanced automated systems resulting in mass-production. The low-skilled work-force consisted mainly of immigrants or rootless rural workers; luxury shoes, meanwhile, were still being made by small manufacturers employing older workers with the appropriate skills.

The proliferation of large mechanised manufacturing workshops explains the melting away of the sector's work-force, with a loss of 500,000 jobs in 20 years. Henceforward work at home was the source of income mainly for the marginal sectors where profits were least predictable, and the majority of central European Jews or Armenians were taken on here.[35]

The limited scale of consumer demand for everyday products also explains why very large numbers of such establishments remained in their rural setting. Sometimes it would be the large factories that decided to cut back part of their rural production, following the pattern described in the preceding chapter; in the Aube, for example, employers considered that beyond a certain size a business became unmanageable because of the high proportion of 'wastage', repeated strikes, and the 'unassailable' efficiency which must be demonstrated to sustain the business. Hence the dispersal of manufacturing to finishers in the area.[36] A rural setting was thus supposed to supply the resources that were lacking in times of unemployment. Until 1930 clockmaking remained a world dominated by small business; out of a national total of 4,700 establishments, 1,200 proprietors worked alone and only two had more than 500 employees. In Besançon, the leading French watch and clockmaking centre, workmen were unemployed from January to March, while in the Aude hat-making industry work was not available on average for more than seven months a year. Even in the Mulhouse wool-spinning and printing works, the classic mid nineteenth-century industries, work slackened in the summer. A

35. Green (1985); also Hyman (1979).
36. Riccomard (1934), p. 143 *et seq*. The late 1920s was also the peak period for the main textile factory in Romorantin (the Normant establishment, with 1,200 wage-earners), a model of paternalism in rural surroundings: 'The worker-peasants began work early in the morning so that they could spend time at the end of the day cultivating their plots of land, and could take days off individually for the heavy work there.' (Bachelard 1978, p. 96).

1936 survey showed that 'in times of prosperity, and when there was no unemployment allowance, spinning and printing employees would work at earth moving from April to the end of August'. In general the Alsace region seems to have retained much on the traditional pattern of multiple employment. 'The Bruche valley, poor in agricultural terms, was not sufficiently productive to sustain farmers through agriculture alone. Thus with few exceptions they all worked in factories or alternatively found supplementary work as lumberjacks.'[37] In the villages round Caudry, in the Nord, in the valleys of the Aa, Avesnois and Cambrésis rivers, where most work was for export, factory-plus-farming made it possible to cope with the vagaries of circumstance through the traditional solution of supplementing agriculture with industrial work.

The last significant type of labour market in France during the 1920s was the 'protected' work-force, very often statute-controlled. It usually included trades with a strong professional inheritance, with an almost complete absence of foreign workers – for example, workers in certain traditional trades, such as printing, successfully preserving traditional corporatist practices which enabled them to control the labour market and benefit from collective agreements. But this protected sector mainly concerned workers in the public sector, working in the arsenals, in state-controlled manufacturing, or in postal communications, and those who benefited from state-backed statutory conditions, such as railway workers after 1920; the railways were a favourite prospective place of work for the rural French.

IV. Working Life

Two central themes characterise workers' daily life in the 1920s: lack of roots, and compartmentalisation.

Profound destabilisation

The specific effects of the 'second industrial revolution' combined with those of the war to achieve a complete transformation in French working life.

---

37. Braun (1938), p. 60.

The influx of population was the first factor contributing to rootlessness. Within the space of 20 years the population of the *départeme.it* of the Seine increased by 35 per cent, and that of Seine-et-Oise by 48 per cent. Although communes near Paris, such as Ivry or Saint-Denis, gained most of their increase before the war, the population expanded sharply in many areas in the post-war years. Between 1921 and 1926 the number of inhabitants in the commune of Bobigny increased by 13.8 per cent per year; the years from 1906 to 1931 saw a sevenfold increase. In the Lyon region the population trebled in the 20 years from 1911 to 1931; the canton of Longwy experienced a similar progression, as did the most heavily-industrialised communes in the Alps.

The population's origins also illustrate this element of rootlessness: 55 per cent of Bobigny's inhabitants in 1930 were born in the provinces, against only 20 per cent born in the Paris region. The disparity was even greater in Vénissieux: in 1896, 70 per cent of the inhabitants originated there, but 35 year later less than one-fifth of the population was native to the Lyon conurbation.

It was frequently the foreign-born workers who made up the bulk of the influx. In Vénissieux they represented 23.4 per cent of the inhabitants in 1921, and nearly 44 per cent in 1931. In many mining communities in the Nord, the steel-working areas of Lorraine, or in Savoie, foreigners outnumbered native inhabitants.

The earlier backwardness in urbanisation and mechanisation and the effects of war damage resulted in truly appalling conditions of daily life, particularly housing, in these industrial zones. In 1920 Saint-Nazaire had living space for 20,000 people but had to supply shelter for double that number. In the ravaged zones of the north and the east the situation was much more dramatic. Reims, for example, had suffered the loss of 7,900 houses out of a total of just over 14,000; in 1921 more than 12,000 people were living in 2,000 barrack-style houses hastily constructed in the aftermath of war, and many were forced to remain in these wretched lodgings until 1930. The other major form of housing, which illustrates the French style of temporary housing, was the furnished lodging. Hotels and barrack hutments were filled primarily with single immigrants but also housed whole families, notably in the Paris area; the expression 'Far West' has been applied to iron-workers in contemporary Lorraine, and it would be equally appropriate to speak of 'pioneers' with reference to housing developments in the Paris suburbs. Between 1850 and 1914 only 3,000 hectares of land

were released for development there, but the more relaxed legislation of the 1920s encouraged an extraordinary passion for this
method of acquiring property: 15,000 hectares, an area equal to one
and a half times the area of Paris itself, were made available for
housing. Buildings were thrown up without regulation or any kind
of advance planning. Inhabitants were usually of modest origins,
seeking to satisfy their dream of property ownership; they bought
the land and used their meagre savings to embark on dwellings
which had more in common with huts than with mansions. In
some communes the wait for electricity, running water, or drain-
age, lasted 20 years. Referring to a development of this type in
Bobigny, one contemporary observer commented that 'the roads
are simply earth tracks and have never seen any attempt at surfac-
ing, so in wet weather they are like running sewers'. He added that
since there were no drains, household water was poured out on to
the ground; hence the evil smells and the proliferation of mos-
quitoes in summer. To add to this, inhabitants had to manage with
water from a well of doubtful quality.[38] Such appalling standards of
hygiene, common in many other industrial areas, were one of the
main reasons for France's backwardness in terms of public health;
holder of the European record for deaths from tuberculosis, France
was also notable for its infant mortality, which was still around 10
per cent in 1926. Immigrant communities were particularly exposed to such unhealthy conditions; at Sallaumines, in the mining
area of the Pas-de-Calais, infant mortality among Polish families
was 167 per 1,000 live births, a figure reminiscent of the worst
years of the Second Empire.[39]

Substantial changes in working conditions were another aspect
of working-class rootlessness during this period. Hundreds of
thousands of workers arriving from rural areas, in France or in
other countries, were suddenly plunged into the atmosphere of the
great factories and the strict discipline which ruled there. Taken on
by an establishment in a Lyon suburb, Jacques Valdour observes
that:

> people coming in or leaving were checked automatically, as happens
> almost everywhere nowadays, by a machine which punched the card
> ready for each one of us in a special pigeonhole. . . . All cards had to be
> punched before the whistle which marked the start of the work session:

38. Quoted by Fourcault (1983).
39. Ponty (1979), p. 200.

machines had to be set in motion as soon as the signal was given. At the end of the session the whistle indicated the moment to stop work. Then everyone had his card punched again and went to the cloakroom to wash and pick up his coat.[40]

Other contemporary accounts describe the repetitive unskilled work, the forerunner of the conveyor-belt system reserved primarily for women and immigrants. A supervisor taken on by Renault underwent the testing experience of a working woman's life:

> Here I am again in front of the grinding-wheel. This is not hard work, but it is dirty. I am completely enveloped in fine black metal dust. I work with enthusiasm, almost feverishly as I begin to pick up the motion: 'My word, I think to myself, since it's got to be done I shall earn my 40 sous an hour or I'll lose my good reputation.' And I work the wheel, I work it desperately, so that when there is trouble, when the wheel breaks or the belt slips, I am ready to cry out 'What a pig of a job' just like my old friends.[41]

Working conditions that had been particularly characteristic of textile factories – dust, humidity, noise – were now characteristic of a wide variety of establishments. Before the war Léon and Maurice Bonneff described the unhealthiness and danger of the new large metal-working and chemical factories. Rubber vulcanisation, for example, required the worker to breathe in carbon sulphur vapour, the cause of extremely serious nervous ailments which were not then legally accepted as 'industrial illness'. Similarly, safety in the mines made no real progress at this time: there were 135 deaths in the Pas-de-Calais in 1929, and the iron-ore mines of Lorraine were still among the most deadly in the world, with rates close to five deaths per 1,000 miners.[42]

Circumstances were less depressing for skilled workers, for this was still a time of transition and Taylorism was in its infancy. As Alain Touraine has shown in connection with the motor industry, until the end of the 1920s the skilled worker was still the backbone of the workshop. Although it was perhaps no longer a question of 'artisan' work as practised by trained labour in earlier years, the

40. Valdour (1934), p. 13.
41. See Fourcault (1982).
42. On the Nord, see Michel (1975), pp. 34–5.

skilled worker still made good use of his intelligence and practical experience:

> He slips a bit of metal in here or there to reduce the play of the machine, resets a horizontal line, tightens up something. . . . He has his own little tool set: adjustable spanner, pair of compasses, set of wedges. He must know how to use his hands, how to use a file. Very many items are of such a complicated shape that they can only be started on the machine and much of the work must be done by hand.[43]

Georges Navel also quotes many examples of the skills of workers trained as mechanics; in a 1930s aircraft factory, for example:

> no item was exactly the same as the next in spite of the machines' accuracy. Things were done by trying the connecting rod against its cap, by judging the degree of pressure needed to interlock them, with a sort of blind man's gentleness, while holding the item up to the light at arm's length to make sure that the fitting was hermetically tight with no light filtering through as if between shutters.[44]

But Navel's book lays equal emphasis on the profound crisis of identity which was then affecting the élite of trained workers. 'The war uprooted us', he comments. This factor, added to the progressive deskilling of work and the disillusionment following the labour movement's setback in 1919/20, engendered a veritable 'race for the future' which explains the turnover of labour described at the beginning of this chapter, and confirmed by Jacques Valdour.

> Economic liberalism has encouraged the French worker not to put down roots; he moves from one factory to another, or from one city or region to another, at a moment's notice. . . . This is what the workers themselves quaintly call 'having itchy feet'. It's an incurable disease; they come and go without notice, they disrupt factory management, interrupt production, add to general costs. And it's the same everywhere.[45]

This instability reflects the urge to escape from less than satisfactory conditions. In the mines at Lens even the long-established mining families, described as 'resigned' by John Condevaux, wanted a better future for their children: 'Mechanised workshops

43. Touraine (1955), p. 60.
44. Navel (1945), pp. 243–4.
45. Valdour (1934), p. 17.

and electricity supplies bring a great increase of job applications from miners' sons, the élite of the mining fraternity. They join the list and wait their turn for a year or two years, or even longer.'[46]

As for workers in the prestige sectors of mechanical or electrical engineering, they often had only one dream: to escape from the world of the 'big factories' for which they were not trained. Such was the work companion described by Valdour who saved one sou at a time in the hope that one day he could make his own living through trade, or the highly skilled worker whom Navel met one day at Berliet, who had led the strikes in 1919 and who had seized on evening classes to rise in the social hierarchy.

A restricted universe

In general terms the industrial expansion had not delivered the benefits of an improved standard of living to the manual worker. The stagnation of average wage rates was striking in comparison with those of the other major industrialised nations, and correspondingly the worker's pattern of expenditure had scarcely changed since the end of the nineteenth century; 60 per cent of total expenditure was still devoted to food in 1930, against 63.6 per cent in 1905 and 65 per cent in 1890, and clothing accounted for 12.6 per cent, the same proportion as in 1890.

These averages, however, conceal very great variations which illustrate the heterogeneous nature of the working world in the 1920s, and which were one consequence of new divisions in the labour market imposed by the managerial class.

Those workers who were still close to the rural world, as in the textile industry, experienced much less of the upheavals described above, and there were still signs of relative continuity from earlier periods. Boys and girls went into the Aube hosiery works at the age of 13 just as others might enter the religious life. Apprenticeship was always 'on the job'. The working man began his professional life as a nap-brusher or messenger, then he became a hosier's assistant. He could not expect to become a hosier himself until he had done his military service.

This particular working world was in great contrast to that of heavy industry. The most 'advanced' workers met together in the big cities; wages in the Paris region were in general noticeably

46. Condevaux (1928), p. 16.

higher than elsewhere, and until 1914 at least car manufacturing workers could earn up to twice as much as those engaged in other forms of metal-work. The habit of 'leisure activities' mentioned in Chapter 3 was on the increase; young workmen who were sport devotees read *L'Auto* regularly, and demanded the introduction of the 'English' working week. At Charonne, in the twentieth *arrondissement* of Paris, 'on Saturday night the enormous cinema in the rue de Buzenval was full to bursting. . . . The orchestra struggled in vain to be heard over the tumult of the enormous crowd who, suddenly fed up with waiting, stopped their chatter and banged loudly on the floor. The curtain rose to great applause.' Works such as Courteline's *Le Train de 9 Heures 47* were very popular, while 'the old-fashioned popular sentimental "moral" drama was out of favour'.[47]

While housing-estates were still like immense building sites there were other districts in the Paris region where longer-established urban settlement made life easier. In his 1928 description, Jacques Valdour speaks of Boulogne-Billancourt as 'a luxury working-class town', even though its inhabitants were 'settled neither in the place nor in their trade'. He adds that the most animated place in the commune, which already boasted 70,000 inhabitants, was the main factory gate; small traders of all nationalities set up stalls, and political militants harangued the crowd:

> A news-stand was set up in front of the Renault factory's main gate with newspapers from Armenia, Rumania, Czechoslovakia, Hungary, Vienna, Berlin, Italy and Spain. When the workshop shifts changed the factory front and the whole rue de Saint-Cloud was transformed into a little street-market where a few French people mingled with Algerians, middle-eastern Arabs, and Jews, to sell such goods as clothing, household linen, shoes, small toilet articles, hardware, paper, polish, fruit and vegetables, cakes, and ice-cream from their modest handcarts.

Sometimes 'revolutionary orators harangued the crowd from the first-floor café windows, or stood on benches or on the car which brought them', inevitably followed by the arrival of the police.[48]

This indicates a socially varied atmosphere; in the world of industrial paternalism things were otherwise. The factory's hold over all sectors of social life prevented organised protest, and the

47. Valdour (1925), p. 61.
48. Valdour (1928), p. 69.

mono-industry system was accompanied by a very homogeneous professional background. It should also be stressed that French and foreign workers lived very separate lives. Although the local work-force held the monopoly of skilled jobs, it knew virtually nothing of the leisured society. The housing estates offered few distractions and in any case work occupied almost the whole of daily life. Among the Lorraine steel workers, for example – especially since the extension of shift working, introduced by employers to counteract the effects of the eight-hour law – the working hours of different members of the family rarely coincided. Some worked every day, others did eight hours without a break and then worked at night one week in three. Thus it was that the family rarely met together as a whole at meal times except on Sundays, and then only if no one had to work that day, which was still a frequent occurrence. Very often the father would come in tired from work, wanting nothing but peace and quiet. And when he was on the night shift he must not be woken, so the children had to go out of the house to play.[49]

All this meant that recreation was limited to visiting a bar with music on Sundays, or fishing or hunting in season; for some there were visits to societies where they would feel 'at home'. Such societies were very numerous in the northern mining communities and indicate the strength of loyalty to home and work. One pastime worth mentioning is pigeon-fancying, which had 45,000 devotees in the Nord and 900,000 pigeons: nine-tenths of the total number in France.[50]

Foreign families were restricted to a veritable ghetto existence. This phenomenon, already described in relation to Lorraine and the north, is confirmed in all mining areas. In Blanzy, in Saône-et-Loire, for instance, the many immigrant workers brought in after the war were considered 'backward', and confined to their own housing estates; 90 per cent of Polish marriages took place within the ethnic group. The same isolation was seen in the mines in the Gard or the metal-works at Rosières in the Cher, where research indicated that 'the ethnic and linguistic isolation of this community was to play a considerable role until 1936';[51] hence the retreat of the

49. Survey carried out by the ACJF at Joeuf (Meurthe-et-Moselle) in 1930; Archives de la Bibliothèque de Documentation Internationale Contemporaine, Nanterre.
50. Michel (1975), p. 76.
51. Pigenet (1982).

different nationalities into the culture of their origin, with the heartfelt hope that one day they would be able to return to their own countries.

5

'Call Me Blum,
Just Like
The Old Days'

The Popular Front marked a turning point in the history of the French working class, both in the victory of the left in the elections of April/May 1936 – an event which was not without precedent – and in the remarkable wave of strikes and factory sit-ins which shook the whole of French society.

The political vicissitudes of this period are well known from the February days in 1934 to the 'pause' decreed by Léon Blum, which led to a fresh breach between socialists and communists, but the social verities of contemporary working-class life, as Jean Bruhat observed a few years ago, have remained shadowy. This does nothing to help modern understanding of the profound causes of worker militancy.

Underlying this paradox is undoubtedly the fact that the history of these years is still too recent and too painful to be calmly assessed by scientific research. Until recently indeed the Popular Front has been for all on the left a genuine 'founding institution', relating more to commemorative practice than historical analysis. In assessing the evocation of events of February 1934 in the post-war *L'Humanité*, Jacques Ozouf stressed the main principles underlying this 'liturgy of repetition', always focusing on serving the political strategy of the moment and emphasising the exemplary role of the communist militants.[1]

1. Ozouf (1966).

The same logic is at work in socialist thinking; this is apparent in the preface written by Pierre Mauroy, then Prime Minister, to Benigno Cacérès's work on the 'birth of the age of leisure' which appeared in paperback at the end of 1981. While recalling the happy moment when – through Léo Lagrange, minister for sport and leisure – workers discovered bicycles and seaside holidays, the purpose is to discredit the notion of any continuity between the Popular Front and the epoch of 'after May 1981'.[2]

Risking apparent sacrilege at this fiftieth anniversary commemorative time[3] – for myth and historical research make uneasy bedfellows – the following pages attempt, with the aid of existing surveys, to set out the sociological causes underlying the working classes' irruption into the public arena.

I. A Break with Tradition

The essential requirement of myth is to eliminate irregularity and discontinuity, to stress a seamless and unfailing chronological uniformity showing each stage as the logical outcome of the preceding step and the precursor of the next. This symbolic striving towards continuity has been apparent since the first days of the Popular Front, from the great demonstration organised at the Mur des Fédérés in the Père Lachaise cemetery, designed to show that the militants of the left were the descendants of the 1871 Paris Commune, to the famous ceremony of 5 June 1936 when the new president of the Council welcomed the union leader and appealed to the militants of the ex-CGTU (the united worker's federation) with the famous phrase: 'Call me Blum, just like the old days'.

The Popular Front, however, can only be understood if it is seen as a complete break with working-class traditions rooted in the early days of the twentieth century, as we shall see.

A war-damaged worker movement

Although worker militancy reached its peak in the opening years of the century, as shown in Chapter 3, it remained extremely vigor-

2. Cacérès (1981).
3. This book first appeared in 1986, 50 years after the Popular Front, the first French socialist government (*tr.*)

ous until the end of the First World War; indeed the fighting spirit of the staff working in armaments factories is impressive in view of the rootlessness and diversity of the labour-force and the close police surveillance. The gunpowder factory at Bergerac, for example, brought together more than 11,000 workers from every kind of background; there were 4,822 men mobilised for war service, 708 civilians, approximately 3,000 women, 2,000 'colonials' – north Africans, Indo-Chinese, and Chinese – and 326 prisoners. Yet in 1917 the union had more than 4,300 members; on almost all sides the CGT militants who favoured the 'Union Sacrée', the formal expression of national unity adopted by all sections of society, were overwhelmed by revolutionaries. Despite the firm attitude of Merrheim, secretary of the metal-manufacturer's federation, pacifist propaganda grew and spread. In 1917 more than 42,000 people were on strike in the Paris area, 90 per cent of them women, and in Bordeaux, according to the *préfet*, 'everyone is talking about Revolution. Everyone says that it is unavoidable.' Fresh strikes broke out in the Gard in June 1918, at the peak of the German offensive; even in the Vosges, at the heart of 'patriotic' Lorraine, 1916 saw the first stoppages, with strikes developing again in May/June 1917. Many factories were paralysed from 1918 to the beginning of 1920. Such activity was largely the result of the deplorable conditions which were then the fate of workers in such establishments; the very rapid rise in prices was accompanied by an official extension of the working day; there were shortages of bread and meat, and frequently workers arriving from other areas were housed in barrack hutments. To this may be added 'the shock associated with an uprooting suffered in dramatic circumstances, with homesickness for lands yielded up to the invaders and great anxiety over the fate of relatives'.[4] But although the will to resist outweighed submissiveness, and despite tremendous national pressure which played particularly on feelings of guilt over those who were fighting in the front line, militancy was also the consequence of collective combative traditions which had hardened since the conflicts of the late nineteenth century.

Turmoil and agitation reached their peak in the international revolutionary conditions which prevailed in the aftermath of war. Millions of people in France were involved in the strikes of 1919/20. On 1 May 1919 half a million demonstrators paraded

4. Huard (1978). See also Gallo (1966).

through Paris; confrontation with the police resulted in one death. Throughout the year there were frequent disputes in building, textiles, and naval construction, although militancy was greatest in the metal-working and chemical industries of the Paris region; 150,000 people stopped work on 1 June and a general strike was narrowly avoided; 1920 was above all the year of the railway-workers' strike; all traffic ceased on 1 May and on the following days they were supported by miners, dockers, metal-workers.[5]

These two years proved not so much a golden dawn, however, as the end of the cycle of the *'belle époque* of strikes', to use Michelle Perrot's expression. The scale of mobilisation, the symbolic choice of 1 May for launching major efforts, the hope of 'the revolutionary dawn', (which would explain the success of the watchword of 'general strike'), the many claims in favour of 'worker control' and against workshop regulations, piecework, and so on – all were reminiscent of past history.

After the repression of the railway-workers' strike, with almost 20,000 dismissals and the CGT threatened with suspension, the worker movement entered a decline from which it did not recover until 1936. There was a spectacular drop in the number of people on strike during the 1920s; from the peak figure of 1.3 million in 1920 it fell to 400,000 in 1921. The trough of the wave was reached in 1927, with a total of 110,000 strikers involved in 396 stoppages, against the 1919 figure of more than 2,000. At the same time the failure rate of such efforts continued to grow, an indication of union impotence. Workers lost 40 per cent of strikes between 1925 and 1935, the proportion increasing to 70 per cent where work organisation was involved, even though the average length of each confrontation was increasing. Contemporary written accounts confirm this growing lack of success.

Thus when Jacques Valdour, who was obsessed by the 'red peril', discussed the revolutionary chants heard in the Levallois factories, he asserted that:

such violent commonplace stuff was all the rage before the war, but now it falls on wage-earners' deaf ears. If we are to learn anything about the people's attitudes from their graffiti, we must remember that before the war all the walls were covered with inscriptions which were anti-

---

5. On the 1919 strike in the Paris area, see in particular Brunet (1980). The indispensable authority on this period is Kriegel (1969).

clerical, revolutionary, or simply political, and observe that today they are extremely rare.

Later he specified, referring to an engine factory set up at Puteaux, on the edge of Paris: 'There are "reds" in all the workshops, little groups of militants, but nowadays they don't have any influence over their companions, and since they are acutely aware of their own impotence, they remain self-contained and optimistic.'[6] The drop in union membership was equally dramatic. In 1920 membership of the CGT was 1.6 million, according to official figures – the union's own figure was 2.4 millions – and the CFTC (the French Confederation of Christian Workers) had some 100,000 members; the total diminished to about 600,000 in later years. Membership of the 'confederated' CGT, the larger union since the split, varied during the 1920s between 500,000 and 600,000. The CGTU's numbers settled at less than 350,000, showing a slight downwards tendency towards the end of the 1920s.

Reasons for decline

The worker movement's growing debility during the 1920s is often ascribed to the ill effects of the political and union split in the development of two often antagonistic poles in the French left: the socialist, 'reformist' tendency, and the communist, 'revolutionary', tendency. This is a justifiable assessment, but the development should also be seen in the light of the economic and social changes already described.

The decline in union numbers was very much less marked in certain regions and sectors of employment. Edward Shorter and Charles Tilly observed that the greatest decline in militancy was in establishments with more than 500 workers; significantly, these were the same large factories where activity had expanded most vigorously in pre-war years. Shorter and Tilly also observed that the zones with the most marked tendency towards urbanisation in the early years of the twentieth century were those where the tendency to go on strike had fallen away most strongly during the 1920s. The Pas-de-Calais was one of the French *départements* where collective disputes diminished most sharply in proportion to total worker numbers; similarly the mining industry, which had been

6. Valdour (1923), pp. 107 and 147.

particularly severely disrupted by the major strikes early in the century, saw its strike rate fall from 15.2 to 6.9 per 100,000 between 1915 and 1935.[7]

After the upheavals of the first years of the century and the 1919/20 episodes, collective disputes became a trivial element in many regions, such as Lorraine's steel-manufacturing zone, until the days of the Popular Front. Even in the immense car factories near Paris militant action virtually ceased after 1920; from then until 1936 there was only one strike at Citroën that lasted for more than 24 hours. After a strike of 15 days in 1926, the Renault factory at Boulogne-Billancourt was characterised by 'extreme weakness' of militant action until 1931.[8] In these sectors union membership fell drastically. The myth of the militant metal-workers had not yet become established. In 1913 the metal manufacturer, Alphonse Merrheim, already saw them as 'pliable and submissive', 'profoundly self-centred' and 'implacably opposed to trade unionism'; indeed, at that time only 2 to 3 per cent of metal-workers were union members, and the federation was described as 'full of holes'. Merrheim was scarcely more generous in 1919, referring to strikers in the Paris mechanical-engineering industry as a 'savage mob'. From 1920 to the beginning of the 1930s union membership in the metal-working industry never grew beyond 5 per cent of the total number of employees, and the situation was similar in the chemical industry. In building, textiles, and the extraction industries, membership of all unions taken together was less than 10 per cent; so that the worker organisations 'had practically no power at all in the true industrial sector'.[9]

The support, even the expansion, of the worker movement in traditional sectors should, however, be emphasised. As Antoine Prost noted in his 1964 survey, 'the most strongly unionised section of the population was in fact the old industrial France, what is now known as "static" France'.[10] A third of the strikes between 1915 and 1935 occurred in only 15 communes. Twelve French cities had at least one strike each year during the same period; four were in the Nord: Lille, Roubaix, Tourcoing and Halluin. These are all textile towns, this being the sector which experienced 60 per cent of all the region's mass confrontations during this period. Such circum-

---

7. From Shorter and Tilly (1974), p. 257 *et seq.*
8. See in particular Depretto and Schweitzer (1984), pp. 92–104.
9. Prost (1964), p. 73.
10. Ibid., p. 95.

stances must of course be seen in relation to the stability already described: no immigration, no radical technological upheaval, a settled population, very often with long-established roots in the neighbouring rural world. All this explains the maintenance of earlier militant traditions, marked not only by a strong fighting spirit but also by the strike atmosphere – communist soup kitchens, exodus of children to supportive communities, massive participation by the women – which was typical of the *belle époque*.

Union activity also found favour during the 1920s in small urban or rural establishments; Charles Tilly stresses the very strong inclination to go on strike among mechanics engaged in small-scale artisan businesses. There too the old tradition was preserved, for it was in these establishments that skilled workers found shelter when they fled from the large factories. Working space and living areas were still sometimes intermingled, reinforcing professional exclusiveness. In the furniture-making industry the small workshops of the Faubourg-Saint-Antoine – the focus for the 'creative workers' who worked to commission on fashionable pieces, whose apprentices would go to improve their technical skills at the Boulle school on Wednesdays – had no connection at all with the factories turning out mass-produced furniture in the nearby Charonne area. Professional independence and pride in well-finished work were still the chief ingredients in their concept of unionisation. 'The spirit of the Faubourg', notes Jacques Valdour, 'is so marked that the furniture workers rarely turn to the CGT or go to its headquarters in the rue Grange-aux-Belles to settle professional matters: each organisation has its own office within the actual district.'[11]

Such trades frequently sustained their corporatist traditions with great firmness; thus the printing federation under the direction of Auguste Keufer based its style closely on American trade organisations affiliated to the AFL (American Federation of Labor). But the closed shop, control of recruitment and of working conditions, were also to be found in many other places, notably in small provincial towns or rural surroundings such as among the tannery workers of Annonay in the Ardèche, or the tulle-makers of Caudry in the Nord. Professional homogeneity, the absence of immigrants, and occupational heredity, all combined in what has been referred to in preceding chapters as the 'protected' sectors of the labour market, including almost all those employed in service industries

11. Valdour (1925), p. 191.

such as public services or transport. It was not therefore purely coincidental that these sectors were the most strongly unionised during the 1920s. Although in 1921 more than 50 per cent of workers in the modern industrial sector belonged to a union, ten years later the figure was only 3 per cent. The worker movement's centre of gravity had shifted towards the railways, telecommunications, the public services; at the beginning of the 1930s all these sectors showed at least 10 per cent union membership, sometimes as much as 20 per cent. Hence also their continuance of pre-war practices and contractual relationships such as collective agreements or worker participation in commissions to debate such matters as the cost of living.[12] It may therefore be argued that the recession in the worker movement after the First World War can primarily be explained by the almost complete absence of long-term organisation in the most dynamic sectors of the working classes – those with the best future outlook and the greatest numbers.

Continued unionisation in stable or protected sectors and regions has been explained here by several references to the maintenance of a 'tradition' of conflict. This expression needs a brief explanation, to give a fuller sense of the break with early twentieth-century 'working-class tradition' represented by the inter-war years.

First it should be stressed that a popular tradition is not to be confused with its written expression, which is often elaborated outside the group concerned. Referring to the 'collective memory', Maurice Halbwachs makes a distinction between history as personal experience and history as something learnt, and it is reasonable to seek a more precise definition of exactly what constitutes working-class 'memory'. It is created chiefly from what has been personally experienced, particularly through events which have affected the life of an individual and which have been shared by a whole social group. Such events remain engraved on the memory – Halbwachs's 'registering equipment' – but they also impregnate all the surroundings in which they happened: the walls, the workshops, the public places which evoke every day, for those who were there, the fundamental episodes of the past. Very often institutions such as clubs and unions are charged with recalling this history through appropriate symbolic means such as songs, flags, and commemorative speeches, which operate like a 'wave-making

---

12. The 1926 collective agreement in the mines of the Nord affected 188,000 workers, i.e. two-thirds of the nation's miners.

machine' capable of 'setting up vibrations on the registering apparatus'. The family is another channel for the independent transmission of tradition, through education and the sequence of identification from parent to child. Finally, 'charismatic' personalities reincarnate important moments of the past because they were the central figures on such occasions and thus embody the local grouping's symbolic self-identification. Factors such as worker militancy, political preference, attitudes to unions and so on stem much more directly from this type of element than from the merits of 'history learnt', what is discovered in books, which rarely evokes anything very concrete.[13]

This general framework of working-class tradition was disturbed between 1905 and 1930 by economic and social upheaval and by the First World War.

Many areas effectively underwent the substitution of one working class for another. Philippe Ariès has shown clearly that metalworkers in the new factories near Paris were not directly descended from the skilled workers of the nineteenth century, for the latter used their education to escape to other social milieux, either in person or through their children. He added:

> Take careful note – this red zone, the rootless and disinherited proletariat, is not, as is often claimed, a consequence of the industrial revolution of the nineteenth century. It developed much later, it dates in general from the 1914 war, when production industry dug itself in on a vast scale round the ancient centres hitherto untouched by large concentrations of the working class.[14]

The physical disappearance of several hundred thousand workers added to the phenomenon. The breakdown of demographic balance in many cases broke the traditional bond of identification between father and son, overturning images of the future projected by former community stability; for, as Halbwachs observes: 'When all jobs were filled and there was very little promotion except through seniority, everyone knew his place and waited his turn, and the young were separated from the old by a dense and unyielding mass, its solidity imposing a sense of stages to be passed through before anyone could attain senior ranking.' It was therefore

13. Halbwachs (1968).
14. Ariès (1971), p. 163.

the whole family philosophy of the transmission of traditional working-class values that was challenged in the 1920s.

The extent of the loss of human life and shifts of population also resulted in the destabilisation of long-established groups; and the social memory that is no longer shared throughout the community soon dies. It is worth turning back to Navel: until the war everyone in his native Meurthe-et-Moselle village of Maidières remembered the 1905 strikes, and there was still support for those in Pont-à-Mousson whose temerity had lost them their factory jobs. But the village was destroyed in 1914 and many of its inhabitants, exiled to Lyon or elsewhere, did not return. Recollection only survived in the memories of individuals who therafter remained scattered. The physical setting too was destroyed in areas occupied by the enemy; Georges Navel did not recognise his village again after the war. At Sallaumines in the Pas-de-Calais the mining company preferred to build new housing rather than restore the old setting, and at the same time there was a completely new population of Polish immigrants. When, half a century later, sociologists attempted to tap the 'collective memory', they discovered that most of the retired inhabitants did not know that there had been a village before 1914.[15] In regions that were newcomers to the world of large-scale industry, such as the Paris suburbs or the Alpine valleys, the workers moved into virgin territory with no history to be evoked.

Sometimes such 'forgetting' was the direct result of action by the management. At Le Creusot, after the 1899/1900 strike, 'the main concern of the management for a long time' lay in 'making people forget, effacing the memory of the strikes from the workers' consciousness at all costs'. This even included obliterating the newsstand which had been the strikers' main meeting point, on the pretext of redevelopment.[16]

The other side of this coin was the strategy of manipulating time to fill the gaps thereby created, through intense commemoration of the war expressed through the construction of a vast number of memorials to the dead. The analysis above of the 'collective memory' shows the effectiveness of this scheme in integrating the French working class. Before 1914 the most notable events in working-class collective existence were all connected with working

15. See Dubar et al. (1980).
16. From Parize (1981), p. 213.

150

life; this might be accidents, such as the 1,200 dead in the Courrières coal-mine in 1906, or a strike bloodily suppressed. In such circumstances the red flag activated the 'wave machine' particularly effectively, producing 'vibrations on the registering apparatus' and welding the group together by pointing a finger at its enemies – the police state and the 'blood-sucking' employers. This element, which was no doubt the trigger of the *belle époque*'s 'worker separatism', changed completely with the war. Henceforward it was the battle against the enemy under arms which lay at the root of national traumas; but instead of being purely worker-oriented, it affected all classes of the nation and so favoured the development of a consensus from which only non-French-born workers were excluded.

These are all reasons for the ease with which all the changes so strongly resisted since the beginning of the century were able to win the day. For the mass of new workers who replaced the older ones – immigrants and rootless French peasants – the tradition of the 'general strike', of 'direct action', of resisting political diversion, or of demands for 'worker control' – none of this was part of their history. Having no qualifications to protect, they accepted the rationalisation of their work the more uncomplainingly in that employment as a machine operator or unskilled worker was highly preferable to the manual work that had been superseded by the machine.

The general instability of the areas of heavy industry before 1930 prevented the entrenchment of a new worker movement, particularly since individual mobility was the most frequent expression of worker dissatisfaction.

For the inheritors of the militant pre-war tradition, the disillusionment following the setback in the revolutionary movement of 1919/20 was added to the work crisis and demographic breakdown. Referring to his workshop companion organising strikes at the Berliet factory in 1919, and as an assiduous pupil at evening classes after the setback in the struggle, Georges Navel wrote: 'He had caught, in advanced milieux, a sort of nostalgia for knowledge and intelligence.' Explaining his own dislike of the factory, the writer-worker added, still referring to the post-war period, 'I had read too much, seen too much.' For those not choosing the path of individual flight to other social settings, political activism would often appear as a lifeline: 'There is a working-class malaise', wrote Navel, 'which can only be cured by positive political activity.'[17]

17. Navel (1945), pp. 75, 52 and 247.

Birth of a new militant worker: the communist

André Siegfried saw clearly that beyond the study of 'the eternal conflict between leanings and parties', political science demanded a sociological approach relating the electoral behaviour of a population to the greater or lesser history of entrenchment in its area, its degree of stability, recent changes in local planning, and other matters. It was realised that in many areas the support of the SFIO (the French section of the Communist Party) or alternatively the setting up of the PCF (the French Communist Party), should be related to earlier economic and social changes. Research has shown that until 1935 the Communist Party had the greatest difficulty in taking root in working-class districts with a positive socialist presence. Although the communists controlled 16 municipalities in the Paris area after the split at the Congress of Tours, most of those elected returned to their 'old establishment' in subsequent years. In the Var too the SFIO, with four deputies out of five in 1914, still retained them in 1928, despite the PCF's activities.[18]

The 'stability' of the textile industry mentioned above explains why in the Nord, and particularly in Lille, the 'Guesdiste tradition' was unchallenged. Among the miners, notwithstanding Polish immigration, the reforming cells of the union movement were already sufficiently solid in 1914 to be able to resist changes in the working classes, at least until the 1930s. It is true to say that developments might vary according to personalities and specific local distinctive circumstances. The place of the Belgian 'second generation' in the textile working class was surely not without relevance to the rapid shift of the town of 'Red Halluin' towards communism; similarly, the pattern of post-war reconstruction explains the continued socialist influence in Noyelles-sous-Lens when the neighbouring commune of Sallaumines elected a communist mayor in 1935. In the first commune the old village had been preserved, and with it the small middle-class sector, descendants of old local families, which maintained their hold over the town despite substantial Polish immigration. In Sallaumines, as has been shown, buildings and population were completely replaced.

It would be wrong none the less to consider the 'old union' as the inheritor of the overall militant tradition of the early days of the century. Although the basic choice between the type of organis-

18. See Girault (1975), particularly pp. 273 and 88.

ation to be favoured – guild chamber or industrial federation – had not yet been settled, the pre-war years hastened the defeat of the craft guild workers. The post-war years brought complete victory for a centralised militant structure based on big industrial unions working largely through delegation of power, and so through bureaucracy. For all those who had acted as the spearhead of 'direct action unions' it was not only a whole concept of collective activity which foundered, but also the appropriate essential body of leaders that encouraged the conservation of professional knowledge and group culture. The partisans of direct action could scarcely recognise themselves in the 'policy of participation' adopted by Léon Jouhaux after the war and later confirmed. Through its role in round-table commissions, in tripartite contractual proceedings, the CGT adopted in their entirety union practices that were formerly the concern of only some of the federations – essentially the mines and the railways. But the worker movement's lack of strong roots in the working world meant that consultation continued to operate only between the national directors of the union. 'Co-management' put down no roots at the most fundamental level, in the workshops, as was happening in Germany at that time. Although CGT reformism thus gained strength through the war, this was due to the decisive weakening of the 'proletarian core' of the working classes. The integration of the organisation into the state system was helped because the majority of union members were employed in public or semi-public sectors.

The communist movement (PCF–CGTU) had even less right to claim descent from the earlier militant tradition, despite the retention of the newspaper *L'Humanité* by the majority group at the Congress of Tours. In the aftermath of the euphoria of 1918–20 they were seeking a worker base, for after the split there were very few leaders of working-class origin in their ranks.

It may be thought that the Leninist strategy favouring action at the heart of the industrial proletariat had certain points in its favour in France, since the proletariat was at that time very poorly represented politically and was virtually unorganised. The SFIO's slow swing to the right, the fact that it was based above all on those social groups which were most integrated into the state, left a large political gap both at parliamentary representation level and at the local level of district and workshop with no history of struggle, or where old values had disintegrated.

This context explains why, until the recession, communist

strategy was more or less deliberately aimed at anything that might be reminiscent of 'tradition': 'Let us make a clean sweep of the past.' Rigid centralisation, narrow subordination of union to party, the lack of interest shown in labour culture, the iron discipline demanded by the militants based on total self-denial in favour of the leaders – all this was opposed to the ideal of the pre-war 'revolutionary trade unionists'. Many of those who belonged to the PCF before the Russian Revolution resigned in later years, and it was the places and militant figures in favour before the war, together with 'Bolshevisation', that were the target. The example of the first communist electoral *département* in the 1928 election, the Cher, is very enlightening in this respect. This region, one of the centres of worker militancy at the end of the nineteenth century, thanks to its rural workers (particularly in the timber industry) and its employees in small artisan industry (such as the porcelain makers in Vierzon), was brought under communist control after the war by the young metal-workers at the Bourges armaments factory; this was the largest company in the area and very hostile to the *Union Sacrée*. With 'Bolshevisation' the nerve centre of the movement shifted from the labour exchange to this major establishment; most of the founders of the first local worker movement, such as Pierre Hervieu, kept aloof or withdrew voluntarily, weary of constantly being treated as 'old social-democrats'. Similarly, although the rural proletariat still had confidence in the communists, the latter were principally concerned with new industrial establishments: 'There is no point in organising ten tree fellers if it means ignoring 2,500 metal-workers', declared one former local communist leader in his memoirs.[19]

The locales favoured by communist organisations were accordingly those that had no history; above all, the Communist Party favoured the suburbs and large factories in the Paris area, with Billancourt the prime objective from the beginning. During the 1920s the Renault factory featured in 720 articles in *L'Humanité*, an average of one every eight days: in 1929 it had 19 factory correspondents. It was there that the militants inaugurated a new political practice of speeches at the main factory gates as workers arrived or departed. The other favoured place for communist activity was the suburban housing estate. Recent research into Communist-Party entrenchment in the Paris area stresses the two main factors

19. Ibid., p. 256 *et seq.*

underlying the organisation's success: separation between home and place of work, as shown by the length of time spent on daily transport, and the novelty of town planning which reached its high point in systematic housing developments. The older part of Montreuil, for example, although more of a working-class district than the new zones, remained hermetically resistant to communist propaganda while the party gained overriding influence in housing development zones. Everywhere it was among the ill-housed that the PCF had its greatest success during the 1920s. Mass disillusionment among people disenchanted with the dream of modest landownership resulted in a 'radical' attitude sympathetic to the communist militants working energetically at the heart of the federation of badly housed workers. The inhabitants were very anxious to protect their modest holdings, and attended owners' gatherings *en masse*. 'The first annual general meetings were very well attended, with discussions and election of officers and management adding to the sense of democracy. Since they were responsible for half the cost of the work, they watched over it with care and discussed it, sharpening their critical senses.'[20] Thus was established a nursery of militants which would be extremely valuable to the PCF at the time of the Popular Front.

The first worker leaders of the new party are also of interest. All witnesses agree in stressing the fact that they were generally young workers; this was a new generation swift to reject tradition, taking over the command posts of the communist system. Much of the opposition between the PCF and the SFIO took on the aspect of a quarrel between the generations, as at the Congress of Tours where the young appeared the determining factor in favour of the Third International, or at a municipal level. In Saint-Denis the old socialist town council was finally defeated by a new team of young communists, members of the JCF (the French Christian youth movement); the most influential members of the local PC did not appear on the list of candidates because they were still too young to be eligible![21]

The growing numbers of local PCF leaders of working-class origin was a further decisive factor – most were skilled metalworkers. At Ivry, near Paris, where the communists triumphed at the end of the 1920s, 65 per cent of those elected were workers; the

20. Bastié (1964), p. 130.
21. Brunet (1980), p. 266.

main group was made up of fitters, turners and mechanics. The higher up the organisational hierarchy, the greater their number; metal-workers at the 1929 Saint-Denis conference, making up 11.3 per cent of members, provided 40 per cent of congress participants. They were, too, the most numerous of those attending classes at the party's central school.[22] Some of these communist leaders may have belonged to the 'mechanic élite' whose great disarray was described by Navel and who sought refuge in political activity.

The PCF was still on the fringes of the political arena, and its militants could therefore take a 'hard line', consistently critical, always increasing the pressure during strikes; this met with the support, explicit or implicit, of all the proletariat excluded from consensus during the 1920s. The PC was favoured by many of the workers in the mines of the Pas-de-Calais, for it appeared 'definitively identified with an aggressive attitude towards the employers. It was the party for those who knew how to speak up and were not afraid of their managers: and of agitators waiting to pounce on the slightest irregularity with cries of injustice'.[23] To this primary image which the militant communist sought to promote must be added another, observed by Jacques Valdour at a meeting in the Paris area: 'The first speaker belonged to the communist youth section. He spoke with perfect diction: he stressed the ends of his words in the style of those who have had good speech-training lessons.'[24] While for the revolutionary union militant it was a point of honour to talk like one of the masses, the influence of educated models seemed much stronger among the new generation; hence the curious mixture of an aggressive 'radical' tone, considered appropriate to defend the most severely exploited, with a polished PCF training-school vocabulary designed to defeat the 'bourgeois' orators on their own ground.

Before the 1930s' crisis the PCF none the less remained a highly marginal organisation in French political life, with only 14 deputies in 1928 and 40,000 members – 15,000 according to the police – in 1930. Given the instability of the world of heavy industry, its recent character (the ghetto in which its member groups, particularly the immigrants, were confined), this chronic weakness is understandable. Yet although the leaders had no troops behind

---

22. Lojkine and Viet-Depaule (1983), p. 241.
23. Condevaux (1928), p. 99.
24. Valdour (n.d.), p. 205.

them they gradually filtered a new militant image into the working world.

The overall strength of the French worker movement was much reduced during the 1920s. Following the 1919 law on collective agreements, most branches of heavy industry abandoned the contractual solution which appeared to be spreading before the war. Similarly, although the militancy of the immediate post-war period was rewarded with the eight-hour law, social legislation slowed down considerably thereafter, and average working-class standards of living ceased to improve.

The other main consequence of reduced militancy was less public representation for the workers; there were far fewer university theses and official or journalistic surveys than before the war, as can be seen from the bibliography. The beginnings of empirical sociological research, concentrating particularly on matters of worker consumerism, were abruptly interrupted. As was noted by Alain Desrosières, 'curiously enough this current of empirical work (which offered important hypotheses immediately before the 1914 war) disappeared, at least in France, during the inter-war years, perhaps as a result of the great loss of life in the 1914 war'.[25] Goblot and even Halbwachs brought out highly literary analyses of the problem of social class. Paradoxically, during the 1920s it was a royalist, an inveterate enemy of the 'reds', who advocated a development of the 'social sciences' based on what is nowadays known as 'participatory observation'; in fact Jacques Valdour was one of the first, if not the very first, intellectual to work in a factory in order to be better informed on the realities of working life. Before Simone Weil established the leftist tradition at the workbench it had been initiated by a representative from the other side.[26]

25. Desrosières (1977), p. 52. Georges Lefranc also mentions the regression in worker initiative, with reference to cooperatives where the original managers were working class, followed by a middle-class 'second generation', and a 'third generation' of technocrats with higher education; see Lefranc (1975), p. 322.

26. J. Valdour defines his system in Valdour (1927). Over a period of 25 years he was taken on for several months each year in various establishments all over France, for 'the only knowledge is that which comes from observation'; elsewhere he says, 'in a survey of this kind it is essential to appear to workers as a worker, which is only possible for someone who genuinely is a worker'. He adds that this thirst for knowledge is not purely abstract, that it should be of use both to society and to workers themselves. His hatred of Rousseau (who, he claimed, was the originator of liberalism and socialism), and his fairly frequent racist and anti-Semitic comments, prove him far from 'progressive'.

II. 1931–1936: Recession

Industrial working-class stability in the first phase of the crisis

The developing crisis in France during the early 1930s led to considerable changes in employment relationships.

Without spelling out all the underlying causes of the economic recession it is worth recalling some that are relevant to the restricted nature of the home market. One of the principal effects of reduced working-class militancy during the 1920s was that the considerable advance in productivity failed to lead to any corresponding expansion in worker consumption; further, tardy nineteenth-century urbanisation, like the severe constraints of heavy industry on the labour market, encouraged major employers to strengthen industrial paternalism based on low wages and the importance of peasant-style self-sufficiency. After the 1920s, processing industries became aware of the obstacles that such a solution imposed on the expansion of capitalism. Citroën and Renault stated their wish for a higher general standard of living in order to improve potential markets for their factories. The resulting conflict with management of heavy industry is well illustrated by a Lorraine ironmaster discussing the workers' circumstances: 'It's not a car for every so-many inhabitants that we need, as you claim – it's a house for each family.'[27]

The leading heavy-industry employers' domination of the business world at that time meant that adoption of the 'Ford' solution was unlikely; stagnation since the end of the 1920s, particularly in light industry, meant dependence on outside markets. The Aude hat industry, which exported nine million hats in 1928, sold no more than 900,000 to foreign markets in 1932, while the home market fell from 15 million to 10 million over the same period. Restricted by national policies on major undertakings, heavy industry suffered a recession which brutally damaged the French economy: steel production dropped by 40 per cent in four years and bankruptcy increased by 60 per cent. The archaic French economic structure was in some respects an advantage, however, since the labour market was still very flexible.

It is essential in this connection to distinguish between two separate phases in the 1930s recession. The initial phase, from 1929

27. UIMM (1928).

to 1932/3, has remained relatively unnoticed because it affected the weakest elements of the working world. First, there was the scope offered by dismissal of immigrant workers. After observing that, 'it is to foreign workers that France mainly owes the prodigious increase in post-war construction, the great hydro-electric development schemes in the mountains, the growth in large-scale metallurgy and mining', Georges Mauco adds that in times of crisis 'the immigrant work-force makes it possible to reduce unemployment and gives our labour market outstanding flexibility'. He even specifies that 'paradoxical though it may seem, it was the reduction in her population that gave France her favoured position in over-industrialised Europe, suffering from both over-production and unemployment. It was the shortage of labour which, by making immigration unavoidable, enabled the nation to tailor its work-force to its needs'.[28]

The use of police department statistics in assessing this problem rather than census counts, which record only part of the situation, appears to indicate that in the most industrialised *départements* the reduction in foreign workers affected up to a third of the total: illegal or unmarried workers were the first to go. By 1936, less than a fifth of the total work-force in construction, a quarter in the heavy-metal industry, and a third in mining were foreigners.

The principle of the 'family' wage packet, earned primarily by the 'head of the family', meant that women were the other chief victims of the reduced labour market; 330,000 were laid off between 1931 and 1936, mainly in textiles and metal-working.

Finally, during this first phase the greatest impact of the recession was felt by workers in rural surroundings who for reasons already shown were frequently involved in the export industries which were the first to suffer. A journalist commented: 'No doubt the enduring importance of the rural population in France compared to many other countries meant that crises of unemployment in France appeared less important.'[29] The contrast in unemployment relief between two *départements* such as the Nord and the Vosges, with similar proportions of active workers, illustrates the difference between urban and rural regions. In the Bas-Rhin, as in the Vosges,

---

28. Mauco (1932), p. 461.
29. Quoted by Marseille (1980). In the author's opinion, sending immigrants back home and the rural world's retreat into itself disguised the extent of the unemployment which affected one million people in 1930–1931 – more than twice the official figures.

many unemployed workers received no relief because there was no unemployment fund in their commune. Thus, 'in the valley of the Bruche [Alsace] there were people who only survived because they owned a few beasts and a field or two where they could grow potatoes'.[30] The dismissal of immigrants and the rural world's withdrawal into its own resources explain the modest scale of a crisis which may perhaps have begun earlier than appreciated but which was hardly noticeable because there was so little unemployment relief. Until 1933, for example, although mines and the chemical industry were already severely affected by reduced employment, very few unemployed were benefiting from municipal aid.

Skilled workers were still relatively sheltered at this time, even in heavy industry, because management wanted to keep them ready for when business picked up again. At Vénissieux, for example, in 1931 three quarters of those without work were foreigners, 58 per cent were manual labourers, and 33 per cent skilled workers.[31] The consequences of this pattern on the structure of the working class can be specified in two words: standardisation and stabilisation.

Between 1931 and 1936 France's working population was reduced by 1.8 million, of whom 1.4 million belonged to the working class; it was, however, the most recent arrivals, the most marginal, who were affected. The reduction in jobs was therefore particularly noticeable in establishments with more than 500 employees, with a reduction of 25 per cent. An examination of the age pyramid shows a contraction in manual work among those in the prime of life, apparent in the reduction of bachelors as a proportion of the industrial worker total (from 42.4 per cent to 39.2 per cent). Similarly, the proportion of workers aged under 40 in extraction industries fell from 67 per cent in 1931 to 65.6 per cent in 1936. In handling and transport the figures are 60.3 per cent and 56.1 per cent respectively. More French, more skilled, more male, more mature, more urban, industrial workers were now also more stable. For the first time since the end of the nineteenth century there was an increase in the proportion of industrial workers employed in the *département* of their birth, from 55.2 per cent in 1931 to 56.4 per cent in 1936; many sources confirm this tendency towards stabilisation. The recession in the labour market brought a

30. Braun (1938), p. 61.
31. Videlier (1982), pp. 368–9.

spectacular fall in the turnover of labour in most sectors; in the Denain-Anzin factory in the Nord the increase in working-class stability was apparent as early as 1930/1. Annual entries in person-nel files fell sharply from several thousand to a few hundred. The turnover rate in the Lorraine iron-ore mines, over 90 per cent at the end of the 1920s according to mining engineers' statistics, barely reached 26 per cent in 1932. After 1932 in particular the skilled metal-workers who had had 'itchy feet' since the end of the war were often obliged to settle down and stay rather than risk failing to find work. In the building trade the crisis brought to an abrupt halt the colossal construction undertakings which were turning the whole Paris region into one vast building site. Manual and seasonal workers were laid off first; other workers had to remain where they were. The collective inquiry into unemployment stressed the stabil-ising effect of the need to prove residence in order to obtain aid. Conditions varied according to district: Boulogne required proof of one year's residence in the area; Amiens required only six months, but specified six years' work for the same employer. Elsewhere workers had to confirm that they were not doing more than one job; in Besançon workers who took on agricultural work in the summer received no relief.[32] It is clear that all such measures operated together to reinforce individual attachment to rigidly defined categories, and thus entrenchment in a fixed work sector and place. At the steel works set up immediately after the war in Saint-Chély-d'Apcher, deep in rural Lozère, the proportion of locally based workers grew from 35.5 per cent to 43.9 per cent, while in Saint-Denis Jean-Paul Brunet notes 'a powerful impulse towards integration on the part of the population of provincial origin. . . . More and more of the younger people were born in Saint-Denis', and civic registers prove that increasing numbers of newly married couples had first met in Saint-Denis itself.[33] The marked slowing down in housing development accentuated the tendency towards stabilisation in the suburbs; housing assistance diminished from 1931 onwards, and ceased in 1935. From 1932 to 1954 there was practically no new construction; out of an increased population of 1.1 million during the inter-war years, 700,000 settled in housing estates.

32. On Besançon, see Daclin (1968), p. 100; on the Nord, Michel (1975), p. 61; for the whole of France, Letellier (1938–49).
33. Brunet (1980) and Maurin (1978).

The developing crisis

Until 1933 large areas of the French salaried sector escaped the depression; those who were still in work suffered no reduction in their standard of living. Miners in the Nord, condemned after 1930 to an average of 60 days without work each year, saw their income reduced by 40 per cent, while those employed in the 'tertiary' sector, protected from unemployment by their status, enjoyed a standard of living that tended to rise. In Paris the nominal working wage index of 100 in 1929 rose to 114 in 1931, and prices frequently dropped. Similarly, civil servants had their pay reassessed and established at a higher level between 1928 and 1930. As shown in figure 5.1, the recession took a firmer hold after the end of 1933; this time there was no 'safety valve', it was the core of the French salaried world that suffered its unrestrained onslaught. Unemployment became increasingly visible as it affected urban workers with no means of support other than their wages.

In Montreuil there were 464 unemployed in November 1931; by November 1933 there were 1,847, and two years later the figure was 4,395. The figure at Ivry rose from ten to 1,000 between 1930 and 1932, and to 3,000 in 1935.[34] Shortly before the Popular Front, the Paris region, with 20 per cent of the working population, had half the nation's unemployed in receipt of assistance. At the peak of the crisis, in February 1935, the country had more than a million unemployed, representing 12.6 per cent of the population. More than 50 per cent of the workers had reduced hours of work. As well as affecting increasing numbers of workers, periods of unemployment became longer; for most people periods of work alternated with periods of inactivity, but the former diminished in length as the recession deepened. All these factors added greatly to the problems of daily life; in 1936 the average unemployed worker's income was less than half that of someone in work.

The solutions applied to this unprecedented economic depression were none the less the traditional ones. Reminiscent of nineteenth-century assistance policies, they were soon seen to be inappropriate. In many communes there was first an appeal to the welfare office for 'bread tickets' and to public generosity to help set up soup kitchens and clothing distribution as well as municipal work sites, but local resources rapidly proved inadequate. In Saint-Nazaire, for example, the amounts paid out as unemployment assistance reached

34. Lojkine and Viet-Depaule (1983), p. 282 *et seq.*

Figure 5.1 Unemployment in France, 1930–1936; percentage shown in monthly surveys by inspectors of employment and mining engineers in establishments with more than 100 employees (ref. Bulletin of the Ministry of Labour)

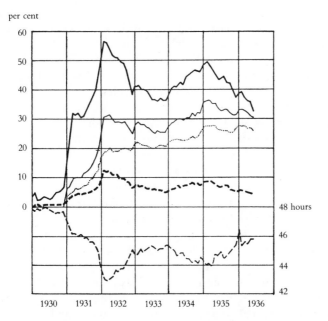

per cent

- Partial unemployment: percentage of workers not engaged in full time work, compared to the establishments' total numbers employed
- Overall reduction in employment compared to the corresponding month in 1930; this adds the percentage of those partly unemployed, converted into full unemployment equivalents, to the total reduction.
- Change in numbers employed: reduction compared to the corresponding month in 1930.
- Partial unemployment converted into full unemployment equivalents: this is obtained by multiplying the number of unemployed workers by the number of working hours missed, and dividing the total by 48.
- Length of average working week

Source: Letellier et al. 1938, vol. 1.

four million francs in 1932 and seven million in 1935. At a national level unemployment relief reached a total of 50,000 million francs in 1935. These circumstances led to ever greater demands on the government; the Saint-Nazaire municipal unemployment fund received a 40 per cent subsidy from central government in 1922, and 60 per cent in 1932, but the bankruptcy of the Compagnie Générale Transatlantique brought crisis to the naval shipyards, unemployment spread with brutal swiftness, and the state was obliged to supply up to 80 per cent of the city's funds allocated for aid in 1935. The increased stability of the working class added to business losses in undermining the paternalist style of labour management. The national survey on unemployment shows that older workers were often the first to be discharged, as being the least 'productive', and the cost of workers' retirement pensions rose in consequence; similarly the reduction in labour turnover increased the number of settled workers who must be cared for. The average individual number of days of sickness acknowledged by the miners' aid fund in the Pas-de-Calais rose from 10.48 in 1930 to 12.27 in 1934, and to 12.81 in 1936.[35] In this way the crisis hastened a development first seen in the late 1920s, that of transferring basic social charges to central state departments; this occurred in the 1928 law on social insurance, and the 1932 law on family allowances.

Yet aid was deeply inadequate. Public departments imposed Draconian conditions, and it was only on the fourth day after discharge that the first allowance could be paid out. Sometimes it was not granted for more than 30 days consecutively, and such payments could never amount to more than half the former income. Garden cultivation, familiar from the growing of modest amounts of home produce, was for many the way to ensure minimum subsistence; this applied not only in the working-class housing blocks of the north and east but also in the many suburban housing developments round the big cities, where people derived the maximum benefit from the little plots bought in the prosperous days of the 1920s. To this was added the humiliation of having to seek work; in many establishments it became customary to bring workers into the workshop for an hour or two and then discharge them. This happened at Renault and the Lorraine metal industry, but also in textiles, as at Romilly in the Aube. 'The workers turned up for work in the morning and waited for the postman. If there were orders in the mail there was work for them; if not, they went home. This was known by the characteristic phrase, "working by the mail".'[36]

35. Michel (1975), pp. 60–1.
36. Riccomard (1934), p. 180.

164

The crisis forced managers to redouble their efforts to improve returns. Frequently they lacked the resources necessary to increase mechanisation, hence the priority given to anything concerning work organisation. This approach became increasingly routine because there was no longer the fear, as in the 1920s, of worker resistance being expressed through turnover of skilled labour. At the same time as reducing wages Renault introduced comprehensive scientific management, notably in the completely new workshops opened at the Île Seguin in 1930. The number of trained men, 46.3 per cent in 1925, fell to 32.3 per cent in 1939. Whereas in the 1920s the factory gates were kept open until 8.00 a.m. to start the day's work, they were now firmly closed at 7.25 a.m. On several occasions staff were discharged and then taken on again at lower wages. In the steel works at Paris-Outreau in the Nord, as at Rombas in the Moselle, it was during the slump that chronometric measurement was introduced and the Bedaux system became widespread. This was also the period when assembly-line work was introduced into the Lip factory in Besançon and the great smelting works in eastern France. To these more constrained working conditions must be added the downgrading suffered by many skilled workers. Discharging immigrant workers and women left many labouring or unskilled posts empty, and someone had to do the work. In the coal-mines in the Nord and Pas-de Calais it was principally the coal-face miners, who included the greatest concentration of immigrant workers, who were laid off, leaving the surface workers largely unaffected; French unemployed workers were invited to take their place. Similarly in the iron fields it has been noted that during the recession workers of French nationality became more numerous, until they made up the largest category.

It was the industrial working class which was chiefly affected, although the national economic crisis had repercussions even for civil servants and workers with official status who were scarcely affected by unemployment. While 1.1 million industrial working jobs had disappeared in five years (400,000 in textiles, 230,000 in metal-working, and 22,000 in construction), the number of 'service' workers remained unchanged, apart from a loss of 46,000, as did that of civil servants – who even grew in number as the army was strengthened. Successive governmental measures led to a reduction between 1933 and 1935 of 13.6 per cent in the income of minor civil servants and of 17.6 per cent in the case of senior civil servants. Pensions of workers and former members of the armed forces were also cut. The entire basic social structure developed by the state during the 1920s suffered from these measures, quite apart from the crisis affecting small commercial trade at the same time, and the difficulties suffered by peasants whose income was cut by three-fifths between 1929 and 1935.[37]

Government employees, being the most efficiently organised, were the first to react on a large scale; in 1933 the unions set up a public services coalition to fight the government measures. The CGT benefited most from this discontent; while in the tertiary sector the CGTU saw its membership melt away, that of the reforming union grew rapidly until in 1935 'the union weight of the tertiary sector is out of proportion to its genuine importance'.[38]

Political motives rapidly came to the fore, however, in justifying employee militancy in this sector. The demonstration of 12 February 1934 was a tremendous success for the CGT; it reproduced very accurately the old divisions within the world of work. Among the 346 places with at least one rally or procession outside the Paris region it was those cities with the most firmly rooted traditional worker movement that saw the greatest activity: Bordeaux, Nantes, Limoges, Toulouse. Elsewhere the CGT redoubled its efforts to ensure that the demonstration should not look like a revolutionary movement. In its appeal it painstakingly avoided such terms as 'worker' or 'working class' in favour of others, more neutral, such as 'employee' or 'ordinary people'. It was absolutely essential to show public opinion that the demonstration was concerned only with defending 'republican institutions'. The CGTU, on the other hand, whose demonstration on 9 February had been severely repressed, openly resisted any middle-class leanings and emphasised its 'proletarian' intentions; but there were far fewer people at the CGTU demonstration than at that of the CGT three days later.[39]

These events undoubtedly formed a turning-point. The communists realised how much they had lost strength. Part of the organisation's social basis had been eradicated by the crisis. The militant Polish communists working in northern France had been expelled, as had the Italians who established the movement in the Lorraine iron-works during the 1920s. In the Paris area skilled workers who had previously been able to express their opinions

37. On this whole topic, see in particular Sauvy (1965–70).
38. Prost (1964) p. 161.
39. Prost (1966).

freely, knowing that they would easily find other jobs, were ruthlessly discharged. In the Batignolles factory in Nantes the CGTU militants took up any trivial job in order to survive.[40] Management took advantage of these new conditions to increase its hold over the work-force. Strikes lasted longer, with an average duration of 34.4 days in 1932, but failed on a hitherto unprecedented scale. The number of strikes, which had already fallen substantially during the 1920s, fell again by half. The Communist Party only survived through its full-time members who harangued the crowds outside the big suburban factories each morning, its militants in controlled sectors such as the railways, and through some town councils where it held control.

Loss of strength and realignment of the underlying social structure combined to favour abandonment of the expression 'class struggle', which gave the PCF 12 deputies in 1932, in favour of a unified strategy. The latter was encouraged by the fighting spirit of the 'reformist' unions, the CGT and the CFTC, in industrial sectors. Strikes fomented by CGT militants (in protest against work rationalisation) broke out in the Lorraine steel industry and at the Lip works. The town of Saint-Nazaire was immobilised by CGT militants opposing a halt in ship construction. Fresh disturbances broke out at the beginning of 1936; 4,500 striking workers, together with salaried office staff, organised a committee of resistance which roused the entire local populace. And in most of the mining areas there was militant activity from 1934 onwards on a scale unknown since 1920.

This activity was also enhanced by the political evolution of a whole section of the Catholic world. The birth of the CFTC in 1920, even though primarily addressed to office and shop workers rather than those involved in the physical labour of heavy industry, nevertheless enabled Catholic militants to be more effective among the common populace, particularly in the northern textile industry. In the crisis of the 1930s the Christian union became involved in long-drawn-out and frequently radical strikes, occasionally even alongside the CGTU. The founding of JOC (the young Christian workers' union) was another unifying element in the working classes, and to this may be added the dynamism of parish activity, notably through church guild work, which was at its peak during the inter-war period.

40. Peneff (1979).

It was, however, undoubtedly the French Communist Party, the PCF, that benefited from such developments. The radical image acquired by its militants in preceding years explains its attraction for so many workers anxious to express their discontent. In the northern mines the reforming generation had not been renewed since the war; in 1930 the five socialist miner-deputies were aged between 52 and 66. Despite their small numbers, with 7,300 members against the CGT's 29,000, the CGTU militants were younger, more ardent, more energetic. Gradually they increased their influence at trade elections: in 1935, 16 out of 23 of their delegates were elected at Anzin, and 32 out of 62 in the Pas-de-Calais.[41] Similarly, their earlier presence among the poorly housed sections of society was considerably strengthened by the profound unrest which affected this sector. Those who were already having difficulty in paying for their land were subjected to ever more severe taxation, all the more difficult to pay because their income was frequently much reduced by the recession. In 1936 only 50 per cent of the least well housed paid such taxes; 40 per cent were brought to court for non-payment of debts under this heading, and 10 per cent were even made bankrupt. Most of them gave their suppport to the PCF.

During the preceding period political and union work achievement in the heavy industrial regions needed constant renewal because of the shifting population and mobility among the militants themselves, but the stabilisation of the working class provided scope for a new tradition of mass struggle. Communist activity at Billancourt, for example, hitherto sporadic, started to develop a more regular pattern. In 1933 the accidental explosion of a boiler in a Renault factory resulted in eight dead and 200 wounded; immediately the communist deputy of the thirteenth Paris *arrondissement* questioned the minister of labour in the Chamber of Deputies, and *L'Humanité* demanded a commission of enquiry. The PCF made great efforts to ensure that as many people as possible attended the funeral of the dead workers, and on the day of the funeral itself the new unifying trend was evident in the presence of intellectuals reading out poems. Above all, however, the ceremony demonstrated to all who cared to look that there were two camps: on one side the mayor of Billancourt, socialist town councillors, Louis Renault, and the minister of labour, and on the other the commu-

41. Michel (1975), pp. 80–4, also Gillet and Hilaire (eds) (1979).

nist militants and 20,000 workers shouting 'murder'. After the minister's speech, the factory CGTU representative addressed the assembly and denounced management responsibility, demanding safety representation. After the ceremony there were scuffles between demonstrators and police, and during the succeeding days and weeks the accident was exploited on a large scale by militants, giving L'Humanité an excuse to increase the number of its correspondents inside the factory. Some months later, during the Citröen strike, between 12,000 and 15,000 people attended a rally in front of the company's main gates. For the first time since 1920 there were large numbers of women present and, also for the first time since then, Renault chose to allow its staff not to work on May Day rather than risk a trial of strength. A year later, in February 1934, there was a genuine turning-point which added a political dimension to the earlier activity: 5,000 demonstrators attended a rally against the extreme right; there were stoppages at Boulogne-Billancourt, and factory membership cells appeared for the first time. In spite of management repression the movement took root steadily, both inside and outside the factory. In May 1936 a L'Humanité newspaper seller was killed by a company security guard. There was a crowd 10,000 strong at his funeral, and a very tense atmosphere. At the parliamentary election, Costes, a Renault fitter, was elected deputy. All the elements needed to establish a genuine worker tradition, to make a mark on the 'collective memory' were clearly present from the beginning of the Popular Front. The Billancourt legend was born.[42]

To this was added the greater popularity of those elected, which stemmed from the social activity of town councils under PCF control. In Ivry, when a council vehicle drove through the streets distributing milk to unemployed workers' children, Maurice Thorez emphasised that such gestures were only possible because of the taxes paid by employers. In 1934 the town council paid out 12 million francs to the local unemployed. Elected representatives set up a special fund to provide aid for those partly unemployed, distributed free school meals, and organised soup kitchens, creating for themselves a fund of trust that rival politicians would not be able to challenge for a long time to come. The politicising of municipal activity was further shown in support for committees for

---

42. All details on the crisis and the Popular Front in Boulogne-Billancourt are taken from Depretto and Schweitzer (1984).

the unemployed, numerous in the Nord and in the Paris area, which organised combined 'Paris marches', with women and children following – another unmistakable indication of the movement's solidity. After February 1934 political 'anti-Fascist' themes provided a means of bringing together social categories with widely differing interests, and multifarious new societies were set up – against war and Fascism, or in favour of defending the USSR, for example; Ivry had 42 such organisations in October 1935. The policy of alliance with the middle classes, demonstrated in rallies in combination with SFIO leaders or with progressive intellectuals, thus underlined the 'respectability' of a party formerly viewed with distrust by the popular classes but which benefited from the reassurance of the new line it had adopted, of 'work, family, nation'.

This combination of elements explains the many successes of the PCF in the 1935 municipal elections. They were victorious in Saint-Étienne, Vénissieux, several of the great cities of the Nord, and above all in the Paris area; indeed so successful were they that this date can be said to mark the second birth of the PCF.

III. June 1936: The Industrial Proletariat Enters French History

An examination of the census carried out shortly before the events of spring 1936 gives the impression that French society had in many respects reverted to its pre-war condition. In the actively employed population only the working class was decreasing in number, from 38.8 per cent to 34.6 per cent. The numbers of employers, office employees and even of 'independent' workers were increasing. Peasants were still the nation's most numerous sector, at more than 35 per cent. Faced with the crisis France had turned once more to traditional artisan and rural values as if unable to cope with industrial development; and yet there were irreversible changes, as the legislative elections were to show.

The logic of mass militancy

The election campaign of April/May 1936 was no tidal wave for the left. As Georges Dupeux has commented, it showed a 'relative stability in public opinion apart from the spectacular growth of the communist vote'.[43] Confirming its 1935 advance, the PCF virtually doubled its 1928 vote, with nearly 1.5 million votes and 72 deputies instead of 12. Such success brought access to parliamentary representation to the working class in heavy industry for the first time in many areas. It was indeed in the most heavily industrialised *départements* that the communist success was greatest, apart from a few rural *départements* where the PCF was able to profit from discontent. Thus the electoral map can be drawn up with its essential elements already in place, even though there would be some additions after the war: the Paris suburbs, the Black Country of the Nord, the Lyon suburbs, the south-east, together with a few cities in the centre of the country, such as Montluçon and Vierzon, all became communist strongholds.

The strikes of June 1936 made clear the other aspect of the irruption of workers in heavy industry into French public life: the birth of mass trade-union membership. Within a few weeks the nation's whole economic life was effectively paralysed; 2.4 million workers stopped production and occupied their premises, completely demoralising the employers who within a few days granted what they had refused for 20 years; membership of the CGT rose fivefold.

The reasons for this extraordinary popular militancy still remain fundamentally unexplained. Analyses in terms of an 'explosion', dear to Georges Lefranc, or expressions such as 'becoming aware', favoured by Jean Lhomme – 'they became aware of their wretchedness and at the same time of their power'[44] – cannot fully explain the specifically working-class reasons behind such events.

A closer look at two particular moments in these strikes may help towards greater understanding. Firstly the initial phase, which was already practically over by June. It was mainly the aircraft factories of Le Havre, Courbevoie and Gnôme-et-Rhône, among others, which were affected, as well as certain metal-working establishments such as Renault and the Longwy steel company at Vénissieux. In each case the work-force was highly skilled. At Renault the movement began in the 'artillery' workshop, the lair of the 'professionals'; and aviation was still then a semi-artisan world. These movements therefore appear to arise specifically out of this particular worker category. Following the logic of what has already

43. Dupeux (1959), p. 126.
44. Lefranc (1966); Lhomme (1954).

been shown concerning the disarray of élite mechanical workers in the post-war period it is evident that attitudes were radicalised by the crisis. After the war labour turnover was for these workers one way of maintaining future flexibility. Expansion had brought hopes of social advancement to many; the economic recession meant a marked split between dreams and reality. The need to remain henceforward bound to their jobs, the humiliations which could follow lowered social status, Taylorism now being applied with full force – all these factors combined to supply the foundations for militancy among the 'worker aristocracy'. Speeches on the 'dignity of the worker', the horrors of the factory 'prison', were typical of this particular social group. Perhaps it is above all their vision of the world – reflected with adjustments through the eyes of an intellectual discovering the workers' universe – that Simone Weil relays when she says: 'There is no intimacy linking workers to their place of work and the objects among which they wear out their lives: the factory makes them foreigners in their own country, exiled and rootless.'[45]

Although few in number these workers performed an 'unleashing' role through their activity and this, combined with the left's electoral success, was to bring the whole of the working class into the struggle. Between 2 and 12 June there occurred what was effectively the second stage in the strike sequence, marked by its spread across the whole of France. After a calm summer, conflict broke out again in the autumn and in some cases lasted until the beginning of 1937. Many sources stress the movement's time-lag in relation to the Paris metal industry, which acted as a role model to be observed and then imitated; it was as though the most advanced sector had begun the acceleration of a process which was not yet ripe elsewhere, introducing a genuine synchronisation of action between the different branches of French industry. Some factories (i.e. those particularly disrupted by the discharge of many immigrant workers, such as the Lorraine steel industry, or by earlier repression, such as the Boucau metal-works) did not join the movement until much later, some of them at the time of the November 1938 strike. There was a ground-swell running through the working class in big industry, building up sometimes very rapidly and sometimes more slowly. The essential point is that this time it was an extremely widespread movement affecting the

45. Weil (1951), p. 34.

unskilled workers, the manual labourers in French big industry, who had no tradition of conflict and no long-established experience of the working world; hence the occasionally violent nature of the conflict compared with the calm atmosphere of earlier strikes. In Clermont-Ferrand, for example, the movement came near to riot, and in many regions of France the police had to intervene from that autumn onwards; hence too the tenacity of the strikers, who frequently refused to follow their leaders' counsel of moderation. In the mines of the Nord the duration of the strike can be explained by the role of new and inexperienced union recruits, drunk on success and hoping to profit from the occasion by winning yet more concessions from the management. Even in the Renault factory 'the mass of the workers was hardly politicised' at this time. Another indication of the recent birth of the movement was the 'spontaneous' nature of many disputes. In Antoine Prost's view:

> By stretching the facts only a little one could say that where there were unions there were no strikers, and vice versa. The railwaymen, post-office employees, public servants, teachers, who made up a large percentage of union members – 22 per cent, 44 per cent, 36 per cent and 25 per cent respectively – remained completely peaceful. On the other hand workers came out on strike in the metallurgical, textile and food industries, which had minimal union membership – 4 per cent, 4.5 per cent and 3 per cent respectively.[46]

There is no clearer way of indicating that it was above all those sectors still completely outside militant life, marginalised in French society, that were hammering at the door. Discussing this wave of strikes Charles Tilly has also noted an exceptionally high correlation between four criteria, providing as many supporting arguments: the large size of an establishment, the absence of previous organisation, the explosion of union activist numbers, and the intensity of the factory occupation movement.

To explain this phase of the strikes it is therefore necessary to look at the problems specific to the mass of workers in these modern industries. The majority, as indicated, moved into large factories during the war or during the following decade, and simultaneously became uprooted. As with all 'first-generation' workers of rural origin, it was not immediately acknowledged that they would continue to live permanently in this new world. Bretons

---

46. Prost (1967), p. 145.

in the Paris area clung together in societies that cultivated the memory of their homes and sent their wages back to the family who remained behind in the village; Polish and Italian immigrants also lived in the hope of returning to their native land – all imagined in a more or less muddled fashion that one day they would abandon the industrial working world. For them too the crisis sounded the knell for many ambitions for the future. Stabilisation brought with it an entrenchment in the working world and a gradual adjustment. Among the Poles, for example, when some members of their group had been expelled, 'the community lived on, reduced in numbers, and grew older, in the sense that it could now look back on an average of more than ten years' residence in France. There was very little renewal from home and in this sense too it took root'.[47] For all such workers it was a time of painful change in overall values, adding to the intensity of the conflict. Since they were there to stay, they should join the struggle to improve the present; hence their growing interest in factory-workshop problems, and in the 'qualifications' to which they were beginning to aspire; hence too their wish for guarantees of security in their professional future. As has been shown by surveys on the sociology of work,[48] the steady deepening of the division of work in a capitalist society explains the appearance of new groups of workers. Initially penalised by their lack of seniority, their interests and values were not represented in collective negotiations because the longer-established groups monopolised union representation. Only exceptionally was it possible to break the old pattern and obtain a complete redefinition of the rules of the game. During the 1930s slump workers in large American industry fought the union monopoly of skilled trade workers; in France, because craft workers were formerly insufficiently organised, antagonism took a different form: it lay more between those working in the 'secondary' sector and those in the 'tertiary' sector. With the Popular Front, however, the interest and values specific to this new worker group emerging from the 'second industrial revolution' were taken under the collective wing. The 'radical' image of the Communist Party, the fact that it had existed in the new production areas since the 1920s, explains why communist words, symbols and reasoning were adopted by such workers to define their collective malaise. It

47. Ponty (1979).
48. See specifically Sabel (1982).

should also be noted that the Matignon agreement was particularly beneficial to the smaller industrial sectors. Wage increases were accompanied by a reduction in differentials, to the benefit of those who earned the least; hence the 'levelling out of the worker hierarchy' noted by Édouard Dolléans, which sometimes annoyed the more favoured groups; and advantages such as collective agreements, which had formerly been the preserve of a few categories, became generally available.

Triumph of a new tradition in the worker movement

At the time of the union reunification members of the 'tertiary' sector predominated, but with the Popular Front this was reversed. 'Some federations (such as postal workers, teachers, civil servants) did not even double their membership, whereas the CGT's alone increased fivefold. Membership in the chemical, glass-working and metal-working industries was multiplied by 20, or very nearly so.' In such circumstances the old worker movement was overwhelmed and, with it, all that remained of the traditions of the days before unionisation. The federation of leather and skin workers, for example, still had its headquarters in Fougères and did not move to Paris until 1937; and the coopers of Périgord were still represented by the CGT, as were so many workers linked to rural life. Henceforward they were swamped by the unionised masses in the big factories, particularly since the leaders of the PCF concentrated on new members in order to impose their dominance. In polemics between communists and socialists under the Popular Front, 'one often sees unitarians and confederationists confront each other like two separate generations': many leaders whom the PCF sought to supplant 'were already militant before 1914'.[49] The Popular Front thus marks the conclusion of the breaking up process already described.

In symbolic terms the equal-representation Matignon negotiations were a completely new chapter in French history. Léon Blum sought to propitiate the CGTU representatives, unused as yet to ministerial palaces and somewhat ill at ease; their lack of self-confidence seemed to reveal the youthfulness of the worker movement they represented, particularly when faced with the self-confidence of someone familiar with the establishment, such as Jouhaux, although the ageing leader of the CGT still remembered

49. Prost (1964), pp. 157–61.

his anarchist past as a matchmaker's son. He was quick to use informal styles of speech and his casual manner contrasted with the formality of the young communists. On 8 June, however, it was Jouhaux's turn to be ill at ease when he was required to record his speech for the radio – he who loved to face an audience and turn its heckling to good advantage. Maurice Thorez, on the other hand, appeared much more adaptable.

The fact that since its birth the PCF had never managed to take root, that its leaders constantly needed replacement, explains why to date the leaders had generally been young. The vast majority of its 280,000 members in December 1936 were discovering political life for the first time with the Popular Front. Sociological analysis of the communists elected in the Paris area at this time show that for most it was the first time they had exercised their electoral responsibility. Only a third belonged to the Seine *département* by birth; 64 per cent were workers, mostly skilled. Out of 144 militant communists in Bobigny there were only five women. Most of the members were young adults, 'generally rootless, newly arrived in the Paris region', 60 per cent from the French provinces, half of them workers and 86 per cent living in a housing estate.[50]

This lack of a settled background explains why to these new-comers the militant activities proposed by the PCF appeared 'normal'. The pattern of strikes offers an example; workshop occupation, during which it was a point of honour to keep the machines in good order, indicates the internalisation of big factory standards, an illustration of the 'workerisation' mentioned above. Similarly, when organising the 30,000 Renault strikers, a highly centralised format was immediately adopted, with a central strike committee demanding a 'striker's card' checking those present. Negotiation rapidly escaped from local and even regional control and was taken on by the national organisation, while new indications of collective identity appeared at the same time. This generation, 'more national and more Jacobin than the last' according to Antoine Prost, was particularly keen to 'reconcile the red flag and the tricolour', both banners being brought out on each demonstration. At Billancourt they flanked the figures of Blum, Cachin and Costes which were borne in procession together with the symbolic figure of the Republic in Phrygian bonnet. Russian groups masterminded the great occasion; in fact all the ingredients of popular communist

50. Fourcault (1983).

culture were on parade.

At the same time workers took over their own suburban district or housing estate. Until now they had been unable to demonstrate their existence as a group in public; hence their delight in the many coordinated celebrations, political rallies, and union processions which continued until 1938. Such local activity also helped to engender local loyalty, encouraged by communist leaders anxious to strengthen workers' ties with their community.

The extent of management's concessions during this period, and the marked contrast with the previous period, explain why these events continue to stand out in the 'collective memory'. This was the beginning of the 'consumer society' as exemplified in the number of cars, which grew from 125,000 in 1920 to two million in 1939. Between the two wars the number of radio sets grew from 1.3 million to 5 million, and by 1939 there were eight million bicycles in France; with the introduction of paid time off, some workers discovered on their first holidays the delights of seaside or mountain – although mythology has exaggerated a phenomenon which affected only the core of the working class. Here was tangible proof for millions of workers that militant action paid off, that it was possible to get whatever one sought from management or government, through collective action. Many were convinced of the need for unions, as were other social groups who in this respect followed the working-class example. In spite of the repression which rained down on the CGT from the end of 1938, this was the beginning of the contractual relationships which formed a permanent addition to the French social landscape.

The Popular Front added a new element, not surprisingly, to the revolutionary slogans of 1848. White-collar workers gave their 'unreserved support to the struggle of their worker comrades'. The cardinal-archbishop of Paris made a 'touching appeal' for greater awareness of the 'workers' distress'. Speaking from his official rostrum Édouard Fuster, a professor of the Collège de France, predicted 'the end of the proletariat' and the 'reconciliation of mankind'. In a country that had had no overall industrial survey since the nineteenth century, people discovered the lack of a French statistical system. The SGF set up 'economic observatories', and sociology was anxious not to be left out; during the crisis the Institut Scientifique de Recherche Economique et Social was established – the 'Social' complemented the 'Economic' aspect – and the extent of the new field was established. Charles Rist, who at the beginning of the century had initiated 'explanations' for strikes based on economic circumstances, supplied the definition of 'social' as it was henceforward to be understood. 'It is right to qualify more precisely as "social" all research relating to living conditions, of well-being and of health, of the various classes.'[51] This was also the moment when, under the impetus of Georges Friedman, the sociology of work was accepted as a discipline.

Collective representation of the new 'proletariat' was established with the encouragement of intellectuals of all shades. 'Journalists are impressed by the unusual nature of the strike, and they have considerably increased the number of their reports.' But the miracles of technology meant that henceforward the new mythology would be disseminated overwhelmingly through pictures. Photographs such as the one sent in by Georges Lefranc in his dossier on June 1936, showing groups of strikers in caps and blue denim working clothes, placards in hand, proliferated in the newspapers. And the cinema, through films and Pathé News, filled hearts and minds with this new concept of 'popular' style. From the beginning of the crisis topics with a 'social' ingredient appeared, for example in René Clair's 1931 film *A Nous La Liberté*. With the Popular Front came a blending of the 'social' and 'popular' themes; the archetype of such films is undoubtedly Julien Duvivier's *La Belle Équipe*, in which, according to Georges Sadoul, the author:

> introduces a new character into the French cinema repertoire, a new hero: the worker. He found the perfect prototype: Jean Gabin presented credibly for the first time the lad in a cap, *sympathique*, brave, tender, quick-tempered, a little rough, a character that was to bring him swift international fame because he represented a particular French character which was highly significant at that time.

This is confirmed by Bénigno Cacérès: 'Jean Gabin did not act the part of a worker, he was the worker, like so many millions of other workers who were coming out on strike in May and June 1936. Workers felt visible for the first time in French cinema; Jean Gabin, unaided, personified the working class.'[52]

Such immense effort aimed at blending together the collective representation of this particular class was accompanied by complete structural continuity, a work of 'perpetuation' of the group.

51. Letellier et al. (1938–49), 'Preface'.
52. Sadoul (1962), and Cacérès (1981), p. 256.

Together with Maurice Thorez's supposed autobiography, the communist mythology of the miner tradition developed, 'from father to son', the basis for a fictional working-class genealogy. The hegemony of the 'Renault *métallos*' depends on the same notion of historicity, of the perpetual militant tradition. In 1932 a pamphlet published by the factory branch of the union was already stating: 'After long months of apparent inactivity, the Renault workers who *have always been* [my emphasis] at the head of the Paris region metal workers regained the place, which they had briefly abandoned, in the lead.'[53]

It is clear to modern readers how they should see this assumed tradition. As for Gabin as the personification of the entire working class, it is worth reading the work of Clément Lépidis, who described the life of an Armenian immigrant in Belleville in the midst of the *Front Popu*. How could people who were nothing but 'bloody foreigners', or as the popular expressions of the time put it, 'wogs, wops, dagoes, blokes with crinkly hair and dark skin', how could they be like Jean Gabin? What could be done with someone who was only a 'foreigner' – described by the French encyclopaedia Larousse as someone 'unfamiliar, from another nationality, not part of a family, not belonging to the unit under discussion, who appears against nature in the form of a man' – how could such a one look like 'the young chap in a cap, *sympathique*, one of us'? Ali could try all he liked in desperation, in these gala days, to enjoy the grand fête in the 'Vel' d'Hiv', the sports stadium, or the accordion music in the bar-music hall playing *Perle de Cristal* or *Le Dénicheur* on the evening of Bastille Day, 14 July, or Fernandel singing *Ignace*. Mademoiselle Françoise, in the name of her Paris childhood, would soon make him understand that he would never be one of the family: 'You must understand, Paris is an instinct.'[54]

---

53. Quoted in Depretto and Schweitzer (1984), p. 172.
54. Lépidis (1973).

6

The Unique Generation

The post-war elaboration of 'socioprofessional categories' by INSEE has had a considerable influence on social science, particularly on the sociology of work; the emphasis is on surveys by questionnaire, dividing the working classes into three tiers – manual operatives, unskilled workers, and skilled workers. Because of the historical approach underlying this book the 'generation' concept already used by Ariès in the wake of Halbwachs has been preferred to the INSEE categories, to include the social behaviour patterns of a well-defined group which could be described as the core of the working class. Quite apart from criteria of age, the term 'generation' is particularly appropriate to research concerning a group of individuals who have lived through the same fundamental experiences and have known the same initial forms of socialisation.[1] In the case of the generation born between the two world wars and involved in big industry, these conditions appear to coincide. The stabilisation of industrial strongholds began in 1930 and continued until the end of the 1950s; hence the renewal of the original group in a second-generation working class, marked by events stretching from the 1930s' recession to the cold war, consisting for the most part of qualified workers, and, through the medium of communist organisations, exercising its hegemony over the world of work until the period from 1960 to 1970. The generation was unique because by destroying its ancestral strong-

1. For a theoretical definition of the concept of 'a generation', see Halbwachs (1968), and Bourdieu (1979), particularly pp. 337–8 and 530.

holds the crisis of the 1970s eliminated any future reproduction of this particular working class.

I. Main Principles of Structuralising a Social Generation

The heroic cycle

The impact of the events of 1936 on the collective memory of the working world was all the greater in that they marked the beginning of a cycle of intense struggle – the strike of November 1938, war-time Resistance, the disturbances of the immediate post-war period – which continued until the end of the cold war. Without going into these events in detail, it would perhaps be helpful to give some indication of how they reinforced the tradition inaugurated under the Popular Front.[2]

The first point to emphasise here is the extreme violence of these social movements. The consequence of the strike in November 1938, which was declared illegal, was terrifying repression. Several thousands of workers, many of them union representatives, lost their jobs, and hundreds were sent to prison. Under the Vichy government the worker movement was reduced to clandestine activity. Leanings towards heroism acquired during previous years encouraged many workers into resisting the occupying forces. In the Nord 120,000 miners stopped work between 27 May and 9 June 1941, and renewed their action in October 1943 in order to protest against the German presence and problems of food distribution. Railway workers began a strike of defiance in August 1944, aimed at paralysing the German forces, and were followed by numerous other bodies. This does not include the manifold acts of sabotage and the Maquis organisation in which workers played a central role. Such activity provoked reprisals in the form of the deportation and execution of several hundred thousand workers, and deeply scarred the memory of all survivors. Scarcely had peace returned when in 1947 the workers' struggle began again, with the same characteristics of illegality and violence as before but this time turned against the French state. In the spring of 1947 the railway workers' strike ended with several deaths and the expulsion of

2. On the role of the workers in the period 1938–1948, see Bourdé (1977); Tollet (1970); and Coutry-Valentin (1981).

some 60 members and, in Marseille, in November of the same year, the crowd invaded the Law Courts and then the Town Hall: the Gaullist mayor was attacked and one worker was killed. The miners' struggle against the Lacoste decrees, which challenged the gains of the Liberation, was even more savage. Men from the CRS (the state security police) and tanks patrolled Montceau-les-Mines and there were brawls in Alès; more deaths, this time in Moselle, at Firminy, and in the Gard. At the Micheville steelworks in Lorraine the workers disarmed a whole company of the CRS; more than 60 people were wounded; workers' wives seized a factory manager. The great strike at Saint-Nazaire in 1955 may be seen as the last episode in this extremely violent cycle.

The central role of the large industrial strongholds is also characteristic of this period. It was only in 1938 that the hitherto marginal naval shipyard union in the Marseille suburb of Port-de-Bouc established its dominance in the local worker movement; this occurred in the wake of the November strike, which provoked intense solidarity with militants who had been discharged. The same shipyard was at the heart of clandestine activity during the Resistance. Again, it was at the metallurgical factory in Batignolles that the secret wartime management of the PC and the CGT in the Nantes area was centralised. With the Liberation the great movement of 'requisitioning' establishments led in several places to the establishment of 'worker control', with the union acting as intermediary. As well as the Berliet works in Lyon, the Port-de-Bouc naval shipyards can again be cited. The leaders of the GCT took control simultaneously of the town council and of the business, which they managed for more than three years, being finally ousted by force.[3] Following the pattern of the occupation movement of 1936 the factory became the principal stake in the struggle. This was the time of miners' sit-ins at the coal-face: blackmail over safety was sometimes used by the strikers to win over the management, another sign of the control that they knew they held over production. Workers in big industry were praised extravagantly during the years of reconstruction because the French nation needed them to recover from the storms of war; it was for this reason that they acquired many new advantages, including miners' and dockers' officially controlled status, and social security.

3. On Port-de-Bouc, see Bleitrach et al. (1981); also Réault (1981), and Molinari (1981).

The third feature, allied to the second, is the decisive role played by the CGT and the PCF throughout these events. The CFTC did not recognise the strike of November 1938, and the CGT militants struggled alone. Nine years later, in November 1947, the CFTC and the supporters of Force Ouvrière (FO – the workers' force) refused to follow the movement led by the CGT and actively sustained by the PCF, and therefore the same professional group-ings and the same industrial locations were involved as in 1936. In April 1947 it was 30,000 Renault metal-workers who gave the signal for action. In all disputes, from the Resistance until 1948, the miners were the most determined. The sociological survey of membership of the FTPF (*francs-tireurs* & French partisans) groups in Valenciennes indicates that three-quarters belonged to the working class; nearly half were in metallurgy, mostly skilled workers, a quarter were miners, and 7 per cent were railwaymen.[4] Compared with 1936 this latter group was undoubtedly the readiest to fight. The generic term 'railwayman' conceals the heterogeneous nature of a world with its own internal rules of opposition. In 1947 it was above all workers in the 'stock and traction' section, in the workshops and depots and therefore in many ways closest to the metal-workers, who led the fight. Conversely, office workers, in general civil servants, clerks, printing or metro workers, were cautious or even openly hostile to the strike at the end of 1947. At the time of the split they provided the founding core of the FO.

It should be emphasised that the claims, both in their expression and in their nature, fell well within the thinking of the Popular Front. They showed the same interweaving of material demands and political objectives, well summarised in the communist key-note words in November 1947: 'The fight of the 25 per cent against the American party'. The violent contrasts over a very short period (1936–48) must be remembered, between moments of intense happiness and considerable gain, and moments of great distress when it appeared that everything that had been gained permanently was suddenly lost again; such factors help to explain the workers' enthusiasm for anything that might look like a guarantee. The miners' or dockers' statute overrode social categories which during the preceding period had been seen as fundamental to the worker hierarchy, at a level which was the envy of many. This factor too would make a profound mark on the generation, and explain its

4. Defromont-Leschevin (1969), pp. 743–55.

enduring faithfulness to the CGT and the PCF through all trials. 'The dockers probably represent the profession that in the space of a little more than one generation has achieved the greatest social advancement', thanks to the statute of 1947, which they perceived as an unassailable charter. 'Since their work and their function were defined by the law they see them as a personal possession, and, as with all those who own something, their intention was to bequeath it to their sons.' Thus the CGT 'gathered in the votes because it led the struggle in difficult times', and because it represented a guarantee of loyalty to the 1947 law – the law which aroused a 'gut attachment' in the dockers who recalled their former precarious position.[5] The same analysis could be applied to explain the car-workers' fight, or that of the naval construction workers, at the time of the Popular Front, in their attempts to win regular work and eliminate slack seasons. Similarly the attachment to the social laws of the time, such as protective measures for dealing with unemployment, old age, and sickness, had its own particular importance for a generation which, in its childhood and adolescence, had lived through the destitution and insecurity of the great recession and the war.

Entrenchment of the working class

The collective tradition of workers in French heavy industry was consolidated between the 1930s and the 1950s through a stable social structure, and above all the stability of the working world. In this respect the Second World War was much less disruptive than its predecessor.

In general terms the balance of social groupings reflected in the 1936 census remained almost unchanged until the mid-1950s; by 1954 the rural and artisan population was still much the same as in the 1930s. During the quarter century from 1931 to 1954 the active industrial working population expanded by barely 500,000, with the increase spread more or less equally between large and small companies. This relative stability explains the persistence of the labour market features mentioned in Chapter 4, with 'protected' sectors, paternalism in heavy industry, the older sectors, textiles and light industry, and the many worker-peasants. Marcel Roncayolo has stressed that 'the main fact still remains the expansion at

5. Lecuyer and Millequant (1984), pp. 55–70.

the margins of the old industrial zones'.[6] Indeed when it came to reconstruction, government and management favoured the same economic zones as before the war; so much so that in the 1950s French big industry appeared to be completing the phase of development embarked upon in the 1920s, in the north, in the east, round Paris, Lyon, and Marseille. At the same time the 'worker orientation' and the homogeneity of the working class grew stronger. Several decades behind Germany, Great Britain and the United States, France reached its peak of industrialisation in 1954, coinciding with the historic peak of workers as a proportion of the industrial population: 87.2 per cent compared with 5.1 per cent in management and 7.7 per cent salaried staff. These figures indicate the place of the working class in the French economy.

Its homogeneity can be explained by the lack of technological innovation since the recession, underlining the level of qualification attained in 1930. The proportion of male workers among those employed in industrial work grew from 64 per cent in 1931 to 69 per cent in 1954, while the number of foreign workers dropped by 1.3 million between 1930 and 1954; most of the 1.7 million who remained had at least 10 to 15 years' residence in France. Finally, this period was also marked by the very low rural exodus, which further intensified the group's homogeneity. These facts prove very clearly that the progress begun after 1931, and which is an essential element in assessing the Popular Front, actually went on developing until the early 1950s. Industrial workers' pursuit of stability intensified the ageing of the labour force in each establishment. In 1951, 40 per cent of the employees at the electrochemical factory at Dives, in the Calvados, constructed at the end of the nineteenth century and surrounded by housing estates built between 1891 and 1926, had been on the payroll for more than 15 years. At SNECMA, an aeronautical business near Paris employing 11,000 people in 1962, the proportion of people leaving to the total number employed was 14.65 per cent; disregarding deaths and retirements, the figure for the worker group is 10 per cent. This underlines the contrast with the 1920s, when Paris establishments led the field in terms of manpower turnover. In provincial aircraft factories, in Toulouse, for example, the rate of leaving was still less than 4 or 5 per cent.[7] At the beginning of the 1970s nearly 40 per

6. Roncayolo (1959).
7. From Jalabert (1974), p. 40 *et seq.* On the Dives factory, see Elhaï (1955).

cent of the employees at the Renault factory in Billancourt had been there for more than 20 years. This entrenchment of employment was matched by entrenchment in the district or in the housing estate. In the thirteenth *arrondissement* in Paris, the 'insanitary block no. 4' in the course of being renovated, was at the beginning of the 1960s mainly inhabited by workers employed in large local factories such as Panhard or SNECMA, or in the multitudinous small businesses clustering round them; while until the end of the 1920s there was a perpetual housing crisis, Henri Coing estimates that in 1936 'the district was complete and would scarcely alter until the present renovation'; 50 per cent of the inhabitants moved in before the Second World War, and 36 per cent in the period 1926–39. In Nantes the population of the housing development at Batignolles was so static that it was considered a genuine 'workers' village'. In the Caen steelworks, in the Lorraine iron fields, or in the industrial north, there were many similar instances.[8]

The stability of the industrial population from the 1930s to the 1950s indicates the importance of that other fundamental factor connected with working-class entrenchment – professional inheritance. Indeed, if it is possible to speak of a 'social generation' with reference to workers born in the inter-war period and attached to the strongholds of heavy industry in the north, the east and the Paris region, it is equally because the majority were of working-class origin. They were the children of that first rootless generation recruited by the great factories during the two decades preceding and following the First World War.

The stabilisation of the 1930s resulted in a change in the scale of values for workers who had hitherto remained outside the factory world. The new system would, however, benefit not so much the members of this group, already too old and insufficiently educated to hope to climb far in the workers' hierarchy, as their children, on whose shoulders rested their hopes of social advancement. Given the stability of the working population at this time, and the sociological uniformity of living conditions in the shadow of the great factories, social success was usually identified with their sons' acceptance into the category of skilled workers. For the young people of the second generation education rarely continued beyond primary-school level; in 1954, 85 per cent of workers' children in Lille aged 15 or over had no education beyond this level. The Vichy

---

8. Coing (1966); on Caen, see Frémont (1981).

government set up apprenticeship training centres in 1941 to act as 'springboards', and these became the best way to attain work qualifications. Whereas in the 1930s only 168,000 had gained their CAP (the diploma obtained after vocational training), the figure passed the million mark between 1950 and 1959.[9] It is true that a substantial proportion of these young people still gained qualification 'on the job', through practical experience, particularly in heavy industry; but henceforward the 'worker élite', particularly the mechanics, could show proof of skills validated by the apprenticeship training school. This system has been described in detail by Philippe Ariès, who observed it as it developed. Evoking the world of the unskilled manual labourer he notes:

> In large working-class suburban areas, experts realise that this untrained and unsophisticated proletariat represents some 30 per cent of the population, mostly born before 1910. Later generations are frequently better educated and more sophisticated in their attitudes; here can frequently be seen the increasingly common type, characteristic of the Paris worker, who is observant, interested, quick to learn, well aware of his intellectual and technical superiority compared with provincial workers. . . . For this second generation suburban worker, social advancement does not follow the same lines as for the Paris artisan of the nineteenth century. In the nineteenth century the most advanced workers left industry independently, to go into offices, or education; it was a sort of creaming off. Nowadays the worker, or rather the skilled worker, is less inclined to change his circumstances. . . . Nowadays the son of the Paris mechanic does not try to leave the factory; he knows that he will acquire certain bourgeois privileges – financial ease, comfort, education – *without changing his way of life as a worker*; his working life gives him power because henceforward it enables him to affect national decisions.[10]

This rise of the second generation at the heart of the workers' world, based on the entrenchment of the first generation, has also been noted in relation to immigrant workers in heavy industry. Here must be emphasised the complete success of the paternalistic strategy in reproducing the labour force: in the coal mines it was

9. Figures quoted in Browaeys and Châtelain (1984), pp. 45–6. The working-class origin of young people working for their CAP is confirmed by the fact that 84 per cent of them entering apprenticeship schools do so direct from primary education, compared with 12 per cent for pupils from the École Nationale Professionelle; from Charlot and Figeat (1985), p. 357.

10. Ariès (1971), pp. 164–5, emphasis in original.

the sons of Poles who to a large extent were to provide the skilled miners after the war, and the statistical survey carried out by Alain Girard and Jean Stoetzel in the early 1950s shows that half the Polish miners' sons were themselves miners, while a quarter were working in associated undertakings, particularly metal-work. The same applied to the Italians in Lorraine, in steel and in the iron-ore mines. Promotion in the alpine electrometallurgical establishments was achieved by immigrants' sons veering towards those areas considered 'better' than the chemical sector where their parents had constituted almost the entire manual work-force. A survey of 217 workers of Italian origin in Val-d'Arve in 1964 showed that 42 per cent of the first generation were employed in the chemical industry and 8.5 per cent in metallurgy; in the second generation only 25 per cent were still in chemical work, 20 per cent had migrated to metallurgy and engineering, and 22 per cent were already salaried office staff. Similarly in the Berliet factory in Vénissieux, among the workers of Italian origin, 'those from the northern provinces [with the longest tradition of migration] and the second generation always held the most highly skilled jobs, hanging on to the least disagreeable work, if not the most highly skilled'. Some dozen years later still Philippe Bernoux affirms that, 'working for Berliet is well regarded in the working world, even if the wages are not necessarily higher than elsewhere. The turnover of staff is therefore low, and people only leave for important reasons.'[11] For many of these workers, who arrived as children with their parents in the 1920s, integration into the working class went hand-in-hand with integration into the French community. The significance shown by the rate of naturalisations in 1947 is, according to Girard and Stoetzel, that it reflects a large-scale granting of French nationality to young people as a reward for their activity in the Resistance, particularly in the mines and the steelworks.

Work on group consolidation

This combination of factors explains why the 1950s undoubtedly marked the apogee of a certain kind of working-class culture in heavy industry. Homogeneity, seniority within a class, and corresponding future expectations contributed powerfully to social

11. Girard and Stoetzel (1953/4), cahier No. 19, p. 60 *et seq*; concerning Italians in the south-east, see Faidutti-Rudolph (1964), pp. 225 and 307; also Bernoux (1973), p. 19.

consolidation through a combined effect which must be observed on two levels.

On a local scale the 1950s encouraged the spread of class norms. These were seen in the consolidation of family values; Anglo-American anthropology has shown the great importance of the family unit for the working classes. As an independent unit in a world so heavily subject to the constraints of work the family is also a haven, a refuge from the group, offering recuperation and restoration, and recent memories of rootlessness intensified such attitudes. The family became effectively a rampart against loneliness, the means to a large element of integration into the local community. Members of the second generation, whether Poles in the Nord or Italians in the eastern regions, integrated themselves through mixed marriages, forming links between French and foreign families which had been very rare in the first generation. Similarly, family events were central to local life: photographs and articles in newspapers with regional or very localised circulation told of weddings, deaths, retirements, pensioners' parties, and so on, often appearing in the companies' own news-sheets.

Outside the core of the family there was a developing sense of belonging to a particular place, a housing estate or a district, which had first become apparent in 1936. Parish-pump loyalty, local patriotism, was frequently mentioned in such working-class communities. Although in broad terms the working class as a whole was not closely involved in social activities apart from those arising from the workers' movement, the local bar or bistro was frequently an important place in such matters. In a small working community such as Villefranche-sur-Saône, for example, the café-bar held a central position in the individual's membership of a group, through its *boules* team. Such teams often operated under the name of the district, with headquarters at a bar where the game was practised in a small yard behind the public bar-room. Thus, 'being a café-bar *habitué*, playing *boules*, being a man, living in a particular district, being a worker – it was all part of the overall picture'.[12]

Many of these cafés were very close to the factories and constituted a kind of bridge between life at work and the world outside the factory; indeed some of the verbal negotiations or collective practices which were begun on the factory floor were concluded in the bars, for there was a complete shopfloor world which extended

12. Bozon (1982; 1984).

far beyond production in the strict sense of the word. Entrenchment in the working class was in theory a 'qualification'; it also opened the way to all customs arising from what Erving Goffman has called, in a different context but one that is none the less applicable to the factory world, 'secondary adaptation'. This includes all the methods used by the individual to fit himself into the business while simultaneously finding his way more or less openly round its regulations. 'Lifting', 'scrounging', or 'pinching' is a good example of this social process. Recent surveys on the topic show that in Lorraine, as in the west or the Paris area, the habit of deflecting work-time, tools or basic materials for personal use was, because of shortages, particularly prevalent during the Second World War. Later such habits persisted for increasingly symbolic reasons.

It was one way of strengthening the ties between members of the local group. Such activity was not permitted to all: it was only possible for workers who enjoyed a certain amount of autonomy in their work, who were sufficiently canny not to be caught, and sufficiently skilful to produce goods from raw materials which were not always appropriate; hence the role of such practices in the consolidation of working-class values such as know-how and courage, which were fundamental to this generation. 'Scrounging' was an important part, in the 1950s and 1960s at least, of 'making a name for yourself', operating in favour of those who were best integrated at the expense of those who could not, or who apparently would not, show themselves capable of such 'tricks'. Materials 'salvaged' or 'picked up' through the business were also the object of a multitude of bartering transactions, responding to the demands of workers who were also highly skilled at domestic repairs and tinkering; many owned houses which were always undergoing some kind of improvement and never quite finished. The social niceties, however, demanded that each 'gift' was balanced as promptly as possible with a quid pro quo for it was unthinkable not to respond in kind. The constraints of the system worked to the advantage of group solidarity, notably in that very often 'scrounging' involved connivance or compromise on the part of the senior employees, particularly the foremen, resulting in modest blackmail and opportunities to extend areas of freedom on the factory floor.[13]

13. On such customs, see 'Les productions symboliques ouvrières' (1984); Lescot et al. (1980), pp. 73–4, and Noiriel (1984), pp. 363–7.

Collective structuralising of the central worker group was also achieved by 'initiation' rituals for new arrivals. The principal element of such working-class rites of passage was that above all they affected young apprentices coming from the same families. Adult power was exercised over them, often displayed through physical aggression and sarcasm on all sides, in the form of teasing and disagreeable practical jokes. The hopeful postulant must learn to cope with all such trials in order to be admitted finally as 'one of the gang' and such rituals also marked him for life as a worker in one particular factory.

Many other rituals formed part of the working life cycle: the rituals of closing down or of retirement were the most prized, providing the excuse for a modest celebration and exchange of gifts and above all the recollection of high points in the group's past in which the retiring worker had played his part, within his own circle and within the setting of the workshop where he had passed a substantial part of his working life. Similarly, group life was calibrated and punctuated throughout by recurrent rites – the annual cycle of holidays, birthdays and patronal feasts such as the miners' Sainte-Barbe, the metal-workers' Saint-Éloi. There were, too, the many symbolic demonstrations designed to show off the factory's 'fertility', such as the inauguration of a new blast furnace in a steelworks, or the launching of a new ship in a naval shipyard.

Business managers frequently encouraged these practices, or at the very least showed no opposition, for it was one way of fostering the workers' attachment to the company they managed, a way of stimulating an investment which also operated through competition to climb the ladder of qualifications validated by the professional classification of 1945, or by the cult of work well done.

A fundamental element linking members of an entrenched community was the CGT union and beyond it, very often, the PCF. Confidence in the organisation was linked to the assiduously maintained principle that what little one has is enjoyed thanks to the union; and the improvements sought will be achieved thanks to the union. Moreover, most of its leaders had themselves risen from the same origins. Very often the elected leaders had won their place through their heroic activity during the 'great age', 1936–48. They gave themselves to the group, were often victimised, showed their courage by saying out loud what others were thinking to themselves. Thus they became charismatic leaders, the embodiment of the whole community's noble deeds. With the population's growing stability they too took root; it is hardly surprising in such circumstances that until very recently a substantial number of elected communist leaders, the 'eminent reds', came from this 'heroic' generation.

All these efforts, aimed at reinforcing mass group identity at a local level, had their political equivalent on a national level in the work of the PCF. As much through parliamentary work as in the political message that it disseminated, it stressed areas of awareness already observed in relation to the Popular Front; these were based on a combination of 'economics', through, for example, speeches on 'the pauperisation of the workers', and simple (not to say simplistic) political exegesis dealing with such topics as American imperialism and the Soviet paradise. At this same time the PCF was refining the collective images of the 'party of the working class'. The miners' mythology now came to full fruition and the home village of the 'son of the people' became the communist Mecca. Party intellectuals lent impressive weight to this approach; from the large range of communist literature the poems of Louis Aragon may be mentioned, collected in a pamphlet entitled *Le Pays des Mineurs*, or André Stil's famous book, *Le Mot Mineur Camarades*, 1949. That same year saw the appearance of Louis Daquin's film *Le Point du Jour*, shot in the heat of the miners' strike in northern France in 1947. The 1950s were also the high point of the great days of 'social realism', offering a new version of the workers' fantasy combining populism and a natural pessimism. The miner thus became, simultaneously, the prototype of the new man, the iconic figure of the proletariat, handsome and noble – and the symbol of the despised working life, with torn hands and ravaged body, and lungs destroyed by silicosis.[14]

It was, however, undoubtedly the *métallo*, the Paris metal-worker, who was in the right no matter what the circumstances. This was the time of Sartrean avant-garde anguish at the thought of 'losing hope of Billancourt', and when industrial sociologists focused their attentions on the major undertakings, the results that included the numerous studies devoted to Renault factories after 1945.

The contemporary influence of the image of the *métallo* on the collective awareness may be better seen in an apposite quotation from the feminine – but not feminist – symbol of popular cinema,

14. For a recent study of this problem, see Lazar (1985).

the actress Arletty: 'I rate the *métallos* above everyone else; they went through 1936. The Paris *métallo* is someone special: they are like engineers, they are perfectionists. I know about the *métallos*, they are not the same as other workers.'[15]

This parallel between the central group of the working class, the CGT and the PCF, explains the enduring success of these organisations at the heart of the working world. Out of every ten workers who voted in the 1956 parliamentary election in the Seine *département*, seven chose the Communist Party and only one the SFIO, the French division of the Workers' International. On a national level, a survey by IFOP (the French opinion-poll organisation) estimated that 50–60 per cent of the workers were communist supporters, against 15–17 per cent who were socialist sympathisers, while a quarter remained faithful to the more conservative parties.[16] A dozen years later the survey of Guy Michelat and Michel Simon, which for once combined the statistical approach with a land survey, showed that working-class heredity operated in favour of increased votes for the left, and above all for the PCF. 'This effect of heredity is such that workers who were sons "of true supporters", and the "true supporters" who were sons of workers, show almost identical electoral patterns of behaviour.' Such a phenomenon stresses the full importance of that first socialisation in childhood in defining ultimate choices. This enquiry also confirms the strength of links between the PCF and the group of workers referred to above as the 'second generation'. In fact it was in the 40–59 age band that it achieved its greatest results; the stronger the feeling of belonging to the working class, the greater the influence of the PCF – and such feelings of working-class solidarity reached their peak among workers aged between 40 and 59.

A mass survey carried out in 1969 of 'the French worker' supported these findings with its own conclusions. It was the workers born between 1920 and 1934 who voted most solidly for Jacques Duclos in the presidential election. They included a majority of skilled workers, particularly those employed in mining, textiles, and steel; and it was precisely this worker group that constituted the most substantial core element of the CGT, both in its votes at trade elections and in the number of members. Elsewhere the CGT

---

15. Quoted in Browaeys and Chatelain (1984), p. 45.
16. Hamon (ed.) (1962), p. 14.

had its greatest influence among workers who were trained and highly skilled. The 35–49 age-group of workers stood out in its particular stability; one-third had been employed for at least 15 years by the company where they now worked, and this age-group also showed greatest attachment to factory and region. Their opinions on the current economic situation cut across those of other categories; they stated, simultaneously, that the condition of the French people had improved overall, and that their own conditions had not improved. This group also expressed the sharpest reservations about credit. All such assessments are understandable only in the light of its own group history, with its hopes and aspirations well represented by the communist organisations; and in return the group remained faithful to those same communist organisations.

> Overall, the cliché image of the unionised worker would tend to describe him as a highly skilled professional who had reached the CAP level of technical competence, a railwayman, electrician or metal-worker, concerned about the future of his trade, aged about 40, working in an establishment with about 1,000 wage-earners, living in a major provincial industrial zone, and with an inclusive family income of between 1,000 and 1,750 francs.[17]

II. The Dominant Worker Group, and Changes in French Society

Unprecedented upheavals

The end of the 1950s marks the beginnings of what economists have analysed as a break with earlier forms of capital accumulation, based since the beginning of the twentieth century on the production of heavy or intermediate capital goods. The 'consumer society' reflects another developmental pattern, that increases in average wages should tally with rises in productivity. Because the extension of capitalism was henceforward very much more dependent than hitherto on the stability of working-class standards of living, a whole series of measures, which were also concessions to workers' militancy, were put in hand to guarantee these resources. According to the principles laid down by Keynes in the 1930s, the state took the initiative through social protection and through

17. Adam et al. (1970), and Michelat and Simon (1977), p. 165.

growth of contractual relationships between 'social partners'.

Beginning notably with the Fifth Republic, the nation's econ-omic structure responded to the effects of a concentration of estab-lishments which was entirely without precedent, and which led to monopolies dominating entire fields of industry. The need for these large groups to export an ever-increasing proportion of their out-put explains the adoption of a policy of free trade, aided by improvements in international transport; hence the development of a new international dimension in the working world, operating at the expense of former colonies which were now independent 'third-world' countries.

French society developed and changed against this background. The rural exodus, modest in scale since the end of the nineteenth century, accelerated sharply; in 20 years the land lost 40 per cent of its farmers and 70 per cent of its wage-earners, so that by 1975 the agricultural population represented less than 10 per cent of the active working population. The new society thus also meant the end of the traditional peasant, as well as of the equally traditional worker-peasant.

The colossal expansion of science and technology after the Se-cond World War, the extension of public services such as edu-cation, health, and cultural amenities in addition to public and private administration, produced over these two decades a very substantial increase in the 'new middle classes': the ranks of the traditional liberal professions and senior managers were multiplied by three, middle management by 2.5, and salaried staff by 1.8.

After reaching its peak in 1954 the working class, as defined by INSEE, diminished as a proportion of wage-earners from 61 per cent in 1954 to 47.7 per cent in 1975; but it grew none the less in absolute terms by two million, to reach 8.5 million in 1975.

One of the most significant elements relevant to this present study is the fresh method of definition within the world of work. In 1954 the strongest category in numerical terms, 46 per cent, was that of skilled workers and foremen, compared to manual operat-ives and unskilled workers, at 41.5 per cent; the balance covered such workers as miners, mariners, etc. Some 20 years later the most highly skilled group made up less than 45 per cent of the total, while the less skilled category had risen to 54.9 per cent. Although the total of manual labourers had grown by half a million, the group that showed the most spectacular growth was the unskilled, with an increase of 1.5 million jobs.

This expansion of unskilled work was chiefly concentrated in new factories producing modern consumer goods. The development of a stable mass market and of new technology encouraged the spread of standardised work in large manufacturing units; these new jobs were created in areas that had hitherto remained rural in character, and the realignment of France's industrial map is a fundamental feature of the period.

In very simple terms French economic areas can henceforth be seen as forming three distinct types. The first is a concentration of 'intellectual' types of work, essentially in the Paris area, with more of the new forms of worker skills than other regions; by 1975 there were as many engineers and technicians as unskilled workers. The second type of region was particularly concerned with 'skilled manufacturing': this covered the bastions of large-scale industry in the provinces, and the core working-class element from earlier times. Here too technological change meant new jobs for highly skilled workers. It was in the third type of area that standardised production was concentrated; the area most affected was western France and areas affected by the 1960s' policy of decentralisation. Improved transport and the fact that these light industries were not primarily dependent on basic raw materials or sources of energy – but above all the great reserves of manpower available – lay behind the development of a new generation of factories in rural areas where 37 per cent of industrial jobs were created between 1962 and 1966.[18]

Basse-Normandie, the area around Caen, is a prototype of the regions affected by such developments. Over a score of years 50 per cent of agricultural workers left the land, and during the same period wage-earning industrial workers doubled in number, while workers in the tertiary sector increased by a third; 70 per cent of the new non-managerial jobs were for unskilled labour. Car manufacturing led the way, with 40,000 new jobs during these two decades, and in Caen, where until the 1950s the only large factory was the SMN (The Normandy Metal-Workers' Society) with its 5,000 steel workers, a new industrial generation arose with, among others, Moulinex, Saviem – 6,000 workers – and Citroën with 3,000.

Western areas enjoyed similar progress; new vehicle manufacturing and electrical industry developments more than made up for stagnation in traditional industry, particularly naval shipyards, and

18. From Lipietz (1983), p. 55.

the number of wage-earners in local industry grew by 11–13 per cent. Growth in the Vendée was even greater than in the Loire Atlantique.[19] Older industrial processes, such as metallurgy, steel-making, chemistry, the 'bedrock' sectors, also shared in and ben-efited from the general dynamism and, apart from textiles and mining, these sectors held their position until the 1970s. The regions in which they and their workers were concentrated, how-ever, were no longer the industrial heart of the nation. Sociological division corresponded to this geographical division of work. New and relatively unskilled jobs were in effect reserved primarily for new workers of rural origin: immigrants and peasants, rootless in the cities, and the new worker-peasants who remained in their villages but who were gathered into the factories by coach, some-times over considerable distances. Within this grouping of workers of rural background should be distinguished two categories par-ticularly concerned with unskilled work.

Firstly, the women. Between 1962 and 1975 the proportion of women employees increased from 33.4 per cent to 38.7 per cent. Much of this increase was absorbed by the tertiary sector, but between 1968 and 1975 the rate of 'feminisation' of the working classes grew from 20.4 per cent to 22.4 per cent. In the same period nearly half the newly created jobs were aimed at women. This did not affect all jobs in all sectors, since in 1975 half the female work-force was employed in consumer industry and 79 per cent of women employees were unskilled.[20]

Immigrant workers represented the opposite pole of unskilled work. The steeper the progressive curve of unskilled employment during these 20 years, the greater the recruitment of foreign labour. From 1.7 million in 1954 the immigrant population grew to 4.1 million in 1975, with Spanish, Portuguese, and Maghreb (North African Arab) workers providing the largest proportion of the newcomers.

In 1968 only 5 per cent of the immigrant workers were employed in mining, with 40 per cent in construction, 10 per cent in agricul-ture, and 20 per cent in metal-work. After 1968, vehicle manufac-turing concentrated particularly on the immigrants, until in 1974 a third of the total work-force in this sector was of foreign origin.

19. Réault (1983).
20. Kergoat (1982), pp. 9–76.

Three-quarters of the immigrants found work in unskilled or manual work.[21]

Of all the profound upheavals experienced by the working class during the 1954–75 period, those that affected its way of life deserve particularly close attention; on average, wage-earners' standard of living trebled over a 20-year period and social-security measures expanded beyond all previous experience. In 1953, 8 per cent of workers owned a car; by 1975 this figure had risen to 73.6 per cent. Television ownership grew over the same period from 0.9 per cent to 88.4 per cent, and for refrigerators the figures are from 3 per cent to 91.6 per cent. Even workers' home ownership increased dramatically, from 19.8 per cent to 37.5 per cent.[22]

There are many other examples of progress which provide a striking contrast with the uncertainty, even destitution, of the preceding period, notably in housing with the spread of standardised council-subsidised housing (HLM units), and other factors such as access to public services. Rates of infant mortality may be seen as a reliable neutral indicator: although the rate among the working class between 1956 and 1960 was still 32.8 per 1,000, by 1969/70 it had dropped to 20.8 per 1,000.

Adaptability

To some extent the upsurge of the consumer society reinforced the acquired attitudes of the dominant worker group. Those who had known poverty and insecurity in childhood were naturally enthusiastic about progress that brought increased material well-being and the added benefit of security. This was enhanced by the fact that such progress was not seen as proof of the virtues of capitalism but of the effectiveness of the collective struggle aimed at 'social gains' and the preservation of such gains. Elsewhere, as already shown in relation to credit, the system of collective group values was strong enough to withstand the pressure of new norms. People accustomed to work since childhood continued in general to work during their leisure hours, either at household 'do-it-yourself' maintenance, employing skills which were less and less in demand within the factory, or in gardening, which was no longer genuinely essential for survival.

21. Granotier (1970), pp. 93–112.
22. Figures taken from tables in Verret (1979), pp. 180–1.

Similarly, the habit of watching television was less passive than frequently alleged, although this social class spent more hours in front of the set than any other; members of middle-management or the professional classes watched television for 8.1 hours per week, on average, against 13.7 hours for farm-workers, while the average rose to 14.5 hours for skilled workers and to 14.7 for the unskilled, manual workers, and service workers.

As Philippe Champagne observed, however, 'messages conveyed by television will only be absorbed if they meet and reinforce favourably predisposed attitudes'. This is why new media models have had only slight impact on a generation that discovered such methods of communication after acquiring the principal elements structuring its habitat and style. As Richard Hoggart had already observed in relation to English workers, it is important to bear in mind that ever-present latent scepticism of the popular classes in the face of messages from outside their own group. Although more than 60 per cent of metal-workers in Toulouse listened to radio news bulletins in the 1960s, they evidently had no illusions about what they were being told: 'I listen to the news', said one of them, 'every night, true or false, good or bad, without believing what they say, just to know what they are trying to make us believe.'[23] These same principles should be applied when seeking to interpret the many setbacks encountered by propagandists for 'Culture', particularly worker-delegate committees trying to convince workers of the virtues of classical theatre, serious music, or modern art.

Increased stability was also an essential lever enabling workers to go on strike against changes that they viewed with disfavour. At the Saint-Chély-d'Apcher factory it was considered that, for the management, 'this relative stability has its drawbacks: when there were takeovers or mergers, when the factory passed into other controlling hands, the fear of losing jobs was extremely powerful – this was the fundamental element that caused strikes, far more than wages or even conditions of work'.[24] This challenge to stability, which began in the mines in the 1960s, was the underlying cause of widespread miners' strikes and coal-face occupation, beginning at

23. Quoted in Larrue (1965), p. 40. According to this author, 70 per cent of workers in the Toulouse aerospace industry in the 1960s took no part in the activities of the Works Committee; on the influence of television, see the Ministère de la Culture (1982), p. 225; and Champagne (1971). The relationship between the working classes and art and museums is considered in Bourdieu and Darbel (1965).

24. Maurin (1978).

Decazeville at the end of 1961 and symbolising the struggle of a whole nation for its survival; it reached its apotheosis with the great 'March on Paris' in 1963. Although the decisions were not challenged, these disputes were a powerful factor in the development of contractual relationships. The 1963 'Round Table' meeting ended in generalised bargaining, confirming the redeployment of miners and inaugurating a form of compromise that was to prove highly successful, that of early retirement. Similarly the general steel works' strike of 1967 ended with the signing of a social agreement, which was also drawn up round a guarantee of redeployment.

Faced with a changing society, skilled French workers (and particularly those who had acquired their CAP) were able to use their seniority to achieve individual solutions and avoid downgrading. Downgrading of jobs in coal-mines, and particularly in textiles, led to such an exodus of skilled workers to other types of employment that industrial managers were obliged to recruit large numbers of immigrants to maintain their work-force. The rapidly expanding French economy put skilled workers in a highly favourable situation and extended their training within the company that employed them. In aeronautics, the birth of the space industry meant substantially higher overall standards – to such an extent that in the 1960s 87 per cent of workers were classified as skilled, 13 per cent unskilled. Engineers, managers and technicians made up as much as 40 per cent of employees. Three-quarters of the workers benefited from supplementary professional training within the company, to keep pace with scientific and technical progress.

> The classic rivetter or welder who worked on sheets of aluminium or duralumin had to learn how to work with adhesives or vacuum-welding, or in a neutral atmosphere, using plasma jet burners on solids of extremely resistant and expensive alloys, perhaps titanium or alloys based on nickel or magnesium. The level of competence was that of the technical *Baccalauréat* with three or four years of factory training, and no longer that of the CAP.[25]

Even in the vehicle-manufacturing sector, the area where assembly-line production was most advanced, 'downgrading' should be considered not in relation to the single large establishment which tended to attract the attention of the sociologists, but on the level of the complex ensemble which it formed with its

25. Jalabert (1974), p. 189.

attendant body of small and medium-sized firms of subcontractors. Indeed, the more standardised the work the more complicated the machinery, demanding advanced skills for its running and maintenance. Similarly, in the large holding companies and conglomerate commercial companies, technological research entailed the creation of small units to develop prototypes, and try out new tools and processes. All this demanded workers capable of showing initiative and solid training. The large survey carried out by Pierre Naville and his team shows that in 1969 Renault employed 80,000 people; but the work-force at Billancourt represented less than half that total, with slightly over 36,000 people of whom 25,800 were factory workers. These last were mostly employed in the manufacture of machine tools, demanding large numbers of skilled hands and lacking any assembly-line element. The actual production lines were set up at Flins and Sandouville, far away from Billancourt, and it is not surprising that the seniority of employees was much greater in the Billancourt workshops than on the provincial factory floor. The dominant group was able to sustain its advantageous position within the working class by resisting attempts at downgrading, often effectively, through professional tradition allied to combative tradition.[26]

The numerous small subcontracting enterprises that gravitated round the big factories were veritable hothouses for the production of skilled workers, of whom some were able to attain craftsman status. Decentralisation of the aeronautical industry into the Cher set up an explosion of small and medium-sized businesses; their 'bosses', with an average age of between 25 and 40, had in general only made the leap to independence after long years of experience as skilled workers. This accords with a broader observation, that access to artisan craftsman status generally involved an interim period as a wage-earning worker. A survey of a group of workers in 1965 who became self-employed in 1970 showed that they had almost all been wage-earners in small businesses, generally skilled, setting themselves up independently at around the age of 30. But this access to managerial status, even for the worker élite, always remained insecure since, during this same period 1965–70, 88,000 small traders and self-employed craftsmen became wage-earners again.[27] This indicates that the ebb and flow between the two

26. Naville et al. (1971).
27. On this point see Zarca (1983); also Mayer (1977).

202

worlds, which was typical of the nineteenth century, had not yet died out.

These few comments indicate that skills or seniority in the working world were the trump cards making it possible to cope with conditions that favoured change. This is confirmed by a 1973 survey of 1,600 workers in the Paris area aged between 55 and 64: 'They are former farm labourers and agricultural workers who went into building trades and unskilled or labouring work. On the other hand, workers who got started immediately after leaving school as trained metal-workers persisted through a network of advanced qualifications.'[28]

Another aspect of this adaptability appears in the strategy deployed by families within the core group of workers to find places for their offspring. The high post-war birthrate meant that hundreds of thousands of young people reached the labour market in the 1960s; of 6.3 million workers under the age of 30 in 1968, 3.6 million began their working life between 1962 and 1968, and more than one person in six had been working for less than six years. In 1968 young workers alone, aged between 15 and 24, represented a quarter of the working class, and many of them were children of the generation discussed above. There too, entrenchment, the strength of family values and stability were appreciable assets. In fact, 'there can be no upward mobility without pre-existing family impetus',[29] and a survey by the CNRS (the national centre for scientific research) indicated the prerequisites that made it possible for a worker's son to improve his social standing. He should have a trouble-free childhood in a large city, or in the Paris area, a reasonably well-educated mother, a father proud of his status as a trained worker, if possible an uncle who was a white-collar salaried employee or a grandfather who was a shopkeeper. He should also be an only child, or at most have only one brother or sister.[30]

Such favourable conditions frequently lay behind scholastic success in training centres and technical education schools leading to the new diplomas in advanced manual qualifications, the BEP (the standard French examination for 16 year-olds) or even the *Baccalauréat*. In industrial cities entrenchment also meant that families had a sound knowledge of the local labour market, helping

28. Vrain and Gautier (1979), p. 450.
29. Darbel (1975).
30. Scardigli and Mercier (1978), p. 149.

them to gain the best places for their children. In Le Havre, for example, the most sought-after establishments today are the Compagnies Françaises des Pétroles, and Goodyear. Technological advances have abolished the more unrewarding aspects of work in the chemical industry. Automation means that actual manufacturing processes, demanding qualifications based on versatility and a sense of responsibility, are more valued than maintenance work. Such companies prefer to recruit young people with a professional diploma, earning wages considerably above the local average. Applicants are assessed with great care, so that only one in ten is taken on; hence the necessity for 'connections' in order to be accepted.[31] Modern steel manufacturing, such as at the automated works at Fos, Dunkirk or Gandrange, looks first to the sons of steel workers when they are recruiting. At La Solmer, Fos, many of the skilled workers come from Lorraine, the 'third generation' of iron-workers. At the end of the 1970s most were in their thirties, with two or three children, a wife who did not go out to work, and good wages, resulting in a stable atmosphere separate from the Marseille conurbation.

It may thus appear that, despite the decline of older industrial regions, the most deeply rooted worker group has succeeded in fitting its children to new dynamic sectors of working-class life. A 1970 INSEE survey questioned the alleged 'disillusionment' of the young with regard to business, a very fashionable theory in anti-establishment university circles; the survey claimed that there were as many young people taking up industrial blue-collar jobs as in preceding generations. A few years later a survey of French workers aged between 16 and 24 showed that 77 per cent were satisfied with the atmosphere in their workshop: 76 per cent were interested in their work; 55 per cent were satisfied with the future prospects offered by their chosen career. Two-thirds stated that they had found their first job within less than a month, and 88 per cent had never lost their jobs.[32]

At the same time some of the values of the earlier generation were being passed on to these young people. The CNRS survey quoted above, covering a sample of workers' sons, showed that in order to explain the factors of professional success, 75 per cent mentioned work and one-third specified honesty; the family was

---

31. See Chopart (1978), p. 44.
32. Mouriax (ed.) (1974).

also a prime asset.[33] The resurgence of the CGT and the PCF after 1968 also contributed to success in the transmission of essential collective values; these organisations tended to appeal to the youngest workers. Within closed professions such as the docks, the union joined protected status as advantages to be passed on to the next generation. 'The legacy also included the entire historic corpus of the confrontations and vagaries that led to this victory, particularly 1936 and 1947.' The strength of the organisation within these professions also enabled the community to survive the profound changes within its crafts, resulting in greatly increased flexibility adapted to technical modernisation.[34] The 1976 enabling law, following the great struggles of the early 1970s, gave print workers a redefined status approaching that of the dockers.

The 'democratisation' of education initiated in the 1960s offered many children from this section of the working class the opportunity to achieve a status beyond the wildest dreams of their parents, let alone their grandparents. Many recent surveys into social mobility indicate a substantial shift from 'blue-collar' to 'white-collar' work: the CNRS survey quoted above gives a figure of 41 per cent of its subject group of workers' sons, mostly moving towards salaried-staff categories.

Table 6.1 gives some indication of the 'democratisation' processes of secondary education from the end of the 1950s until the present time; it also shows up its limitations, which will be referred to later. In essence it shows that workers' children tended to find it more difficult to continue with secondary education in the 1970s. Elsewhere working-class children were over-represented in the 'drop-out' streams, the CPPN, CPA and CEP classes (See Table 6.1), and also in the shorter technical education streams.[35] A closer look into the problematics of working-class generations and skills would doubtless show that it is the children of the most highly qualified and solidly entrenched generation of workers who gain access in greatest numbers to extended secondary education.

Slow disintegration of the group

The process of changing social status from one generation to

33. Scardigli and Mercier (1978).
34. On this flexibility of the 'protected' professions, see Segrestin (1984).
35. From Charlot and Figeat (1985), p. 468.

Table 6.1 Workers' children in Secondary Education as a percentage of total numbers per year-class

age	1958–1959	1961–1962	1963–1964	1967–1968	1973–1974	1976–1977	1980–1981
13–14 (public sector)	21	24.4	28.1	35	38.3	38.3	35.7
13–14 (private sector)		12.3			21	21.3	22.5
15–16 (public sector)		18.8		25.7	25.3	25.9	27.3
15–16 (private sector)		5.9			10	11.1	14.6
16–17 CAP★ (public)	48.6	50.4	50.2	54.3	51.2	53	52.3
16–17 BEP★ (public)				38.7	41.1	43.3	44.4
13–14 practical or CPPN★				55.6	53.2	53.5	54
CEP★					56.2	55	56
CPA★					51.4	50.4	50.4

Source: Charlot and Figeat 1985, p. 468.

CAP: Certificat d'Aptitude Professionelle
BEP: Brevet d'Enseignement Primaire
CEP: Certificat d'Education Professionelle
CPPN: Classes Pré-Professionelles de Niveau
CPA: Classes de Pré-Apprentissage

The two year-classes CPPN followed by the CPA are for the least able pupils aged 13–15 who cannot cope with standard classes. Most leave at the end of the CPA without any examination successes and do not find employment.

another, however, entails a slow loosening of the ties linking the members of this working-class community, even though remaining a limited phenomenon until the beginning of the 1975 crisis.

Development starting in the 1960s was based on 'bypassing worker strongholds', progressive deindustrialisation of the old bastions of employment leading to creeping marginalisation of workers in such sectors. In textiles and coal-mining the decline began in the 1950s; between 1947 and 1980 the number of coal-miners fell from 330,000 to 33,000 and complete coalfields, such as the Loire, were wiped off the map. Textile industry in the Vosges lost half its work-force between 1954 and 1980, and in the Nord the loss was 40 per cent between 1954 and 1974. The Nord and Lorraine, the two bulwarks of heavy industry, were in decline from the end of the 1950s despite dynamism in the metal industry; many workers could find new jobs only by moving away, by uprooting themselves again. Between 1954 and 1962 the balance of migration was already slightly negative – the loss in the Nord was 23,000 and in Lorraine, 38,000; the tendency increased between

1968 and 1975, leading to a loss of 98,000 from the Nord and 53,000 from Lorraine.

Diminishing industrial vigour in these regions marks the beginning of a collective crisis of identity for a group whose self-image was constructed round work as the central factor of social value. Positive strategies of social advancement were replaced by defensive struggles to preserve jobs. At first sight the great mining strikes of the early 1960s may look like group victories, with the embattled worker appearing as a television hero for the first time, making a forceful contribution to the positive effect of such movements on public opinion; the abiding image is of the Decazeville miners spending Christmas 1961 at the bottom of a mine shaft. However, the irruption of television into the collective representation of the working class introduced a new image of the 'defeatist' worker, which is still dominant today.

The 'self-confident production worker' of the 1950s was overtaken by technological change. Automation did away with the last remaining congenial manual tasks in the textile industries; in the Nord, 'the textile tradition of a regional labour-force, the whole corpus of custom and knack which passed more or less by word of mouth from father to son, lost much of its strength'. Decentralisation had a similar effect on the old skills of light industry, ranging from hat-making in the Aude to pottery manufacture in Gien, on the Loire. Artisans had no successors, for their children preferred more modern sectors; and in any case, where such work still existed it was heavily mechanised and had lost all attraction – hence the massive recruitment of immigrant workers.[36]

Having concentrated all their efforts on encouraging their labour-force to put down roots, business managers now favoured mobility; relocating production required many workers to move from their home towns to more dynamic centres and played an important role in the physical disintegration of the group. For the steel workers in Saint-Chély-d'Apcher, whose parents had 'emigrated' from the Massif Central during the 1920s, 'their entrenchment had become so deep-rooted that any transfer was seen as akin to deportation'.[37] The same attitude was seen in Denain steel-

---

36. See Battiau (1976), vol. 1, p. 340. The end of craft workers in rural surroundings is well analysed with reference to central France in Bachelard (1978) pp. 309–11; and for the Aude, in Moscovici (1961).

37. Maurin (1978).

workers transplanted to Dunkirk, 60 kilometres away, or those in the De Wendel factories sent to Fos-sur-Mer. Early retirement enabled many of the 'second generation' to remain where they were, for good or ill, but such means of sustaining the community were attenuated by departures and the effective continuity of un-broken collective memory was destroyed. This was intensified by new forms of urbanisation entailing new patterns of work, based on the dispersal and segregation of living zones which dominated the modern 'monopoly-cities';[38] the new working-class generation had to start afresh to recreate its communities. Even without the relocation of industrial employment, the rapid development of the consumer society brought with it new styles of collective housing, which crowned the triumph of housing developers. In most cities the central zones lost all their working-class element; workers were relegated to large housing developments on outlying estates, 'ZUPs' (urban priority areas) and 'new towns' running into each other. Where industrial paternalism once reigned the 1960s saw managers in retreat; henceforward Michelin chose to rent flats in Clermont-Ferrand for its workers rather than build new housing blocks. Almost everywhere management entered into joint agree-ments with central government to finance fixed-rent housing de-velopments in zones well away from the old working-class blocks which huddled close to factory chimneys. In Caen, for example, the close identification of the SMN steel-workers' housing was challenged: 'The collective identity of localised groups could be seen in the territorial cohesion supporting that identity. In 20 years the cohesion vanished.'[39] For the workers from the thirteenth *arrondissement* in Paris, removed from their 'insanitary blocks', the move resulted in a profound crisis in their collective identity because the pattern of daily life, custom, street layout and the surrounding buildings, all was familiar and reminded each individ-ual of the age-old shared past. People in large housing estates had to adjust to anonymity, their living space structured entirely differ-ently not only in the surrounding district but in their own dwell-ings.

Indeed, the controlled low-rent housing developments were built to consumer standards that were completely alien to earlier

---

38. This has been described with reference to the steel industry in Dunkirk by Castells and Godard (1974).

39. Frémont (1981).

working-class districts. A survey carried out among inhabitants of a large housing estate in the Paris suburbs showed that 60 per cent of households considered their furniture inadequate, and 44 per cent had been forced to take out a loan immediately after moving there, to set themselves up. Moving to the new housing quickly entailed fresh budget planning, with increases in rent, transport, and loan repayments.[40]

The old ties linking members of the earlier local working-class groups were dissolved; not all members of the group were re-housed in the same block, and the daily collective tasks which tended to reinforce group identity no longer existed. Formerly the collective eye kept keenly focused on each individual, notably through local gossip, prevented independence of action or behaviour that ran counter to the interests and norms of the group, helping to integrate the more marginal elements into the broad structure of local society. Economic and cultural inequality, allied with the developments already described, brought irretrievable rupture. The more fortunate members of the working-class world, seeking upward mobility, enjoyed living next to people of a higher social status – since most large housing developments encompassed a wide range of social classes – and release from the watchful eyes of their original community. Conversely, the least well off could no longer count on the effective support of others; further, they were often much less capable of coping with the seductions of 'an easy life' or resisting credit, particularly when their modest resources were roughly shaken out of balance by unaccustomed essential expenditure. All the big housing developments therefore rapidly developed a hierarchy based on three groups:

— low income: unskilled workers, immigrants, frequently the uprooted rural incomers, of whom some quickly became insolvent. This was the group with the greatest number of 'social cases' dependent on aid;

— skilled workers, salaried staff, technicians, with sufficient resources to adapt to new material and cultural standards;

— managers, generally young, for whom the housing estate or block of flats represented only a step along the road to higher status living accommodation.[41]

Similarly, many surveys show progressive weakening of the

40. See the survey of Chamboredon and Lemaire (1970).
41. Pialoux and Théret (1980).

factory-floor customs described earlier, whether they concerned 'scrounging' or the various 'rites of passage'. This can be explained by evolving social attitudes and by young people's emancipation from adult control among the popular classes, while in a consumer society, 'salvaging' material from the factory was of less interest. But above all automation frequently challenged old autonomous factory-floor working customs. Using computers to keep track of the steelworks' stocks will often make it impossible for workers to misappropriate materials, quite apart from the considerable extension of shift work which disrupts the daily rhythm of family life and traditional methods of group organisation. It is increasingly difficult for unions to fix a time and a place convenient for everyone to meet together.

In seeking the greatest possible advantage from the general changes in French society over the last 20 years, the central worker group has itself helped to loosen the ties between its members. As was clearly seen by Andrieux and Lignon as early as the 1950s, resignation and submission to fate are persistent elements of working-class life, even for skilled workers;[42] but mass compulsory education offers fresh notions of future expectations, previously limited by class constraints. 'Pride in one's work' is exalted, but at the same time all family efforts are concentrated to ensure that the children's life 'will be different from ours'. The extended years at school and the consequent delay in embarking on the working life, prolonging the childhood period of 'social irresponsibility', reinforce the establishment of 'working-class youth' – 'youth' being a category formerly reserved for the wealthier layers of society. The consumer society has latched on to this new class of consumer, particularly by means of new models diffused through the media, and has created a whole new working-class generation ignorant equally of war, of the heroic days of the PCF, and of the pangs of famine. What used to be a 'victory' at work, or in a work-related struggle, shows an increasing tendency to become normality for young people who have grown up in the affluent society.

Even for the children of skilled workers who leave school with a recognised training qualification, the 'democratisation of education' – as has been shown by Claude Grignon in his ethnographic survey undertaken in a technical training centre – marks in fact the

42. Andrieux and Lignon (1966), p. 85.

appearance of a new system of training which tends to identify an 'élite of outcasts'.[43] This phenomenon accelerates the devaluation of popular localised models through the diffusion of new images to all homes.[44] Even for those families who have moved only at the cost of heavy sacrifices so that their children 'can get on as much as possible', disillusionment is not slow to develop. Between 1965 and 1970, 16 per cent of technical *baccalauréates* were eventually taken on as ordinary workers; 35 per cent underwent this downgrading between 1972 and 1977, and although between 1965 and 1967, 60 per cent of those holding a BTS (the higher technician's certificate) were taken on as technicians, only 45 per cent were still holding such a job between 1972 and 1977. The work of Pierre Bourdieu and Jean-Claude Passeron has shown that the popular classes discovered education at the same time as they encountered relegation, for the effect of the shift in general social structures was inflation in educational qualifications. Hence the disillusionment, perhaps the most unifying factor of socialisation for the new generation, provoked by the discrepancy between what members of that generation had a right to look forward to, as they embarked on their education, and what they actually received – frequently a return to their place of origin which was seen as a setback.

Access to the world of the skilled worker, which for the preceding generation had often been the means of effective integration into the heart of French society, was accompanied for these 'downgraded' individuals by a profound questioning of their social identity. This collective experience, affecting not only working-class youth, is one of the chief reasons for the anti-establishment humour often encountered in the new generation. It took concrete form in the generation gap of the late 1960s, expressed in the fashion of shoulder-length hair contrasting with their parents' 'short back and sides' and the passion for rock music and electric guitars which relegated the accordion and the dance band to the ranks of entertainments for the 'old has-beens'.

This combination of circumstances – technological change, diminishing collective memory, violent contrasts in forms of basic socialisation – explains new youth attitudes towards the factory world.[45]

43. Grignon (1971).
44. The increasing number of dissertations after May 1968 on 'worker alienation through work' has certainly played its part in this downgrading.
45. Bourdieu and Passeron (1970), also Clot (1982).

The SNCF, the state railway corporation, offers a useful illustration of the whole phenomenon. The early 1960s challenged the cohesion of the entire old-style 'railwayman' society. Instability among railway personnel increased sixfold between 1950 and 1973; between 1980 and 1982, 45 per cent of new probationary recruits resigned despite the recession. Industrial accidents, seen by managers as a sign of reduced interest in work, have increased since the 1970s. Trying to identify the causes of this 'profound change', Georges Ribeill cites the abandonment of traditional forms of staff integration by managers applying methods of work rationalisation and, increasingly, the new patterns of management inspired by American-style business management. To this should be added the crisis in traditional recruitment which developed during the 1960s. 'A major and unprecedented phenomenon', modern railway workers were not in general the product of the rural world but were mostly townspeople. 'For these new generations of recruits, young, urban, with more years of education, being taken on by the SNCF means much less than it did for earlier generations.'[46]

III. Marginalisation and the Difficulties of Escaping It

The core group of workers was not entirely successful in its efforts to pass on the community's collective mores to its children. The reproduction of class values in new categories of workers was understandably not easy, because of their lack of long tradition and their radically different circumstances.

From the 1960s onwards most new recruitment to the lower levels of the working world was achieving by drawing on rural manpower either from foreign immigrants or from the French countryside.

Most recent sociological surveys show that these new worker groups remained marginalised in society and in the worker movement. This is primarily the result of deliberate policy on the part of business managers and of a government particularly anxious to reinforce internal divisions within the working world after the events of May 1968. The recruitment of some millions of immigrant workers, radically different in their culture, history, and

46. Ribeill (1984), p. 100.

aspirations from French workers, the establishment of new factories in zones far removed from the old industrial manufacturing centres – none of these factors were likely to encourage *rapprochement* between the various elements of the working class. Furthermore new districts were allocated to industry even in the oldest industrial cities, well away from the town centre and the 'old factories'. Economic activity was now concentrated in the 'industrial zone'; consequently, in regions such as western France there is no communication between the old working class of the naval shipyards or metal-works and the new electronic industry. 'The separation of these two working nations intensifies material isolation and cultural and historical alienation.' The two successive stages of industrialisation in Caen likewise reflect the two separate working classes which ignore each other; the SMN steel workers who, after the melting-pot effect of the 1920s constitute the most fully integrated community, have little to do with the thousands of former rural workers who fill the fixed-rent housing estates of the new-town development schemes and who supply the squads of unskilled labour for Savem or Moulinex.[47]

There are, however, some specifically working-class reasons for this separation between the two worlds. In the old industrial centres the task of consolidating the central group, particularly in times of recession, worked against the interests of newcomers who were vaguely resented as posing a threat. At first the latter, often alone and lacking seniority, were unable to insinuate themselves into the practices of skilled workers such as 'scrounging', which required deftness and independence, or family interaction; nor were they invited to join in the commemoration of a past which in any case was not their own. Yet it must be emphasised that this 'externalisation' was an active process. This may distress the proponents of working-class social cohesion – who often conform unawares to the ecumenism of populist mythology – yet it must be stated that the collective effort which welds the group together operates simultaneously to prevent any growth of social cohesion among newer arrivals. It is already 20 years since Norbert Elias demonstrated this process, when describing 'gossip' in operation in an English industrial town.[48] The flow of words and rumours

47. Réault (1983), and Frémont (1981). On the new workers from rural backgrounds, see also Eizner and Hervieu (1979), and Baudoin and Collin (1983).

48. Elias and Scotson (1965). The quotations are taken from a chapter translated and introduced by Muel-Dreyfus (1985).

continually circulating in the community helped to sustain reputations and weld individuals into the group, to 'keep the wheels in motion'; hence the importance of strategic settings such as the café, the market, or the public wash-house. At the same time, however, gossip operated 'to reject individuals and break up relationships. It could be used as a highly effective method of exclusion.' Those who already had the least developed network of friends or family were therefore reinforced in their marginality by the community's investment in sustaining group values – hence the importance of commemorative functions celebrating anything from the Resistance down to the smallest party marking retirement from the factory floor, underlining the lack of merit in those outside the group. 'Everywhere the attribution to oneself of group charisma and the attribution to outsiders of associative demerits are complementary phenomena.' This social phenomenon, which is not limited to the working-class world, explains why the established metal-workers round Nantes label welders of rural origin 'the yokels', why in the Longwy coalfields second-generation immigrant steel workers consider the Meuse peasant-workers, recruited *en masse* after 1945, as 'muscle men' with 'nothing between the ears'. All surveys, even well before the recession, show that immigrant workers accumulate on their narrow shoulders the weight of shame allocated by others.

This approaches the root of the problems experienced by the worker movement in bringing different sectors of the working class together within the same organisation, including the conflict of self-interest, with the discrediting of new workers providing the pretext for giving them the most wearisome and least well-paid jobs.

There is no difficulty in listing some of the criteria which for 20-odd years have operated to marginalise new worker categories: youth, foreign nationality, rural origin, being female; one such factor alone may not necessarily create a victim, but not all are required together to be operative.

If youth can appear to be a handicap, particularly since the 1974 crisis, this is primarily because the negotiations and compromises between unions, government, and management often take effect at the expense of the young. The practice of early retirement helps towards a kind of rearrangement of job losses, favouring those who are not yet part of the labour market, such as school pupils and apprentices, who will find it increasingly difficult to launch themselves into the work-force when economic circumstances become harsher.

Young people from the most humble backgrounds, particularly with rural origins, are the chief victims of such selection. Indeed, if there is a working-class rationale of advancement up the social scale there is also, as shown in the CNRS survey already quoted, a working-class rationale of decline. During the 1970s poor families were recruited particularly from western and southern France, from the countryside and the small towns. Father out of work, living in a rural area, coming from a large family – any of these elements, often seen in combination, tend to result in poverty.

> The responsibility accorded to 'accident' as an explanation for the development of poverty should be severely reduced. . . . Chance misfortune does not initiate or aggravate poverty except in two sets of circumstances – if it comes as a final burden adding to other incidents, or if it affects an individual who is inherently predisposed to it, putting him in a situation that is increasingly difficult to resolve in material terms.[49]

A deprived upbringing is commonly cited in this type of catalogue. In the large establishments on the edge of the industrial zone at Fos-sur-Mer, with a preponderance of unskilled workers, those forced into such a 'choice' have frequently been affected by family breakup such as divorce, emigration, or death of one or both parents. Only the fact that life has been particularly hard for them since childhood can explain why they should be resigned to taking on the worst and most despised jobs.[50]

A rural background is often the determining factor in developments of this type; in fact uprooting to move to large housing estates, with the isolation and disturbance of old values which that entails, renders individuals particularly susceptible to new consumer expectations. The impossibility of planning an often very uncertain budget and the temptations of credit and advertising work together to precipitate a blind plunge into the immediate present which can be the first step towards failure in society. Surveys on how workers of rural origin behave in business also show up the handicaps of such a background in efforts to rise through the social hierarchy. Again, it is important to make

49. Scardigli and Mercier (1978), p. 173.

50. For full details on Fos, see in particular Bleitrach and Cornu (1979), p. 82 *et seq.*

distinctions according to background circumstances and the locale of arrival. The exploitation of natural gas and oil at Lacq in the Pyrenees after 1956 led to the establishment of a complete industrial complex built up within a very few years in a zone that was previously entirely rural. Although skilled workers were imported from the old industrial areas of the Nord, Lorraine, or the Paris region, the manual labourers and unskilled workers were either immigrants or came from the local countryside. Yet the former craft workmen and farmers' sons, who often held a BEPC qualification, progressed much faster up the professional ladder than did former farm labourers. Similarly in the Toulouse region, it is those with an agricultural background, most strongly rooted in the rural world, who find the greatest difficulty in integrating into the industrial world. On the other hand those who fled the countryside where they felt uncomfortable are more easily assimilated even when their rise through the working hierarchy is less impressive than that of the newcomers with an urban background, and they swiftly adopt professional attitudes; it appears, however, that the SNCF is less welcoming than the aeronautics industry.[51]

Such problems of assimilation are all the greater for immigrant workers, since to rural uprooting must be added all the factors deriving from differences of language and culture. Many surveys have shown the isolation of these workers, treated as 'bachelors', lodged in supervised 'Sonacotra' hostel-type centres no better than the old hutments. As for foreigners' families, the paternalistic workers' estates would surely have seemed like paradise compared to the housing they were familiar with after the Second World War. In 1968, 100,000 people lived in shanty towns in the Paris region alone, and a few years later a secretary of state acknowledged that between 700,000 and 800,000 immigrants were still housed in such shacks. Ghettos have tended to develop in all the major cities, particularly in the poorest development zones.

Immigrant workers were primarily used for manual labouring jobs in the 1920s, but after about 1960 they were mainly recruited for unskilled work, particularly in the car-manufacturing industry. Many authors, but most notably Robert Linhart, have described the isolation of foreign unskilled workers compared with the qualified French worker, the stultifying effect of their jobs, their

---

51. On workers of agricultural background in Toulouse, see Curie (1974); on Lacq, Larbiou (1973).

disorientation when faced with patterns of industrial life which they are poorly equipped to deal with.[52]

Although nationality remains, as three-quarters of a century earlier, the prime factor justifying the reservation of such jobs for immigrants, it may also be observed that the ideology of 'supplementary work' provides a consistent pretext for steering almost all young working women towards repetitive work of this type. In 1975 half the unskilled jobs were taken up by women or foreigners.

This labour force is particularly numerous in large establishments concentrating on standardised mass production; but it can also be found in many small businesses with modest capital and low mechanisation, existing on the fringes of the market and where most jobs combine low wages and lack of qualifications. As shown in the survey carried out in the Vitrolles area near Marseille, physical effort is still a considerable element provoking complaints from the workers: 'Nearly all interviews turned almost constantly round discussion of how the interviewee was affected physically. Backs strained by carrying heavy burdens or standing up for long periods, hands crushed in a pasta cutter, armpits inflamed by allergy, tears from peeling onions, exposure to extremes of temperature, burns from chemicals or molten metal, eyes and lungs full of dust.' Added to all this is the constant presence of the foreman or the small businessman, always most fiercely aggressive towards the Arabs who are never called by their own names, or towards the women, obliged to suffer all kinds of sexist or patronising humiliation – in short, all the attitudes of 'ordinary Fascism' which is practised continually in such surroundings, without any kind of collective worker defence to restrain it.[53]

While the economy prospers it must be remembered that many such marginalised workers put up with the situation because they assume it to be temporary. Immigrants and women are in fact sufficiently numerous to undertake all the unskilled work because, for these social categories more than for others, the factory is seen as only one stage in life. Following a sequence already observed in the nineteenth century, labouring work is seen as a means of reinforcing customs and ways of life that are imposed from outside. Describing the three stages of Algerian emigration after the Second World War, Abdelmalek Sayad has shown how it was originally

52. Linhart (1977).
53. Bleitrach and Cornu (1979), p. 103 *et seq*.

seen as a solution to the problems faced by communities of village origin. Each sent one of its number to the large French factories, to bring back sufficient for the peasant group's survival in the face of changing capitalist agriculture; hence the practice of alternating migration and the 'protection' afforded to the immigrant worker, since his vision of the world, his scale of values, remained those of his peasant community and protected him against xenophobia.[54]

In the same way the factory often appears as a single episode in the life of women workers, lasting until marriage or the birth of the first child; this was why the average age of women electronics workers at the beginning of the 1970s was only 23. Undoubtedly such arrangements on the part of the marginalised sectors of the labour force fitted in very well with management plans, but the temporary nature of such work was also one form of protection for the popular classes.

In the decade after the Second World War the unifying image of the working world, based on its two symbolic figures of the miner and the metal-worker, was already a limited class vision which devalued its other elements, such as the colonial Algerians who were recruited in large numbers after 1948, women, or the hundreds of thousands of worker-peasants; the latter, with their double status, were never represented or protected under either guise, as was clearly shown by Étienne Juillard in his survey focusing on Alsace.[55] But with the sociological breakup of the world of work which began in the 1960s, the myth of the 'party of the working class' corresponded less and less accurately to reality. At a union level it was chiefly the CFDT that managed to seize some of the aspirations of the new layers of society. The survey of the French worker published in 1970 showed that this particular organisation primarily included all the technicians, the new worker-peasants taken on as unskilled workers, and trained workers in the new industrial zones. From the first the CFDT actively supported the struggles of the unskilled workers. The Caen region offered the spectacle of two worker groups representing two industrial eras, one in steel based on the CGT including the older workers, more masculine and more highly skilled, and the other, particularly at Saviem, centred on the CFDT and the unskilled workers.

---

54. Sayad (1977); on the difference between plans according to differing working-class categories, see also Bernoux (1973).
55. Juillard (1953).

Looking only at their relevance to the working class, the events of May 1968 undoubtedly reflect this discontent among workers of rural origin, condemned to remain unskilled all their lives. The movement appears more complex, however, and full consideration would require precise analysis of the background for each one of the component parts of the working class, and their relevance to their own problems in each struggle. The major role played by technicians and salaried staff might be explained, in the light of what has already been indicated, by the conjunction of two circumstances; social origin, frequently as a qualified worker and so favourably disposed to the struggle, and a sense of being 'downgraded' in comparison with what combined family efforts might have led him to expect. The precursor steel strike in 1967 illustrates a third aspect of the workers' part in May 1968, the militancy of traditional industries in decline. In a final comparison with June 1936 the criterion of youth must be stressed, adding its own somewhat confusing slant to traditional analyses of workers' struggles. In fact, as Charles Tilly noted, the movement of May 1968 is characterised by the exceptional involvement of young people, regardless of social background.[56]

The fact remains that these happenings and the subsequent strikes, such as that in Le Mans in 1971, made a powerful contribution to the renewal of collective working-class protest. For several years the unskilled worker was king, and manifold sociological works were devoted to this new figure. Minister Edgar Faure said in 1971: 'Our grandchildren will be as revolted by the current constraints suffered by unskilled workers as nineteenth-century public opinion was when it discovered what work in these factories involved.'[57] The cinema played its part in all this: Karmitz's *Coup pour Coup* is a good illustration of the new fashion: the union is despised for compromising while the hard, violent, relentless strike is applauded unreservedly.

After May 1968 it was the noble figure of the unskilled worker who took up the baton of the metal-worker of earlier days: 'untamed' 'untrammelled', 'the mass worker', resisting 'the system', preferring sabotage and absenteeism to traditional methods of struggle.

---

56. Shorter and Tilly (1974), p. 140 *et seq.*
57. Quoted in Dumont (n.d.), p. 71.

7

Collapse of
the Class System

Perhaps only the techniques of 'pop art' would be equal to providing an accurate representation of the working class in a state of turmoil, torn apart by an unprecedented range of experience and by an increasingly fragmented sense of collective identity. On a more prosaic level it will be sufficient to show here how this collapse was a product of the 'crisis'[1] accentuating the contrasts between different social categories and disturbing areas of traditional mass representation. Much can be deduced from the 1982 census; its implications are only now becoming evident, and it provides a prime checklist on French society after ten years in recession.

I. 'The Working Class in a State of Distress'

Under this heading a recent issue of Le Monde's 'Dossiers and Documents' series described the most visible consequences for the working-class world of the state of crisis since the end of the 1970s, that of de-industrialisation.

---

1. This ambiguous expression appears to indicate the world-wide changes in economic, technological and social circumstances currently facing modern Western society.

De-industrialisation in France

New industrial regions were developed between 1954 and 1975, weakening the central strength of the old bastions but not threatening the industrial working class as a whole because it was still growing in numerical terms.

For some ten years now a new pattern has been apparent: a reduction of the industrial population in both relative and absolute terms. It is clear that although the rural population dwindled by a further 100,000 between the two census counts of 1975 and 1982, the proportion is substantially greater among those working in the secondary sector, where numbers fell by nearly a million. Even consumer-goods manufacturing, the largest employment sector before 1975, has lost approximately 20,000 jobs each year since then. In the major traditional areas of industry the loss has been severe: between 1976 and 1983 steel-manufacturing jobs have been reduced by more than a quarter, with losses of more than 28 per cent in textiles and 27.5 per cent in machine-tools. Analysis of establishments according to size for the same period shows large companies – with more than 500 employees – reducing numbers by between 20.6 per cent and 16.5 per cent, while those with fewer than 50 wage-earners, who employed 43.1 per cent of the total industrial work-force in 1976, increased their share to 49.1 per cent in 1983.

Such changes should be seen in the light of very strong growth in the tertiary sector, which grew by 1.3 million jobs between the two most recent census counts and thus provided for the future of the active working population. Today (1986) 60 per cent of French wage-earners are employed in this sector, the greatest growth being registered in large retail stores – up by 134 per cent – and in social work, where case-related services increased in number by 119.9 per cent, and others by 87 per cent.[2]

The further realisation that the 1982 census showed a decrease in the urban population and a corresponding increase in rural areas, for the first time since the nineteenth century, adds a sense of the approaching end of an economic and social cycle, dating from around the beginning of the First World War and devoted to the triumph of the large factory and massive concentrations of humankind.

Before over-hastily accepting the concept of 'change', it must be

2. Figures taken from articles by Huet and Schmitz (1984; 1985; 1985a).

recalled that this same cycle – including the reduced industrial population, and workers' retreat into small business – was also part of the 1930s crisis, as if a 'slack-water' phase may be a necessary part of abrupt transformations, giving society a breathing space in which to adjust to the changes.

Over the last two or three years, however, the accelerated dismantling of French industry has proved that the current changes are irreversible. More than 200,000 jobs in industry, including construction work, have disappeared each year since 1982; and sectors hitherto more or less immune, such as naval shipyards and particularly car manufacturing, have felt the full force of the cold winds. 'After the enduring bottomless pits of steel and chemicals, all or nearly all the big names of French multinational companies have been affected: Renault, Peugeot, Michelin, Dunlop-France, Creusot-Loire. Refineries, paper pulp and products, construction and public works – all are devastated areas. In electronics almost all the warning lights are flashing red.'[3]

Obviously this does not mean that matters will never improve; but such businesses can only recover by cutting severely into job numbers to increase productivity. Today, therefore, it is general industrial employment, as recognised for decades, that is aware of a mortal wound.

For several years whole regions were in decline as industry was reconstructed. Without retracing the end of steel manufacturing in the Longwy basin, the example of Valenciennes may be quoted, one of the central elements of French economic development in the twentieth century. In 1962 the three pillars of local industrial development – coal, steel and primary metal processing – still employed 50,000 people; by 1980 the figure was less than 10,000, and has since dropped even lower – there are now more teachers than steel workers in the area. The 3,000 unemployed in 1975 became 18,000 by the end of 1981.[4]

It is an everyday truism that the failure of a large company brings down the city or the district that depended on it: ARTC in Roanne, Creusot-Loire, Issoire-Valéo, the naval shipyards of La Seyne-sur-Mer, Dunkirk, Saint-Nazaire, to give only the most recent examples.

Without further debating the causes of the crisis, which have been the subject of many studies, it is worth noting current

3. *Le Monde*, 25 August 1984; see also 'Les restructurations industrielles' (1985).
4. Veltz (1982), p. 141.

technological developments, dictated by international competition but established in the short term by a sharp cut in numbers employed. Production that required 300 looms in 1979 would now keep only 120 looms in operation; similarly in metal manufacturing, the operation of rolled strip has doubled in speed; continuous casting has meant redundancy for most of the work-force in traditional steelworks. Steel manufacturing employed 160,000 workers in 1974; the current figure is no more than 80,000 and technological progress is considered responsible for a third of this reduction. In car manufacturing, the assembly time for a Renault 5 has been reduced from 28 hours in 1980 to 20 hours in 1985.

Computer science and robotics, the two axes of the 'new technology' in industry, introduced radical changes in the pattern of working life quite apart from their general effect on the job market. Although it may still be too early to judge, in the car industry it seems that the classic trades of adjusters and mechanics are likely to suffer most from the introduction of robots.[5] The wholesale introduction of computers in steel-manufacturing workshops has meant a complete redefinition of traditional crafts, with most operators at work stations watching their electronic screens all day long. Compared with the 1930s, when the crisis put a stop to technological innovation, the contrast is radical.

Unemployment – a specifically working-class fact of life

Unemployment has been the most dramatic consequence of French deindustrialisation for the working class. In 1975, 3.9 per cent of workers were without jobs; in 1982 the proportion was 7.7 per cent, representing more than 620,000 individuals, while overall the rate of unemployment was running at 6.7 per cent of the active working population. This scourge can be seen to perpetuate other social inequalities: at the same time unemployment affected 3.3 per cent of middle management and 2.2 per cent of senior managers and qualified professional practitioners, compared with 8.7 per cent of unskilled or manual workers.[6]

These figures show that unemployment strikes unevenly at the very heart of the working world, affecting the most vulnerable elements more severely. In October 1980, for example, 5.3 per cent

5. See Coriat (1984).
6. Huet and Monnier (1985).

of male workers were unemployed, while for female workers the proportion was 11.4 per cent. Immigrant workers suffered similarly: in March 1979, 9.8 per cent were without work, and the proportion rose to 11.7 per cent in March 1983.

But above all the mechanism of social guarantees acquired by the preceding generation of workers, notably the system of early retirement as a compromise solution in the face of job suppression, had terrible effects on the younger workers as the crisis deepened. In 1983 half of those without work were under the age of 25, and the lower the educational standard the greater the risk of unemployment. In fact, 'for those with the lowest standard of skills, the labour market became gradually more unattainable'.[7] As education plays an ever-growing role in introducing young people to the labour market, so workers' 'qualifications' increasingly depend upon it; yet despite the successive reforms of the last 20 years, schools remain incapable of adapting to the problems of the working-class world. In 1980 the proportion of children entering the educational system at the age of six and subsequently required to repeat their first school year was 29.9 per cent for the children of agricultural labourers, 23.9 per cent for the children of manual labourers, 22.5 per cent for those from an unskilled background, 21.4 per cent from service industry backgrounds, and 14.9 per cent from skilled working-class homes, but only 2.4 per cent for those whose parents belonged to senior management or 'the professions'. Although between 1972 and 1980 a greater proportion of children from all social groups in normal education continued their education beyond the obligatory elementary level, the gap between the various social categories was as great as it had been in 1972–4.[8]

In recent years it has been increasingly difficult for young people to find work. In 1973, 10 per cent of them had known unemployment for at least nine months since leaving school; by 1980 the proportion had risen to 29 per cent.

For the unemployed in general, the average length of each period without work has tended to increase, and the proportion of workers without jobs for two years or more rose from 6 to 14 per cent between 1975 and 1981. When it is realised that the longer an individual remains unemployed the lower his chances of finding a job, the anguish of individuals condemned to such an existence, or

7. 'Emploi: la fin des débutants', *Le Monde*, 11 June 1985.
8. Levasseur and Seibel (1985).

the fear of it, may be imagined. Insecurity, material deprivation, the feeling of uselessness, all combine to explain the findings of a medical survey: that in all social categories the death rate is higher among the unemployed than among those in work.[9]

The problem is more serious for younger adults since increasingly the work they are offered is not permanent; in order to evade the rigidity of the labour market, businesses have tended in recent years to favour temporary employment and contracts of fixed duration.[10] In addition to part-time work, which particularly concerns women, and new governmental programmes such as the TUC job opportunity scheme, such unreliable forms of employment, which mostly affect the working class, contribute powerfully to its breakdown into manifold divisions. It is also undeniable that a whole generation's attitude to work has been profoundly affected.

No section of the working class is entirely shielded from the crisis, although its younger members are most directly affected. Forced early retirement is frequently a painful experience for workers whose value system is founded on work as the central element of social usefulness, and who are thrust roughly into inactivity without any preparation for their changed circumstances or their preferences. Similarly, for those who are still too young for early retirement, and particularly in sectors that are in decline, business closures mean accepting lower-grade jobs. Assembly lines in western France are recruiting workers with the now-obsolete CAP, or with outdated practical qualifications, for unskilled jobs. More than a third of the sons of skilled workers are themselves unskilled or manual labourers.[11] The problem is particularly serious for skilled workers in heavy-metal industries, in glass, or ceramics; in 1982 two-thirds were aged over 35 and had been employed by the same company for more than ten years, but only one in four possessed a CAP-validated skill. It was they above all who had to undergo the humiliations of 'retraining' for the sake of future prospects. The 'know-how' which, some years earlier, had been a matter of pride was now seen as a handicap by specialists in the new technologies. Thus Unimétal, a subsidiary of the steel-manufacturing group

9. Huet and Monnier (1985). See also Lecomte (1986).

10. In 1979, 180,000 people were engaged in temporary work, of whom 72 per cent were working-class, mainly unqualified, young people. For some years now numbers of jobs of fixed duration have increased: see Huet and Monnier (1985a).

11. Réault (1983).

Sacilor, estimated at the beginning of 1985 that 15 per cent of its staff due for 'retraining' could be considered as 'handicapped'. This included workers who showed the 'consequences of sickness or accident, but also a broader inadequacy relating to work situations' resulting chiefly from 'cultural backwardness' where immigrants were concerned, or from skills related to internal promotion, in the case of craft workmen.[12]

Unemployment and the 'new poor'

Over ten years the crisis has considerably aggravated various social phenomena whose origins and principal patterns were established in the preceding period.

The most vulnerable individuals or families, particularly on the big housing estates, become disastrously entangled in events that gradually turn them into what are politely referred to as 'social cases'. In 1980, for example, 45 per cent of rent in controlled low-rent housing was not paid on time; hence the expulsion of the least solvent into temporary housing, new ghettos of poverty.

Such places represent a 'subsistence economy' at the heart of the 'consumer society', which is not unlike conditions at the beginning of the nineteenth century. A recent survey shows that in most cases the total resources of the family unit consisted of 'bits of earnings and unemployment allowance: 25 to 45 per cent; social security allowance: 55 to 75 per cent; black economy: 5 to 10 per cent'.[13] Here the distinction between 'the poor' and 'the poorest' lies in possession or lack of furniture, which represents material proof that one can pay rent, that the bailiffs would find something to seize. 'Furniture is often sold, exchanged, taken in payment of services rendered. It circulates on housing estates as fast as individual people and becomes a form of currency and, more than money, a measure of value and equivalent value in relation to other possessions.' Apart from furniture the chief element of the internal hierarchy in 'temporary housing' is the BAS: the 'Bon de l'Aide Sociale', a social-security food voucher; quite apart from its value for acquiring food, it renders its holder eligible for free medical treatment. And above all the BAS confers a status: that of the accepted pauper, acknowledged, 'registered as such; officially accepted and consequently

12. Quoted in *Libération*, 1 April 1985.
13. Laé and Murard (1985).

more or less protected'. In a society completely structured by rules and regulations, the worst condition of all is clearly not to belong to any particular category.

Another element of social marginalisation that has been severely aggravated by the crisis, and which is frequently associated with temporary housing units, is delinquency. This too is a development noted by sociologists since the early 1960s, shadowing new standards of housing and consumption. With the loosening of bonds linking members of solid and long-established working-class communities the most vulnerable elements no longer benefit from protective group mechanisms. It is no coincidence that even today crafts within big industry are relatively free from delinquency; it is most strongly associated with the construction and public-works industries, with their disproportionate numbers of salvage and scrap dealers. Thus the Longwy region is still one of the least delinquent in the whole of France compared with similar urban regions, despite its current level of unemployment.

It is clear that the crisis has done no more than accentuate weaknesses established in earlier days, and it is possible to assess its severity by measuring it against the growth of the prison population. The number of people held in French prisons rose from 26,000 in 1975 to 39,000 in 1981, an increase of 50 per cent over six or seven years. Sociological research into those going into prison illustrates the underlying causes with maximum clarity: 60 per cent of first-time prisoners were aged less than 26; nearly 40 per cent were out of work at the time of their arrest; among those of working age, 56 per cent were from the working class; 45 per cent had no qualification, and 31 per cent had fathers who were themselves workers. The over-representation of young immigrants, 26 per cent of the total, illustrates the particular zeal of police and courts in dealing with a social category that arouses all racist instincts, and also proves that the new 'second generation', both immigrant and working class, lacks the capacity for integration into the community shown by those born in the inter-war period.[14]

To such 'handicaps' of nationality or qualification are added the contributory factors indicated in the previous chapter: more than a third of prisoners observed in the study had at least five brothers and sisters, and two-thirds were from homes broken by parental

14. Fize (1985), and Aubusson de Cavarlay (1985); on delinquency, see also Chamboredon (1971).

separation, or the death of one or both parents, or were ignorant of who their parents were. In assessing the social causes of delinquency the culminating factor is status lower than the father's professional occupation, a circumstance that exercises enormous psychological damage. The survey quoted above on those entering prison estimates that, in the most favoured hypothesis, 'prisoners retained membership of their class of origin but in many cases they could not replicate their parents' social standing and many had already embarked on the process of downward mobility'.

II. The Old and the New

Maintaining traditional differentials

There are those who claim that there has long been a gradual levelling out of class inequality in France: it is, however, certainly true that despite 150 years of struggle and confrontation the working class is still a distinctly subordinate group within French society, most notably in areas concerning professional life. Even if not to be compared with the nineteenth century, the disadvantages of working conditions continue to brand the group. Workers remain by far the most liable to industrial accidents; although the incidence had diminished since 1955, particularly where it had been highest, in construction, mining and steel manufacturing, the rate has remained virtually static since 1972. The number of industrial accidents with stoppages has stabilised at around one million for the last 30 years. The safety aspect, or lack of it, is not often discussed today, yet it is the single greatest cause of death: accidents at work correspond effectively to 'approximately one death per hour worked, a serious accident every minute, an accident with work stoppage every six seconds, based on total numbers of wage-earners'.[15] The survey carried out by INSEE on conditions at work for the period 1978–81 gives plentiful further illustrations of workers' disadvantaged status in the wage-earning world. While 73 per cent of salaried staff can stop work during the day without authorisation, this applies to only 38 per cent of manual workers, and similarly, of all employed categories, it is the latter who suffer most from 'no talking' regulations imposed by the management.

15. These statistics do not include wage-earners outside the general social-security system, such as the miners: see Molinié and Volkoff (1985).

229

Workers also make up the greatest number of those 1.3 million whose activity is subject to 'severe time constraints', with 'assembly-line work' the most obvious example of this type of restriction. More than 2.5 million workers are also familiar with the delights of shift work which, according to medical surveys, causes digestive and nervous upsets for 20 per cent of them.

The shift-working pattern appears to be spreading; the number of those working at least 100 nights per year has grown by 68.4 per cent and, those who are subject to 'clocking-on' represented 19.1 per cent of male workers in 1978 and 21.9 per cent in 1982.[16]

Thus the 'novelty' of improved conditions for those who are the chief victims of modern society still lies in the future, and further proof can be seen on examination of each category within the working class.

As with vulnerability to unemployment, it is the young, the women, and the immigrants who are worst served in their conditions of work.

Young people suffer disproportionately from 'severe time constraints'; the 1978 survey showed that this was the main problem for 40 per cent of workers aged between 18 and 29. On average, immigrant workers earn 25 per cent less than their French equivalents, although their working days are longer. As for women workers, the differential separating them from male factory workers is as great as that which separates skilled and unskilled workers. There is evidence: more than 11 per cent of women, skilled or unskilled, are not allowed to talk while they work, a restriction applied to only 2–3 per cent of men. More than one female unskilled worker in four is on an assembly line, against one in 13 of male workers. A third of the male unskilled work-force is engaged in repetitive work against two-thirds of women in the same category. The most depressing aspect is that here too the situation has deteriorated over the last several years. Between 1978 and 1982, night work increased by 19.5 per cent for women, by 11 per cent for men. For men too, the proportion with working days of more than 11 hours (including breaks and mealtimes) has decreased by 26.2 per cent, while for women the proportion has gone up over the same period by 17.6 per cent.[17]

There is an additional factor in this depressing situation: some

16. Molinié and Volkoff (1981; 1980).
17. Ibid.

members of marginal groups coped more easily with exploitation during the prosperous era because their worker status was only temporary, but with the crisis this 'voluntary flexibility' was considerably weakened by the downturn in the labour market. In the early 1980s only 17 per cent of workers engaged in jobs with little security of tenure stated that they had sought this type of work, while 60 per cent would have preferred more settled employment.

Such circumstances explain the ageing of the immigrant working class in French companies: 'The foreign worker population has clearly aged between 1972 and 1978; among those under 30 their proportion has tumbled, while in the older age-groups they are more strongly represented.' The ending of recruitment of foreign workers and their frequent refusal to return to a home country where economic circumstances were still worse than in France explain why in 1978 the average age of male industrial immigrant workers was higher than that of French men; in the construction industry the difference between the two groups was nearly four years.[18]

Women workers are similarly affected. As Jacky Réault observes, in western France marriage no longer means giving up work: having children is delayed ever longer, and there is an increase in the number of children born before the working mother remains entirely housebound. The same pattern is clearly apparent on a national scale; instead of acting as a reserve labour force to cushion chance irregularities, female workers tend to become a permanent part of the business. This entrenchment on the part of women and foreign workers is not unconnected with their new militancy, as seen in recent strikes inspired by unskilled foreign workers; it was the female clothing workers who were responsible for the most significant strike of 1981/2 in the Nantes area.[19] The sequence of events here is similar to that described above in respect of the 1930s.

Figure 7.1, based on the factorial analysis of five variables – qualifications, sex, nationality, seniority, age – defining the work-force in French industry in 1978, gives a particularly clear illustration of the oppositions that are characteristic of the modern professional working world.

Following François Eymard-Duverney's analysis,[20] each axis of the graph is based on two poles reflecting the opposing sectors of

18. Willard (1984).
19. Kergoat (1982); and Réault (1983).
20. Eymard-Duverney (1981).

Figure 7.1 Industrial Sectors and their Work-Force

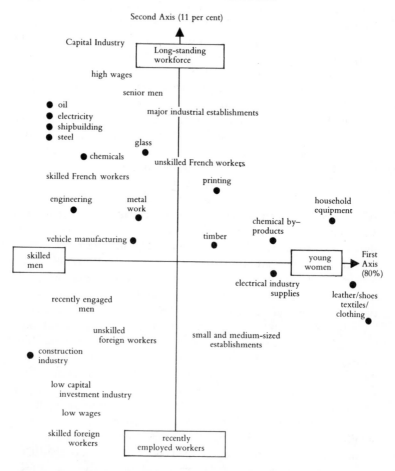

This diagram displays visually the characteristics of the work-force in each section. Engineering, for example, employs skilled male workers with little seniority. The first axis shows primarily the proportion of men and secondarily their skills (the further to the right along the axis, the fewer skilled men) and the age of women workers (the further to the right, the younger the women).
Source: Based on Eymard-Duverney 1981.

the industrial working class. On the first axis lies the important criterion of sex as a factor of internal discrimination, with men lying overall towards the skilled end of the scale and women, whether skilled or not, placed towards the least well-regarded sectors of the labour market. In fact the businesses that prefer to employ skilled, male, French workers, are those that now dominate the market: oil and gas; the nationalised electricity and gas-supply companies; basic chemical and synthetic-fibre manufacturers; and naval, aeronautics and armaments manufacturers. Manual workers represent only a modest proportion of the total number employed in these branches of manufacturing; between a third and half at most. Such industries are also responsible for many of the new worker skills, such as employees trained to maintain and regulate production-line equipment or carry out trials and checks on highly sophisticated machinery. Steel manufacturing and companies associated with primary metal processing follow close behind this first group, even though the labour force is in general perceptibly less highly skilled. The vertical axis shows that this first group of companies is also characterised by greater seniority in the work-force and by higher wages. This combination of elements makes it the most highly privileged sector of the working class, with express or tacit protected status.

The opposite pole is made up of the low-skilled female work-force, usually young, and fairly new to the company. Here may be found the types of business mentioned in the preceding chapter, particularly those supplying household equipment, often based on the edge of rural areas, and noted for assembly-line work. The placing of the construction industry should be observed: it stands out from the two poles in representing elements of both – generally low wages despite being a masculine industry, yet also demanding significant skills. This is the preferred sector for foreign workers hoping to rise in the worker hierarchy.

While the larger businesses favour an older French-nationality labour force, the smaller enterprises are still characterised by a greater turnover of labour, with lower wages and greater dependence on immigrant workers. Construction and public works are the most typical sectors of such small businesses, which still have much unrewarding manual work, allotted to the most recently recruited foreigners. The insecurity of employment in such small and medium-sized companies is all the greater in that they frequently remain outside collectively negotiated agreements. This should not, however, conceal the survival of many undertakings of an artisan nature; they are often family-run, rooted in their region and employ a highly skilled work-force subcontracting for the major shipyard or car-manufacturing corporations. As noted above, such small companies nowadays represent a surviving refuge for skills no longer required in the larger establishments.

The sccial inequalities of working conditions touch on most aspects of daily life. A theoretical example, such as life expectancy at the age of 35, is eloquent: while a teacher today can expect to live a further 43.2 years, a working man has an expectation of six years less. Apart from industrial accidents, the cause of this disparity must lie in class-related inequality of access to health. Workers, together with the peasant class, are characterised by under-consumption of medical care and by a lower rate of visits to specialist care. Nineteenth-century historians make abundant use of height to illustrate the drawbacks of worker status at a time when workers were often turned down for military service because they were too short. A century and a half later the victories of the worker movement are certainly visible in improved average height among the popular classes, but there is none the less a continuing and close correlation between social hierarchy and masculine phys-ique; the average height for members of the liberal professions is 5ft 9ins, against 5ft 7½ins for skilled workers and foremen, 5ft 7¼ins for unskilled workers, and 5ft 6½ins for farmers.[21]

These differences are apparent in all areas of the consumer society. Out of the whole range of actively employed adults, workers and peasants go away least often for summer holidays: 53.2 per cent. Of those who do go away on holiday, workers are the most likely to stay with friends or relations or go camping: 60 per cent of the total. The working class, together with white-collar workers, represents the highest proportion of credit customers for consumer goods; and the 'democratisation' of car ownership should not hide the fact that 76 per cent of the working class owners buy a second-hand car, compared with scarcely a third of senior managers or members of the professions; and the value of the second-hand 'bargain' may be questionable.

A survey undertaken by the National Institute of Agronomic Research shows that the gap between the differing professional categories persists right down to daily food consumption. Beer, bananas, pork, potatoes, and pâtés, are favoured by the French working class much more than by salaried staff and managers. The reverse applies to ready-prepared dishes, whisky, and lamb.[22]

---

21. Charraud and Valdelièvre (1985).
22. Grignon and Grignon (1980).

Table 7.1, which covers some of the most significant results of the survey published in 1982 by the Ministry of Culture on 'French Cultural Habits' relating to the working class, illustrates the enduring divisions between France's different social groupings, in terms of reading and of sport or access to varying forms of recognised cultural activity. In practical terms the only areas in which the working class is more actively engaged than its managers are do-it-yourself work, bingo and betting. This underlines one of the fundamental characteristics of working-class culture: that entertainment is frequently combined with other objectives, such as practical necessity or the hope of material gain, placing it in opposition to the 'gratuitous' element emphasised by bourgeois cultural activity. These statistics also reflect the differences within the working-class world itself, dividing it into its various component segments. In all respects it is the unskilled and manual operatives who come lowest.

It is a problem that resurfaces elsewhere in social life. Not only do unskilled and manual workers have the lowest life expectation – at age 35 it is on average 37 years for the former and 34.3 for the latter – but this social category has enjoyed the least progress over 20 years because workers are at greater risk of industrial accidents and work-related illness, and their daily lives are subject to the lowest standards of hygiene. Material and intellectual poverty can push some into concentrating only on the present moment, as shown by the ravages still caused by alcoholism in France. 'Cirrhosis of the liver and alcoholism are almost unknown among managers and teachers. These two causes of death chiefly affect manual workers and farmers; the risk of death from alcoholism or cirrhosis of the liver is ten times greater among working-class men than among salaried managerial staff.'

The most underprivileged sectors of the working world are also those who suffer most from loneliness, a factor particularly marked in old people who end their days abandoned in welfare institutions. A survey among retired people aged over 60 shows that the majority of those who pass the last stages of their life alone in institutions are former agricultural workers and unskilled or manual workers; 54.6 per cent of the retired in the survey spent more than half their time in their single or shared rooms, 47.4 per cent of them without moving from their armchair. In fact 'the family' is an asset that becomes rarer as one descends the social ladder; at the beginning of the 1980s, among the active population aged between

Table 7.1 Workers' Leisure Activities in 1982 (per cent)

Activity	senior managers, professions	skilled workers, foremen	unskilled labourers, service personnel
Newspapers:			
Never read a daily paper	23.9	29.5	32.0
Read one every day	46.6	43.0	37.4
of these readers:			
– read a national paper	50.3	19.3	13.2
– read a local paper	41.6	58.8	59.5
Regular reading of magazines:			
– current affairs	32.6	8.9	6.6
– women's or family magazines	14.7	12.5	16.2
– literary, scientific, historical	25.3	12.5	5.9
Musical instruments:			
Owning at least one instrument	56.1	31.7	31.3
of which one is – piano	17.2	2.8	3.2
– guitar	23.1	15.2	15.7
– wind instrument	30.2	19.4	17.5
Taken part within the last twelve months in:			
– Bingo	38.1	65.1	63.7
– horse-race betting	6.9	26.0	29.5
– National Lottery	10.8	14.7	17.5

Done the following within the last twelve months:			
– dressmaking, knitting	12.6	9.0	28.5
– minor household repairs	35.1	49.7	33.4
– major household maintenance	22.7	34.5	17.6
Regular sporting activity:			
– walking	33.6	18.3	17.7
– football	6.4	15.8	12.5
– skiing	14.3	6.5	5.4

Source: Ministère de la Culture 1982.

35 and 54 and excluding farm workers, 20 per cent of manual workers, 10 per cent of unskilled workers, and 9 per cent of skilled workers were unmarried. Loneliness is also apparent in the lack of social life in the least prosperous members of the working population; of all socioprofessional categories, those who go out least are the unskilled and manual workers. They visit friends particularly rarely – 59 per cent, against 69.1 per cent of skilled workers and 86.4 per cent of salaried staff and members of the professions. This is additional evidence, similar to that relating to immigrant populations, of their marginalisation at the heart of society.[23]

Some changes in everyday working-class behaviour

The preceding section shows that in times of crisis the differences between social groups tend to become more marked by virtue of the elementary principle of social science that those who defend themselves most successfully against challenges to their interests are also those who occupy the most favoured rungs of the social ladder. Such 'conservatism' or 'corporatism' does not mean that the overall social structure is static; in the working-class world, and particularly among young people, new styles of behaviour and values are adopted, which should not be seen as indicative of what the world of work will be like tomorrow, but which give further proof of class breakdown, caught between a retreat into traditional values and a search for new ways of life.

Quite apart from all the well-known elements of the true youth culture, notably in such spheres as music and entertainment, the results of the 1982 census identify some examples of working-class behaviour that depart sharply from previous habits and indicate that, at least in the development of custom, the younger members of the working class are taking an active part in current changes in French society.

The decline of marriage, seen by demographers as a particularly significant element in this respect, is evident in the appreciably greater numbers of unmarried working-class women aged between 30 and 34, rising from 9 per cent in 1975 to 13 per cent in 1981.

---

23. On the effects of alcoholism on health, see Desplanques (1985); on loneliness among former workers in hospital, A. and A. Mizrahi (1977); the figures on frequency of social outings are taken from the survey of the Ministère de Culture (1982).

Similarly, youthful cohabitation, relevant to only 5 per cent of couples in 1975, applied to 12 per cent in 1981; this put the working class in second place, behind those working in service industries and equal with senior salaried staff. Another indication of changing family norms is seen in the spectacular increase in 'illegitimate children acknowledged by their father'. In 1968 this was rare; it has now grown from 14 to 45.8 per cent among unskilled workers and from 15.5 to 52.9 per cent in skilled workers. Finally, it is known that half the number of legal abortions now relate to working-class wives.[24]

Another element to be stressed here is that the working-class world no longer appears to be shut in on itself, as was still the case in the 1950s. Even now social mobility usually means only a very small shift, but there are none the less very few families whose members all still belong to the working class; by 1970, 35 per cent of technicians, 22 per cent of primary-school teachers, and 18 per cent of women in medico-social services, were from working-class backgrounds.[25] The 1982 census indicates that if three workers out of four have a working-class or non-working spouse, 44 per cent of female commercial employees have a working-class husband. This points more to a redefinition of the working class than a genuine change in social class: the work of a supermarket checkout assistant differs very little from assembly-line work, yet it is a further factor in the collapse of the older generation's homogeneity.

III. The Inadequacy of Working-Class Images

New scientific approaches

Two decades of sociological change in the working-class world and advances in the presentation of scientific data encouraged INSEE to draw up a completely new system of professional classification for the 1982 census; the categories included in the working class were based on the central image of the metal-worker, so that the small artisan business was overlooked and attention focused on the large factory.

Henceforward, as shown in figure 7.2, two main categories of workers were defined: the artisan type, mostly skilled, constituting

24. Boigeol et al. (1985); and Villac (1985).
25. Quoted in Bleitrach (1981), p. 296.

Figure 7.2 Patterns of Worker Distribution in 1981 according to new INSEE employment classification

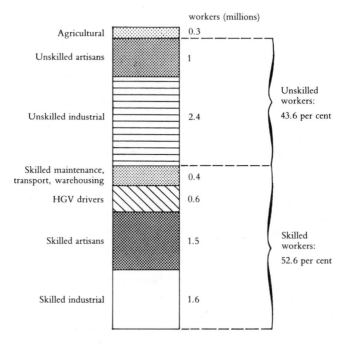

Source: General population census, 1982 (employed population).

2.5 million individuals, and the industrial type, generally without qualifications, totalling 4.4 million excluding agricultural workers and heavy-goods vehicle drivers. In industry, unskilled workers are mainly wage-earners engaged on standardised production lines, while the skilled workers are considered such if their trade skills are the basis for their job – such as an engineering mechanic or electrician, or if they show aptitude for responsibility in running valuable installations, such as in the chemical or oil industries. To avoid the risk of yet again compressing a whole group into a few specimen figures, recent census counts define a core in each case, assembling professions that most nearly conform to the definition and the crafts that differ from it to a greater or lesser degree.[26]

Proliferating surveys – sociological, anthropological, or econ-

26. See further explanation in Desrosières and L. Thévenot (1979); and Seys and Gollac (1984).

omic – have also helped considerably to diversify definitions of the working class. The multidisciplinary approach, including the historical element of the individual's personal background as an explanation of his current social style, offers more detail than earlier industrial sociological classifications based on the occupation at the time of the survey. Thus it has been possible to compare recently, with reference to working-class nutrition, workers of peasant origin who prefer a small market town to a big city, the suburbs to the centre, who work in their gardens and retain links with the countryside, especially all methods of self-sufficiency such as jam-making and home freezing, with workers of working-class origin with more varied tastes – derived from long-term familiarity with the diverse urban markets – who have very little free time because their wives also work, and who are almost completely ignorant of any kind of rural self-sufficiency. A monograph survey on a generation of workers aged 38 in 1980 in Amiens illustrates the complexity, even at a local level, concealed by the overall classification of 'working class'. Four subgroups can be distinguished: workers who are urban by birth, city dwellers, generally more highly skilled and usually working in public corporations or small businesses; rural workers of country origins, providing a high proportion of skilled workers in large local companies; and two intermediate categories – those with urban origins and living in the country, often on housing estates; and those of rural background living in the city in controlled low-rent housing in industrial-development zones, supplying the great majority of unskilled workers. These variations must be seen in conjunction with the industrial history of the region, since a new generation of business establishment took over in the 1960s from the old network of the Amiens textile industry. Twenty years after the establishment of new factories the fusion between the old and the new workers is still incomplete, while young workers face a radically new situation connected with the problem of finding a job in their area.[27]

Diversity of political representation

The severe crisis in the worker movement since the end of the 1970s has also exacerbated the divisions in working-class political representation.

27. Desrosières and Gollac (1982).

This is particularly apparent in organisations linked to the Communist Party. Between 1968 and 1978 the CGT's share in professional elections to the workers' council dropped steadily, from 55.6 per cent to 44.9 per cent; and although there has been official silence on the subject, union membership has fallen away considerably in recent years. This is less apparent in other organisations, in particular Force Ouvrière, but the drop in numbers has become a very serious problem for the worker movement as a whole: it must indeed have fallen to a very low level for the French government, representing the nation of the 'revolutionary union movement', to consider compulsory deduction of union dues from wages.

For the Communist Party, the slow erosion of the past 20 years has become a veritable rout: in the municipal elections of 1983, the PCF lost control of 22 of the 72 towns it held with over 30,000 inhabitants, and the parliamentary election of 1986 did nothing to alter this tendency.

Apart from any points of political strategy underlying this diminution of power, there may be factors that are more precisely 'sociological', thus more 'objective', behind this decline in communist fortunes. The collective working-class memory was profoundly affected by the perfectly balanced fusion of a generation, an organisation, and a series of seminal events; this group influence did much to foster political representation combined with group militancy in support of the Communist Party, but the succeeding generation remained outside this influence, and indifferent to it. This undoubtedly played a large part in the PCF's loss of power and the diversity of organisations currently enjoying a share of working-class confidence. It may be helpful to distinguish between the communist worker electorate, which was dominant until the 1960s, and that which succeeded it. All sociological electoral surveys show that until that pivotal epoch the communist worker vote was not a particularly youthful element but mainly represented workers of mature years. Conversely, at the parliamentary elections of 1978 it was the under-40s who became the decisive force for the left, in particular for the PCF. As Albert Hirschman stresses, the simple act of placing a voting paper in the ballot box does not in itself provide insight into the strength of an individual's commitment in favour of his or her chosen candidate. For the older generation tenacious fidelity to the PCF was linked to the history of a particularly powerful collective militancy; but the young worker who has supported the communists in the last decade expresses his approval of the party's tribunal function rather than the heroism of its class-war militants. During the crisis the protest vote coincided with the workers' fervent wish for profound social change, to be achieved through the 'common purpose programme'. Although this political strategy briefly proved capable of gathering in plenty of votes, the greater vulnerability of a worker vote based on waiting passively for change is also comprehensible; such change was scarcely apparent in the working world after May 1981, hence the scale of disenchantment and the crisis of confidence suffered by the entire left.

Sociological and political causes are therefore both relevant to an understanding of reduced worker identification with collective representation. This reduction was clearly illustrated in a recent SOFRES (an opinion-poll organisation) survey showing that the proportion of French people who felt they belonged to the working class dropped sharply between 1976 and 1983, from 27 to 22 per cent of all socioprofessional categories, and by nine points among workers.[28]

It is not for the researcher to judge whether such a development bodes well or ill for the working world. The whole of this study indicates that when individual members of the subordinate classes are left to themselves their interests have little chance of being protected, indeed of being perceived, by the society in which they live: hence the need for collective action. It has also been shown, however, that group militancy backing a central organisation could achieve, through the force of circumstance – the need to present a single image subsuming individual interests – a reduction both in problems considered worth standing up for, such as wages and conditions of work (though rarely matters relating to private life) and in the number of social categories capable of identifying themselves as specifically part of the official worker movement.

The collapse and disintegration of contemporary working-class organisational patterns into conflicting paths is perhaps the best way to draw public attention to these specific problems, similar to the domination familiar to other categories – women, young people, or workers of foreign origin – which could only survive in traditional organisations by undergoing a more or less substantial transformation.

---

28. Opinion poll 'Les Français et L'État', carried out in March 1983, with detailed results published in *L'Expansion*, 6 May 1983.

Conclusion

Finally, the burden of past working-class history should not be undervalued: for a working class crystallised as much in its legal definitions, its institutions and its collective image, as in the territory it has carved out for itself, its past continues to affect the way in which the whole of society sees its future. To this end it is worth turning to various comparative studies covering France, Great Britain, and West Germany.

Great Britain demonstrates the full strength of mass working-class identity, militant in the face of upheavals that challenge its very existence. The 1984 miners' strike is the best illustration of this aspect, in its length, its resolution, and the role played by the movement's leader – himself a former miner, and son and grandson of miners. More generally, studies comparing France and Great Britain have shown that negotiating practices at factory-floor level are much more firmly established on the English side of the Channel than in France, leaving little scope for managers seeking to impose change. 'The working community has the means to defend its prerogatives, and it exercises them, thereby accentuating rigid departmentalisation of work and reducing internal mobility of the work-force.' In France, despite spectacular conflicts, reduction of employee numbers is easier and more systematic.[1] Questions of professional training offer a basis for comparison with Germany and also show the scale of the contrast. In West Germany the power of worker status, known to sociologists as *Arbeiterschaft*, means that

1. Segrestin (1984), p. 106; see also P. Dubois (1980).

the basic group enjoys a large degree of autonomy in the workshop, and managers depend on employee cooperation to gain the greatest benefit from workshop skills. Their workers are also much more flexible than those in France, the result of an education policy supporting mass vocational training separate from general education. Apprenticeship is frequently the basis for genuine social advancement within the company, and the workers' collective identity is strengthened by greater stability among skilled workers, as seen in their high rate of social reproduction. In France, on the contrary, the company is based on the wage-earners' performance characterised by compartmentalised and low-skilled work, and weighed down by meddlesome and bureaucratic supervision on the part of the overseers. Similarly, where in West Germany collective negotiation occurs chiefly at branch or regional level, in France the fundamentals take place at a confederate level. The depth of dispossession affecting the basic group in France is perceptible.[2]

The whole of the working-class world's social history must be called in evidence to explain these differences. In Great Britain the very strong worker identity derives from the group's considerable seniority. As has been shown by E.P. Thompson, the decisive economic, social, and political developments underlying the formation of a genuine 'class' date back to the beginning of the nineteenth century. Around 1870, 'three or four generations after the Industrial Revolution', according to Eric Hobsbawm, Great Britain 'was first and foremost a nation of workers'; 77 per cent of the working population consisted of 'manual labourers', and the small peasant class had virtually ceased to exist.[3]

Progress has been slower in Germany, but the development of the working class occurred abruptly under the rule of an authoritarian state directed by Bismarck, who in exchange accorded the workers a degree of social protection unparalleled elsewhere. This revolution 'from above', to quote Gramsci, was a powerful unifying factor for later working-class generations, a factor that explains the strength of the *Arbeiterschaft*.

France represents the other side of the coin; indeed, it is scarcely possible to identify the precise 'birth' of the working class, since it is characterised by constant renewal and considerable heterogeneity. One of the basic reasons for this is the resistance derived from

---

2. This analysis is taken from Maurice et al. (1982).
3. Hobsbawm (1977), vol. 2, p. 141.

the French Revolution which, in this respect, should be seen as much more than a bourgeois revolution. At the level of economics (consolidation of modest rural land ownership) and of politics (rights linked to citizenship) the popular classes were able to oppose industrial upheavals effectively after the middle of the nineteenth century. Their inheritance from the French Revolution included two further elements: on the one hand, the militant tradition of the 'sansculottes' – the élite of urban craft workers, against whom the government is the more vulnerable because Jacobinism left the nerve centres of power concentrated in Paris, in the realm of the craft workers; on the other hand, the early introduction of universal suffrage, evidence both of the ideology of 1789 and of an attempt to circumvent the revolutionary combativity of workers in the great cities. Until the beginning of the twentieth century all these factors operated together to strengthen working-class resistance to the industrial revolution.

Countering recent theses, which questioned the backwardness of French capitalist development illustrated by David Landes, it should be emphasised, in company with Karl Polanyi, that no industrialised society whatever has been able to evade the rigour of the laws of the 'self-regulating' market. France saw the delayed consequences of the Industrial Revolution taking full effect in the 1920s; this was when backwardness in urbanisation, collective structures, and social protection, brought their full weight to bear on French society. The 'consequences of the war' have been exaggerated in considerations of the structural modifications in French capitalism: this immaturity has also been masked by the fact that the inter-war period is still the black hole of French social history, but above all because the most radical proletarianisation turned the spotlight on immigrant workers in an atmosphere of exaggerated nationalism.

The history of the working class and, on a larger scale, the whole history of French society, thus appears dominated by a central question: how to impose the inevitable upheavals of the capitalist system – which no 'first generation' of workers has ever accepted willingly[4] – on working classes in possession of democratic means of opposing them? Numerous intellectual minds have wrestled with the problem from the late nineteenth century onwards, turning France into the 'laboratory of political ideas' described notably

---

4. This is stressed by, among others, Marglin (1973).

by Zeev Sternhell, with the invention of many twentieth-century techniques of power. Nationalism is an important factor here as a mechanism to counter the 'Rights of Man', applying the weight of the heaviest social and economic constraints to 'non-citizens'.

The heterogeneous nature of the world of work and the slow progress of proletarianisation also explain the chronic weakness of the worker movement. The craft unions have never succeeded, as in the United States or Great Britain, in imposing their rule on the working class as a whole; this is also a result of the unique political experience developed since the Revolution by the élite urban worker, particularly in Paris. The tradition of 'direct action' was scarcely compatible with the rules of the representative system based on delegation of powers.

The Popular Front marked the definitive end of this worker movement stage, and the emergence of the hitherto marginal industrial working class into the political arena. Lacking established traditions, it immediately accepted the new rules and saw the PCF and the CGT as capable of defending its interests. Its struggles were to occupy the front of the stage until the 1960s, although they now appear to be languishing for lack of champions.

The 'eternal youth' of a substantial section of the French working class should be emphasised, and is no doubt relevant to the famous 'revolutionary tradition' of the French worker movement. Here it is important to avoid confusing two very distinct processes:

— the nineteenth-century revolutionary *journées*, days of protest linked with the genuine history of the urban craft world since the time of the *ancien régime*;

— the high points of collective militancy in the twentieth century, in 1906, 1936, and 1968, which belong to the history of big industry. On each occasion a new generation of workers, with few roots and without genuine traditions, was at the heart of the most radical conflict.

One explanation of the contrast between the 'reforming' tendency of the British and the 'revolutionary' tendency of the French may be found here. It would be possible to offer numerous examples proving that a genuine worker tradition contains the 'sense of potential limits' – knowing what can be obtained and what is unobtainable – principally through awareness of setbacks which can in a few months efface years of communal effort to establish a durable organisation; it is known that for the rest of his life Jouhaux regretted having thrown the whole of the CGT into the adventure of the 1920 general strike. The class's lack of long tradition persuades its members in moments of euphoria that anything is possible, at the price of ever-recurrent disillusionment.

Bibliography

Ackerman, E. B. (1977), 'Industrialisation et mutations sociales dans une commune rurale au XIXe siècle: Bonnières-sur-Seine', *Annales d'Histoire du Mantois*, pp. 17–27

Adam, G., F. Bon, J. Capdevielle and R. Mouriaux (1970), *L'Ouvrier français en 1970*, Paris, Colin

Aguet, P. (1954), *Les grèves sous la monarchie de Juillet (1830–1847)*, Geneva, Droz

Agulhon, M. (1970), *Une ville ouvrière au temps du socialisme utopique: Toulon (1815–1851)*, Paris, Mouton

—— (1979), *La République au village*, Paris, Éditions du Seuil

Angelis, A. de (1982), *Blue collar workers and politics: a French paradox*, London, Croom Helm

Andréani, É. (1965), 'Les grèves et les fluctuations de l'activité économique de 1890 à 1914 en France', Paris, law thesis

Andrieux, A. and J. Lignon (1966), *L'Ouvrier français aujourd'hui*, Paris, Gonthier (reprint)

Ansart, P. (1970), *Naissance de l'anarchisme*, Paris, PUF

Ariès, P. (1971), *Histoire des populations françaises*, Paris, Éditions du Seuil, 'Points Histoire' series, (reprint)

Artisans et ouvriers d'Alsace, (1965) (collected work), Strasbourg, Librairie Istra

Asselain, J.-C. (1984), *Histoire économique de la France du XVIIIe siècle à nos jours*, vol. 2, *De 1919 à la fin des années 1970*, Paris, Éditions du Seuil, 'Point Histoires' series

Aubusson de Cavarlay, B. (1985), 'Condamnations et condamnés' in INSEE, q.v.

Audiganne, A. (1860), *Les populations ouvrières et les industries de la France*, 2 vols, Paris, Capelle

Auduc, J.-L. (1980), 'La grève des boutonniers de la région de Méru en 1909', *Annales d'Histoire Compiégnoise*, pp. 53–62

Auffray, A. et al. (1978), *La grève et la ville*, Paris, Bourgois

Bibliography

Aumont, M. (1956), *Monde ouvrier inconnu: carnets d'usine*, Paris, Spes

'Aux origines de la révolution industrielle: industries rurales et fabriques', (1979), *Revue du Nord*, January (special issue)

Bacconnet, D. (1956), 'Industrialisation d'une grande vallée alpine (le Grésivaudan) et conséquences démographiques et rurales', *Revue de Géographie Alpine*, pp. 99–166

Bachelard, P. (1978), *L'Industrialisation de la région du Centre*, Paris, Gilbert Clary, geography thesis

Barbance, M. (1948), *Saint-Nazaire, le port, la ville, le travail*, Moulins, Crépin-Leblond

Barberet, J. (1886–90), *Le travail en France: monographies professionnelles*, 7 vols, Paris, Berger-Levrault

Barbéris, F. (1973), 'Les ouvriers-paysans', *Études Rurales*, January

Barral, P. (1967), *Le Département de l'Isère sous la IIIe République*, Paris, Colin

Barthes, R. (1957), *Mythologiques*, Paris, Éditions du Seuil, 'Points' series (reprint 1970)

Bartuel, C. and H. Rullière (1923), *La mine et les mineurs*, Paris, G. Doin

Bastié, P. (1964), *La croissance de la banlieue parisienne*, Paris, PUF

Battiau, M. (1976), 'Les industries textiles dans le Nord-Pas-de-Calais', Université de Lille-III, geography thesis

Baudant, A. (1980), *Pont-à-Mousson (1918–1939): stratégies industrielles d'une dynastie Lorraine*, Paris, Publications de la Sorbonne

Baudoin, Th. and M. Collin (1983), *Le contournement des forteresses ouvrières*, Paris, Librairie des Méridiens

Bédé, J.-E. (1984), *Un ouvrier en 1820*, manuscript published by R. Gossez, Paris, PUF

Belleville, P. (1963), *Une nouvelle classe ouvrière*, Paris, Julliard

Berger, G. (1973), 'Aspects anciens et récents des activités industrielles rurales en Forez', *98e Congrès des Sociétés Savantes, Section d'Histoire Moderne*, Saint-Étienne, vol. 2, pp. 181–204

Bergeron, L. (1978), *Banquiers, industriels, négociants parisiens du directoire à l'Empire*, Paris, Mouton

Berlanstein, L. R. (1980), 'Growing up as workers in 19th century Paris', *French Historical Review*, no. 4

—— (1981), 'The formation of a factory labour force: rubber and cable workers in Bezon (Val -d'Oise) 1860–1914', *Journal of Social History*, pp. 163–86

Bernard, Ph. (1953), *Économie et sociologie de la Seine-et-Marne (1850–1950)*, Paris, Conin

Bernoux, P. (1973), *Trois ateliers d'OS*, Paris, Éditions Ouvrières

Berstein, S. (1980), *Histoire du parti radical*, Paris, Presses de la Fondation Nationale des Sciences Politiques

Bertaux, D. (1977), *Destins personnels et structure de classe*, Paris, PUF

Berthier de Sauvigny, G. (1976), 'Les ouvriers d'industrie sous la Restoration', *Bulletin de la Société d'Histoire Moderne*, no. 10

Bezucha, R.-J. (1974), *The Lyon uprising of 1834: social and political conflict in the early July monarchy*, Cambridge, Mass., Harvard University Press

Blanqui, A. (1849), *Des classes ouvrières en France pendant l'année 1948*, 2 vols, Paris, Pagnerre

Bleitrach, D. and A. Cornu (1979), *L'usine et la vie*, Paris, Maspero

Bleitrach, D. et al. (1981), *Classes Ouvrière et social-democratie*, Paris, Éditions Sociales

Boigeol, A. et al. (1985), 'Le Divorce', in INSEE, q.v.

Bois, P. (1971), *Paysans de l'Ouest*, Paris, Flammarion, 'Champs' series (reprint)

Bonnault-Cornu, P. (1981), 'Élements pour une histoire ouvrière de Port-de-Bouc', *Cahiers de recueil de la mémoire du chantier naval de Port-de-Bouc*, June

—— (1983), 'Du charpentier-bois à l'ordinateur: le traçage des navires', *Travail, Idèologie, Pratique*, no. 2

Bonneff, L. and M. (1984), *La vie tragique des travailleurs*, Paris, ÉDI (reprint)

Bonnet, S. (1975–85), *L'homme du fer*, 4 vols, Metz, Éditions Serpenoise

Bourdé, G. (1977), *La défaite du Front populaire*, Paris, Maspero

Bourdieu, P. (1979), *La distinction*, Paris, Éditions de Minuit

Bourdieu, P. and A. Darbel (1965), *L'amour de l'art*, Paris, Éditions de Minuit

Bourdieu, P. and J.-C. Passeron (1970), *La reproduction*, Paris, Éditions de Minuit

Bouvier, J. (1964), 'Mouvement ouvrier et conjoncture économique', *Le Mouvement Social*, July

Boy, D. (1978), 'Origine sociale et comportement politique', *Revue Française de Sociologie*, January

Boyer, R. (1985), 'Les approches en terme de régulation: présentation et problèmes de methode', *Documents du CEPREMAP*, July

Boyer, R. and J. Mistral (1983), *Accumulation, inflation, crises*, Paris, PUF, 2nd edition

Bozon, M. (1982), 'La fréquentation des cafés dans une petite ville ouvrière: une sociabilité populaire autonome?', *Ethnologie Française*, no. 2

—— (1984), *Rapports sociaux et vie quotidienne d'une petite ville de Province: la mise en scène des différences*, Lyon, PUL

Bozon, P. (1943), 'L'industrie du Seuil-de-Rives', *Revue de Géographie Alpine*

Braun, A. (1938), *L'ouvrier alsacien et l'expérience du Front populaire*, Paris, Sirey

Brelot, C.-I. and J.-C. Mayaud (1982), *L'industrie en sabots*, Paris, J.-J. Pauvert aux Éditions Garnier

Bresle, A. (1963), 'Les ouvriers viennois en 1936', *Cahiers d'Histoire*, pp. 209–26

Brody, D. (1960), *Steelworkers in America: the nonunion era*, Cambridge, Mass., Harvard University Press

Browaeys, X. and P. Châtelain (1984), *Les France du travail*, Paris, PUF

Brunet, J.-P. (1980), *Saint-Denis: la ville rouge*, Paris, Hachette

Burdy, J. P. (1986), 'Le soleil noir: formation sociale et mémoire ouvrière dans un quartier de Saint-Étienne, 1840–1940', doctoral thesis, Université de Lyon, typescript

Bibliography

Buret, É. (1840), *De la misère des classes laborieuses en Angleterre et en France*, 2 vols, Paris, Paulin

Cacérès, B. (1981), *Allons au-devant de la vie: la naissance du temps des loisirs en 1936* (preface by P. Mauroy), Paris, Maspero

Capdevielle, J. et al. (1979), *France de gauche, vote à droite*, Paris, Colin

Carbonnel, M. (1946), *L'adolescence ouvrière: essai de psychologie*, Paris, Éditions Ouvrières

Caron, F. (n.d.), *Histoire économique de la France, XIXe–XXe siècle*, Paris, Colin, 'U' series.

—— (1973), *Histoire de l'exploitation d'un grand réseau: la compagnie du chemin de fer du Nord, 1846–1937*, Paris, Mouton

Carré, J. J., P. Dubois and E. Malinvaud (n.d.), *Abrégé de la croissance française*, Paris, Éditions du Seuil, 'Points' series

Caspard, P. (1979), *La fabrique neuve de Cortaillod*, Paris, Publications de la Sorbonne

Castells, M. and F. Godard (1974), *Monopolville: l'entreprise, l'état, l'urbain*, Paris, Mouton

Cazals, R. (1978), *Avec les ouvriers de Mazamet*, Paris, Maspero

Centre d'Étude Lyonnais d'Études Féministes (1984), *Les femmes et la question du travail*, Lyon, PUL

Certeau, M. de (1980), *L'invention du quotidien*, 2 vols, Paris, UGE

CFDT (1977), *Les dégats du progrès*, Paris, Éditions du Seuil, 'Points Politique' series

Chamboredon, J.-C. (1971), 'La délinquance juvénile: essai de construction d'objet', *Revue Française de Sociologie*, July

Chamboredon, J.-C. and M. Lemaire (1970), 'Proximité spatiale et distance sociale dans les grands ensembles', *Revue Française de Sociologie*, no. 1

Champagne, P. (1971), 'La télévision et son langage: influence des conditions sociales de réception sur le message', *Revue Française de Sociologie*, no. 3

Charlot, B. and M. Figeat (1985), *Histoire de la formation des ouvriers, 1789–1984*, Paris, Minerve

Charraud, A. and H. Valdelièvre (1985), 'La taille et le poids', in INSEE, q.v.

Chassagne, S. (1971), *La manufacture de toiles imprimées de Tournemine-les-Angers (1752–1820)*, Paris, Klincksieck

Chassagne, S., A. Dewerpe and Y. Gaulupeau (1976), 'Les ouvriers de la manufacture de toiles imprimées d'Oberkampf à Jouy-en-Josas (1765–1815), *Le Mouvement Social*, October

Chatelain, A. (1977), *Les migrations temporaires en France, 1800–1914*, 2 vols, Lille, Atelier de Reproduction des Thèses

Chevalier, L. (1950), *La formation de la population parisienne au XIXe siècle*, Paris, PUF

—— (1978), *Classe laborieuse, classe dangereuse à Paris pendant la première moitié du XIXe siècle*, Paris, Hachette, 'Pluriel' series (reprint)

Cheysson, E. (1911), *Oeuvres choisies*, 2 vols, Paris, A. Rousseau

Chombart de Lauwe, P.-H. (1956), *La vie quotidienne des familles ouvrières*, Paris, Éditions du CNRS

Bibliography

Chopart, J.-N. (1978), *Vivre pour travailler, travailler pour vivre*, Paris, CSU

Clause, G. (1970), 'L'industrie lainière rémoise à l'époque napoléonienne', *Revue d'Histoire Moderne et Contemporaine*, July (special issue)

Clot, Y. (1982), 'Jeunes et travail', *La Pensée*, no. 255

Codaccioni, D. (1971), *Lille 1850–1914: contribution à une étude des structures sociales*, Lille, PUL

Coing, H. (1966), *Rénovation urbaine et changement social*, Paris, Éditions Ouvrières

Collinet, M. (1951), *L'ouvrier français (essai sur la condition ouvrière 1900–1950)* Paris, Éditions Ouvrières

Condevaux, J. (1928), *Le Mineur du Nord-Pas-de-Calais: sa psychologie, ses rapports avec le patronat*, Lille, Imprimerie L. Danel

Coornaert, E. (n.d.), *Le compagnonnage en France du Moyen Age à nos jours*, Paris, Éditions Ouvrières

Corbin, A. (1975), *Le Limousin, archaïsme et modernité (1845–1880)*, 2 vols, Paris, Marcel Rivière

Coriat, B. (1978), *L'atelier et le chronomètre*, Paris, Bourgois

—— (1984), *La Robotique*, Paris, La Découverte

Cosson, A. (1978), 'Industrie de la soie et population ouvrière à Nîmes de 1815 à 1848', in 'Économie et société en Languedoc-Roussillon de 1789 à nos jours', *Actes du colloque de Montpellier*, Montpellier, Publication de l'Université Paul Valéry

—— (1985), 'L'industrie textile à Nîmes, 1790–1850', *Le Mouvement Social*, October

Cote, L. (1903), 'L'industrie gantière et l'ouvrier gantier à Grenoble', Grenoble, thesis

Cottereau, A. (ed.) (1983), 'L'usure au travail', *Le Mouvement Social*, July (special issue)

—— (1985), 'The distinctiveness of working-class cultures in France, 1848–1900', in I. Katznelson and A. A. Zolberg (eds), q.v.

—— (1987), 'Justice et injustice ordinaires sur les lieux de travail d'après les audiences prud'hommales (1806–1966), *Le Mouvement Social*, October–December

Courougues, C. and M. Pialoux (1984/1985), 'Chronique Peugeot', *Actes de la Recherche en Sciences Sociales*, no. 54, 1984, and nos. 57–8, 1985

Coutry-Valentin, M.-R. (1981), 'Les grèves de 1947 en France', Paris, Institut d'Études Politiques, thesis

Crebouw, Y. (1967), 'Recherches sur l'évolution numérique de la main-d'œuvre industrielle depuis en siècle', 3 vols, Paris, thesis

Crossick, G., R. Floud, and P. Thane (eds) (1984), *The power of the past*, Cambridge, Cambridge University Press

Curie, J. (1974), *Le devenir des travailleurs d'origine agricole*, Paris, Champion

Cuvillier, A. (1914), *Un journal d'ouvrier: 'l'atelier' (1840–1850)*, Paris, Alcan

Daclin, M. (1968), *La crise des années 1930 à Besançon*, Paris, Les Belles Lettres

Dalotel, A., A. Faure, and J.-C. Freiermuth (1980), *Aux origines de la commune: les reunions publiques à Paris, 1868–1970*, Paris, Maspero

Darbel, A. (1975), 'L'évolution récente de a mobilité sociale', *Économie et*

Statistique, October

Dauby, J. (1977), 'La vie du coron à l'époque de Jules Mousseron', *Le Pays noir vu par Émile Zola et Jules Mousseron*, Lille, CRDP

Daumard, A. (1963), *La bourgeoisie parisienne de 1815 à 1848*, Paris, SEVPEN

Daumard, A. and F. Furet (1959), 'Méthodes d'histoire sociale: les archives notariales et la mécanographie', *Annales ESC*, October

Daumart, A. (1963), 'Une référence pour l'étude des sociétés urbaines en France au XVIIIe et au XIXe siècle: projet de code socioprofessionnel', *Revue d'Histoire Moderne et Contemporaine*, July

Dauphin, C., and P. Pizerat (1975), 'Les consommations populaires dans la seconde moitié du XIXe siècle à travers les monographies de Le Play', *Annales ESC*, pp. 537–52

Decottignies, G. (1950), *La betterave à sucre et l'industrie sucrière dans l'Aisne de ses débuts à nos jours*, Soissons, Imprimerie Saint-Antoine

Deforges, Y., (1981), 'Éléments pour une génétique de l'objet technique', Compiègne, Université de Technologie

Defromont-Leschevin, A. (1969), 'Le mouvement FTPF dans le Valenciennois', *Revue du Nord*, pp. 743–55

Degenne, A. and J. Duplex (1984), 'Une qualification industrielle actuelle: les OHQ de Port-de-Bouc', *Terrain*, no. 2

Dejonghe, É. (1971), 'Les problèmes sociaux dans les mines du Nord-Pas-de-Calais pendant la deuxième guerre mondiale', *Revue d'Histoire Moderne*, pp. 124–47

Dejours, C. (1980), *Travail, usure mentale*, Paris, Centurion

Delesalle, E. (1950), 'Le travail de la femme dans l'industrie textile et du vêtement dans l'arrondissement de Lille', Lille, thesis

Delpech, H. (1938), *Recherches sur les niveaux de vie et les habitudes de consommation chez les ouvriers toulousains, 1936–1938*, Paris, Sirey

Démier, F. (1982), 'Les ouvriers de Rouen parlent à un économiste en juillet 1848', *Le Mouvement Social*, April–June

Depretto, J.-P. and S.-V. Schweitzer (1984), *Le communisme à l'usine, vie ouvrière et mouvement ouvrier chez Renault, 1920–1939*, Lille, ÉDIRES

Dereymez, J.-W. (1981), 'Les usines de guerres (1914–1918) et le cas de la Saône-et-Loire', *Cahiers d'Histoire*, no. 1

Désert, G. (1975), *Une société rurale au XIXe siècle: les paysans du Calvados (1815–1895)*, Lille, Atelier de Reproduction des Thèses

—— (1981), 'Aspects de la criminalité en France et en Normandie', in 'Marginalité, déviance, pauvreté en France, XIXe–XIXe siècle', *Cahier des Annales de Normandie*, no. 13

Desplanques, G. (1984), 'L'inégalité sociale devant la mort', *Économie et Statistique*, January

—— (1985), 'La mortalité masculine selon le milieu social', in INSEE, q.v.

Desrosières, A. (1977), 'Éléments pour une histoire des nomenclatures socioprofessionnelles', in INSEE, q.v.

Desrosières, A. and Gollac, M. (1982), 'Trajectoires ouvrières: système d'emplois et comportement social', *Économie et Statistique*, September

Desrosières, A. and L. Thévenot (1979), 'Les mots et les chiffres: les nomenclatures socioprofessionnelles', *Économie et Statistique*, April

Destray, J. (1971), *La vie d'une famille ouvrière*, Paris, Éditions Ouvrières
Dommanget, M. (1953), *Histoire du Premier Mai*, Paris, Société Universitaire d'Éditions et de Librairie
Dourdan (1982), (symposium), *L'emploi, enjeux économiques et sociaux*, Paris, Maspero
Dubar, C., G. Gayot and J. Hédoux (1980), 'Sociabilité minière et changement social à Sallaumines et Noyelles-sous-Lens (1900–1980)', in 'Sociabilité et mémoire collective', *Revue du Nord*, April (special issue)
Dubois, P. (1977), *Le sabotage dans l'industrie*, Paris, Calmann-Lévy
—— (1980), 'Niveau de main-d'œuvre et organisation du travail ouvrier: étude des cas français et anglais', *Sociologie du Travail*, July
Duby, G. (1978), *Les trois ordres ou l'imaginaire du féodalisme*, Paris, Gallimard
Duchemin, Ph. (1955), 'L'industrie moderne à Tarbes: ses origines', *Revue de Géographie Pyrénénne*, pp. 176–89
Duharcourt, P. et al. (1977), *Développement du capitalisme, politique urbaine et habitat ouvrier: l'exemple de l'agglomération de Reims, de la première moitié du XIXe siècle à nos jours*, Reims, A. Rallet
Dumay, J.-B. (1976), *Mémoires d'un militant du Creusot (1841–1905)*, Paris, Maspero-Presses Universitaires de Grenoble
Dumont, J. P. (n.d.), *La fin de OS?*, Paris, Mercure de France
Dunham, A. (1953), *La Révolution industrielle en France (1815–1830)*, Paris, Marcel Rivière
Dupeux, G. (1959), *Le Front populaire et les élections de 1936*, Paris, Colin
—— (1972), *La société française*, Paris, Colin, 'U' series
Durand, C. (1978), *Le travail enchaîné: organisation du travail et domination sociale*, Paris, Éditions du Seuil
Durkheim, E. (1967), *La Division du travail social*, Paris, PUF (reprint)
—— (1983), *Le Suicide*, Paris, PUF (reprint)
Duveau, G. (1947), *La vie ouvrière sous le Second Empire*, Paris, Gallimard
—— (1948), *La pensée ouvrière sur l'éducation*, Paris, Domat-Montchrestien
Eizner, N. and B. Hervieu (1979), *Anciens paysans, nouveaux ouvriers*, Paris, L'Harmattan
Elhaï, H. (1955), 'L'usine de Dives (Calvados)', *Norois*, pp. 67–80
Elias, N. and J. L. Scotson (1965), *The established and the outsiders*, London, Frank Cass
Éric, A. (1972), 'La vie de l'usine', *Les Temps Modernes*, July
Etcherelli, C. (1971), *Élise ou la vraie vie*, Paris, LGF, 'Le Livre Poche'
Eymard-Duverney, F. (1981), 'Les secteurs de l'industrie et leurs ouvriers', *Économie et Statistique*, November
Faidutti-Rudolph, A. (1964), 'L'immigration italienne dans le Sud-Est de la France', 2 vols, Université de Nice, thesis
Fize, M. (1985), 'Les entrants en prison', in INSEE, q.v.
Flonneau, J.-M. (1970), 'Crise de vie chère et mouvement syndical: 1910–1914', *Le Mouvement Social*, April
Fohlen, C. (1956), *L'industrie textile sous le Second Empire*, Paris, Plon
Foucault, M. (1974), *Surveiller et punir*, Paris, Gallimard
Fourcault, A. (1982), *Femmes à l'usine en France dans l'entre-deux-guerres* (anthology), Paris, Maspero

—— (1983), 'Bobigny: banlieue rouge: de la crise des lotissements aux années du Front populaire', *Communisme*, no. 3

Frémont, A. (1981), *Ouvriers et ouvrières à Caen*, Université de Caen, CERA

Frey, M. (1978), 'Du mariage et du concubinage dans les classes populaires à Paris (1845–1847)', *Annales ESC*, pp. 803–29

Freyssenet, M. (1977), *La division capitaliste du travail*, Paris, Savelli

Fridenson, P. (1972), *Histoire des usines Renault*, vol. 1, *Naissance de la grande enterprise*, Paris, Éditions du Seuil

—— (ed.) (1976), 'L' autre front', *Le Mouvement Social*, vol. 2

—— (1979), 'Les premiers ouvriers de l'automobile: 1890–1914', *Sociologie du Travail*, July

Friedman, G. (1964), *Le travail en miettes*, Paris, Gallimard, 'Idées' series

Furet, F. (1978), *Penser la Révolution française*, Paris, Gallimard, 'Folio' series

Furet, F. and J. Ozouf (1977), *Lire et écrire*, 2 vols, Paris, Éditions de Minuit

Furon, B. et al. (1978), 'Aspects médicaux: sociaux et professionnels du travail en équipe chez les femmes', *Archives des Maladies Professionelles*, no. 3

Gadrey-Turpin, N. (1982), *Travail féminin, travail masculin: pratiques et représentations en milieu ouvrier à Roubaix-Tourcoing*, Paris, Éditions Sociales

Gaillard, J.-M. (1974), 'Un exemple français de "villeusine": la grand' combe dans le gard et sa compagnie des mines 1830–1921', Université de Paris X, typescript thesis

—— (1977), *Paris, la ville (1852–1870)*, Paris, Champion

—— (1981), *La vie quotidienne des ouvriers provençaux au XIXe siècle*, Paris, Hachette

—— (1981a), 'La petite entreprise en France aux XIXe et XXe siècles', *Rapport français à la commission internationale d'histoire des mouvements sociaux et des structures sociales*, concentrating on small businesses and world industrial growth, Paris, Éditions du CNRS

Gallo, M. (1966), 'Quelques aspects de la mentalité et du comportement ouvrier dans les usines de guerre en 1914–1918', '*Le Mouvement Social*, July

Ganne, B. (1983), *Gens de cuir, gens de papier, transformation d'Annonay depuis les années 1920*, Paris, Éditions du CNRS

Gaudemar, J.-P. de (ed.) (1980), *Usines et ouvriers: figures du nouvel ordre productif*, Paris, Maspero

Gillet, M. and Y.-M. Hilaire (eds) (1979), *Le Nord-Pas-de-Calais, 1936–1939*, Lille, PUL

Girard, A. and J. Stoetzel (1953/4), *Français et immigrés*, 2 vols, Paris, PUF, Cahiers INED

Girault, J. (1975), *L'implantation du parti communiste dans l'entre-deux-querres*, Paris, Éditions Sociales

Gistucci, J.-B. (1979), 'Un exemple de désarticulation régionale: le cas provençal, 1800–1850', *Peuples méditerranéens*, pp. 75–103

Godard, J. (1899), 'L'ouvrier en soie, monographie du tisseur lyonnais,

1899', Lyon, law thesis

Goetz-Girey, R. (1965), *Le mouvement des grèves en France*, Paris, Sirey

Goody, J. (1977), *The domestication of the savage mind*, Cambridge, Cambridge University Press

Gordon, G., R. Edwards, and M. Reich (1982), *Segmented work, divided workers: the historical transformation of labor in the United States*, Cambridge, Mass., Cambridge University Press

Gossez, R. (1967), *Les ouvriers de Paris*, Paris, Bibliothèque de la Révolution de 1848, XXIV

Granotier, B. (1970), *Les travailleurs immigrés en France*, Paris, Maspero

Green, N. (1985), *Les travailleurs immigrés juifs à la Belle Époque*, Paris, Fayard

Gribaudi, M. (1988), *Itinéraires ouvriers: espaces et groups sociaux à Turin au début du XXe siècle*, Paris, Ed. de l'EHESS

Grignon, C. (1971), *L'ordre des choses*, Paris, Éditions de Minuit

Grigon, C. and Ch. Grigon (1980), *Consommation alimentaire et style de vie: contribution à l'étude de goût populaire*, Paris, INRA

Griner, M. (1950), 'La famille ouvrière dans la région de Nancy, étude économique et sociale', Nancy, law thesis

Guéhenno (1961), *Changer la vie*, Paris, Grasset

Guerrand, R.-H. (1967), *Les origines du logement social en France*, Paris, Éditions Ouvrières

Guglielmi, J. (1953), *Salaires et revendications sociales en France, 1944–1953*, Paris, Colin

Guibert, J. (1983), 'La vieillesse ouvrière', *Cahiers du LERSCO*, Nantes, March

Guilbert, M. (1966), *Les fonctions des femmes dans l'industrie*, Paris, Mouton

—— (ed.) (1976), *Femmes à l'usine et au bureau: enquête sur la condition des femmes travailleuses (ouvrières et employées)*, Paris, Centre Confédéral d'Études économiques et Sociales

Guin, Y. (1974), *Histoire de la Bretagne*, Paris, Maspero

Halbwachs, M. (1933), *L'évolution des besoins dans les classes ouvrières*, Paris, Alcan

—— (1968), *La mémoire collective*, Paris, PUF (reprint)

—— (1970), *La classe ouvrière et les niveaux de vie*, Paris, Gordon Breach (reprint)

Hamon, L. (ed.) (1962), *Les nouveaux comportements de la classe ouvrière*, Paris, PUF

Hanagan, M. (1980), *The logic of solidarity: artisans and industrial workers in three French towns 1871–1914*, Chicago, University of Illinois Press

Hardach, G. (1969), *Der soziale Statuts des Arbeiters in des Frühindustrialisierung (1800–1870)*, Munich, Duncker und Humblot

Hardy-Hemery, O. (1983), 'Une nébuleuse en expansion aux XIXe–XXe siècles: l'espace de l'usine sidérurgique de Denain', *Le Mouvement Social*, October

—— (1984), *De la croissance à la déindustrialisation: un siècle dans le Valenciennois*, Paris, Presses de la FNSP

Hatzfeld, H. (1971), *Du paupérisme à la sécurité sociale*, Paris, Colin

Hemlich, Y. (1977), *Arbeiterskämpfe in Frankreich: Ein Beitrag zur social- und*

Bibliography

Rechtegeschichte 1789–1939, Meisenheim-am-Glan, A. Hain

Heywood, C. (1981), 'The market for child labor in 19th century France', *History*, no. 216

Hirschman, A. (1982), *Shifting involvements: private interest and public action*, Princeton, NJ, Princeton University Press

Hobsbawm, E. (1962), *The age of revolution: Europe 1789–1848*, London, Weidenfeld & Nicholson

—— (1977), *Histoire économique et sociale de la Grande-Bretagne*, vol. 2, Paris, Éditions du Seuil (French edition)

—— (1978), 'Sexe, symbole, vêtement et société, *Actes de la Recherche en Sciences Sociales*, September

Hoggart, R. (1957), *The uses of literacy*, London, Chatto & Windus

Houssel, J.-P. (1984), *La Province loin de la métropole: sur la crise du Roannais*, Lyon, PUL

Huard, R. (1978), 'Les mineurs du Gard pendant la guerre de 1914–1918', in 'Economie et société en Languedoc-Roussillon de 1789 à nos jours', *Actes du colloque de Montpellier*, Montpellier, Publication de l'Université Paul Valéry

Hubscher, R. (1985), 'La petite exploitation en France, XIXe–XXe siècle', *Annales ESC*, January

Huet, M. and Monnier, B. (1985), 'Le chômage', in INSEE, q.v.

—— (1985a), 'Les nouvelles formes d'emploi', in INSEE, q.v.

Huet, M. and Schmitz, N. (1984), 'La class ouvrière en détresse' (1984), *Le Monde*, 'Dossiers et Documents', December

—— (1985), 'La population active', in INSEE, q.v.

—— (1985a), 'L' évolution des emplois', in INSEE, q.v.

Hurpin, G. (1975), 'Fileurs cauchois à la fin du XIXe siècle', in *Le textile en Normandie*, (from 1972 Symposium in Rouen), Publication de la Société Libre d'Émulation de la Seine-Maritime

Hyman, P. (1979), *From Dreyfus to Vichy: the remaking of French Jewry, 1906–1939*, Columbia, Columbia University Press

'Industrialisation et désindustrialisation', (1984), *Annales ESC*, September

INSEE, (1977), *Pour une histoire de la statistique*, Paris, Imprimerie Nationale

—— (1985), *Données sociales* (collected work), Paris, Imprimerie Nationale

Isambert-Jamati, V. (1955), *L'industrie horlogère dans la région de Besançon*, Paris, Éditions Ouvrières

Jacoby, B. (1983), 'De l'objet à l'homme: rivets et riveurs à travers la société industrielle', Strasbourg, dissertation

Jacquemet, G. (1982), 'Belleville ouvrier à la Belle Époque', *Le Mouvement Social*, January

—— (1984), *Belleville au XIXe siècle*, Paris, EHESS

Jalabert, G. (1974), *L'industrie aéronautique et spatiale en France*, Toulouse, Privat

Johnson, Charles H. (1979), 'Patterns of proletarianisation: Parisian tailors and Lodève woollen workers', in J.-M. Merriman (ed), *Consciousness and class experience in 19th century Europe*, London, Holmes and Meier, pp. 65–84

Jonas, S. (1977), 'La fondation de villages ouvriers des mines de potasse dans le Haut-Rhin (1908-1930)', *Revue des Sciences Sociales de l'Est de la France*, pp. 71–148

Jones, G. S. (1983), *Languages of class: studies in English working class history 1832–1982*, Cambridge, Cambridge University Press

Juillard, É. (1953), *La vie rurale dans la plaine de Basse-Alsace: essai de géographie sociale*, Paris, Le Roux

Julliard, J. (1965), *Clemenceau: briseur de grèves*, Paris, Julliard

—— (1988), *Autonomie ouvrière: études sur le syndicalisme d'action directe*, Paris, Gallimard/Éditions du Seuil

Kahan Rebecq, M.-M. (1939), *La classe ouvrière en Alsace pendant la monarchie de Juillet*, Paris, Les Presses Modernes

Katznelson, I. and A. R. Zolberg (eds) (1985), *Working-class formation: nineteenth-century patterns in Western Europe and the United States*, Princeton, NJ, Princeton University Press

Kergoat, D. (1982), *Les Ouvrières*, Paris, La Sycomore

Kieffer, L. (1974), 'La culture de la Garance en Bas-Rhin, jusqu'en 1870', *Saisons d'Alsace*, pp. 7–30

Klatzman, J. (1957), *Comportement électoral et classe social: le vote OC et PS à Paris et dans la Seine*, Paris, Cahier de la FNSP

Kocka, J. (1983), *Lohnarbeit und Klassenbildung, Arbeiter und Arbeiterbewegung in Deutschland 1800–1975*, Berlin, Verlag J. H. W. Dietz Nachf

Kriegel, A. (1969), *Aux origines du communisme français*, Paris, Flammarion, 'Champs' series (reprint)

Kriegel, A., R. Gossez, and J. Rougerie (1962), 'Sources et méthodes pour une histoire sociale de la classe ouvrière', *Le Mouvement Social*, July

Kuczynski, J. (1961–7), *Die Geschichte der Lage der Arbeiter unter dem Kapitalismus*, 37 vols, Berlin, Akademie-Verlag

—— (1969), *Les origines de la classe ouvrière*, Paris, Hachette

Kulstein, D. (1964), 'The attitude of French workers during the Second Empire', *International Review of Social History*, pp. 226–36

'La France sous le Premier Empire', (1970), *Revue d'Histoire Moderne et Contemporaine*, July (special issue)

Laé, J.-F. and N. Murard (1985), 'Formes de consommation populaire: l'économie de survie', *Le Temps Modernes*, April

Lamy, Y. (1984), 'Travail du fer, propriétés foncières, sociétés paysannes en Périgord (1789–1930)', Université de Paris X, typescript thesis

Landes, D. (1982), *The Prometheus unbound: technical change and industrial development in Western Europe from 1750 to the present*, Cambridge, Cambridge University Press

Lantz, P. (1983), 'De la banalité de la vie quotidienne', symposium on *Le sens de l'ordinaire*, Paris, Éditions du CNRS

Larbiou, S. (1973), 'Industrialisation-urbanisation? l'exemple de Lacq', *Études Rurales*, January

Larrue, J. (1965), *Les loisirs ouvriers chez les métallurgistes toulousains*, Paris, Mouton

Lartigue-Vecchié, M. (1960), 'Les grèves des dockers de Marseille, 1890–1913', *Provence Historique*, pp. 146–79

Lasserre, A. (1952), *La situation des ouvriers de l'industrie textile dans la région lilloise sous la monarchie de Juillet*, Lausanne, Imprimerie H. Jarmin

Bibliography

Latreille, G. (1980), *La naissance des métiers en France*, Lyon, PUL
Lazar, M. (1985), 'Le mineur de fond: un exemple de l'identité du PCF', *Revue Français de Sciences Politiques*, no. 4
Le Bot, M. (1967), 'Machinisme et peinture', *Annales ESC*, January
'Le mouvement ouvrier en mai 1968', (1970), *Sociologie du Travail*, July (special issue)
Le Play, F. (1856–1913), *Les Ouvriers des Deux Mondes*, revue
—— (1877–79), *Les ouvriers européens*, 6 vols, Paris, Mame et Fils
Lecomte, T. (1986), 'Les demandeurs d'emploi: morbidité et consommation médicale', CRE-DES
Lecuyer, B. and F. Millequant (1984), 'Les dockers: quelques traits d'une corporation charnière dans la chaîne des transports', in G. Ribeill (ed.), 'Frontières et identités professionnelles dans les métiers des transports', *Journée du 16 novembre 1984, GRECO travail et travailleurs*, typescript
Ledrut, R. (1966), *Sociologie du chômage*, Paris, Éditions Ouvrières
Lefranc, G. (1966), *Juin 36, l' 'explosion social'*, collected work, Paris, Gallimard, 'Archives' series
—— (1975), *Histoire du travail et des travailleurs*, Paris, Flammarion
Lefranc, J. (1959), 'Un intérieur ouvrier au XIXe siècle', *Études Ardennaises*, pp. 3–16
Leménorel, A. (1982), 'Minerai de fer de sidérurgie en Basse Normandie, dans la Mayenne et dans la Sarthe de 1835 à 1925', *Annales de Normandie*, March and June
Léon, P. (1968), 'Point de vue sur le monde ouvrier au XVIIIe siècle', *3e Conférence internationale d'histoire économique de Munich*, Paris, Mouton
Léonard, J. (1981), *La médecine entre les savoirs et les pouvoirs*, Paris, Aubier-Montaigne
Lépidis, C. (1973), *L'Arménien*, Paris, Éditions du Seuil
Lequin, Y. (1974), *Les ouvriers de la région lyonnaise (1848–1914)*, 2 vols, Lyon, PUL
—— (1982), 'De crises en avancées: la croissance de la classe ouvrière', Chapter IV of the collected work, *La France contemporaine de 1789 à nos jours*, Paris, Éditions Sociales
—— (ed.) (1983), *Histoire des français (XIXe et XXe siècles)*, vol. 2, *La Société*, Paris, Colin
'Les migrations', (1980), *Ethnologie Française*, April (special issue)
'Les productions symboliques ouvrières' (1984), *Ethnologie Française*, April (special issue)
'Les restructurations industrielles' (1985), *Le Monde*, 'Dossiers et Documents', January
Lescot, J., G. Menahem and P. Pharo (1980), 'Savoirs ouvriers, normes de production et représentation', Boulogne-sur-Seine, ACT, rapport CORDES, typescript
Letellier, G. et al. (1938–49), *Enquête sur le chômage*, 3 vols, Paris, Sirey
Levasseur, E. (1907), *Questions ouvrières et industrielles en France*, Paris, Ed. Arthur Rousseau
Levasseur, J. and C. Seibel (1985), *Réussite et échec scolaires*, in INSEE, q.v.
Lévêque, P. (1983), *Une société provinciale: la Bourgogne sous la monarchie de*

Juillet, 2 vols, Paris, EHESS-Jean Thouzot

Lévy, A. (1957), *Sociologie de l'entreprise, un atelier au travail*, Paris

Lévy-Leboyer, C. (1968), 'La croissance économique en France au XIXe siècle', *Annales ESC*, July

Lévy-Leboyer, M. (1971), 'La "décélération" de l'économie française dans la seconde moitié du XIXe siècle', *Revue d'Histoire Économique et sociale*, no. 4

—— (ed.) (1979), 'Le patronat de la deuxième industrialisation', *Le Mouvement Social*, vol. 4

Lhomme, J. (1954), 'Juin 36', in A. Siegfried (ed.), *Aspects de la société française*, Paris, Librairie Générale de Droit de Jurisprudence

—— (1968), 'Le pouvoir d'achat de l'ouvrier français au cours d'un siècle, 1840–1940', *Le Mouvement Social*, April

Linhart, D. (1981), *L'Appel de la sirène*, Paris, La Sycomore

Linhart, R. (1977), *L'Établi*, Paris, Éditions de Minuit

Lipietz, A. (1983), 'Croissance et salariat industriel', in F. Ginsbourger (ed.), 'Le travail ouvrier', *Cahiers Français*, January

Lojkine, J. and N. Viet-Depaule (1983), *Classe ouvrière, société locale et municipalité en région parisienne: le cas d'Ivry-sur-Seine*, Paris, Centre d'Étude des Mouvements Sociaux

Lorenz, E. H. (1987), 'L'offre de travail et les stratégies d'emploi dans la construction navale en France et en Grande Bretagne (1870–1970)', *Le Mouvement Social*, January–March

Louis, P. (1927), *Histoire de la classe ouvrière en France de la Révolution à nos jours: la condition matérielle des travailleurs*, Paris, Marcel Rivière

Lucas, P. (1983), 'Les travaux et les jours (à propos des enquêtes orales faites à Montceau-les-Mines)', *Cahiers Internationaux de Sociologie*, no. 74

Maillard, F. (1953), 'L'industrialisation de Montbéliard', Nancy, law thesis

Maillard, J.-L. (1980), 'La construction navale du Havre de 1830 à nos jours', *Études Normandes*, pp. 41–68

Marcellin, J. (1969), *Étude comparative d'ouvriers de 40–45 ans travaillant à la chaîne*, Paris, CNAM

Marglin, S. (1973), 'Origines et fonctions de la parcellisation des tâches', in A. Gorz (ed.), *Critique de la division du travail*, Paris, Éditions du Seuil, 'Points Politique' series

Marillier, J. (1954), 'Les serruriers du Vimeu et la terre', *Société d'Émulation Historique et Littéraires d'Abbeville*, pp. 371–95

Marliave, Ch. de (1955), *Les mines d'anthracite de la Mure, 1806–1946*, Paris, Arthaud

Marseille, J. (1980), 'Les origines inopportunes de la crise de 1929', *Revue Économique*, July

—— (1981), *Une famille d'ouvriers de 1770 à nos jours*, Paris, Hachette

Marty, L. (1982), *Chanter pour survivre: culture ouvrière dans le textile sedannais*, Lille Fédération Léo-Lagrange

Marx, Karl (1971), *Un chapitre inédit du 'Capital'*, Paris, UGE, (translation and introduction by R. Dangeville)

—— (1975), *Le Capital*, Paris, Éditions Sociale, (reprint)

Matton, R. (1927), 'L'industrie métallurgique à Maubeuge', *Annales de Géographie*, pp. 309–27

Bibliography

Mauco, G. (1932), *Les Étrangers en France*, Paris, Colin

Mauger, G., and C. Fossé-Poliack (1983), 'Les loubards', *Actes de la Recherche en Sciences Sociales*, no. 50

Maupéou-Abboud, N. de (1968), *Les blousons bleus*, Paris, Galilée

Maurice, J.-P. (1968), 'La commune de Saint-Juéry et les usines de Saut-du-Tarn 1825–1945', *Revue du Tarn*, pp. 69–85

Maurice, M., F. Sellier and J.-J. Sylvestre (1982), *Politique d'éducation et organisation industrielle en France et en Allemagne: essai d'analyse sociétale*, Paris, PUF

Maurin, J.-R. (1978), 'Le personnel de l'usine sidérurgique de Saint Chély-d'Apcher (1916–1969), in 'Economie et société en Languedoc-Roussillon de 1789 à nos jours', *Actes du colloque de Montpellier*, Montpellier Publication de l'Université Paul-Valéry

Mayer, N. (1977), 'Une filière de la mobilité ouvrière: l'accès à la petite entreprise artisanale et commerciale', *Revue Française de Sociologie*, January

Mayeur, J.-M. (1973), *Les débuts de la IIIe République*, Paris, Éditions du Seuil, 'Points Histoire, Nouvelle Histoire de la France Contemporaine' series

Mazoyer, L. (1938), 'Catégories d'âge et groupes sociaux: les jeunes générations françaises de 1830', *Annales d'Histoire Économique et Sociale*

—— (1946), 'L'ouvrier de 1830 et sa vision du monde social', *Revue Socialiste*

Mer, J. (1977), *Le parti de Maurice Thorez*, Paris, Payot

Michaud, R. (1967), *J'avais vingt ans*, Paris, Éditions Syndicalistes

Michel, J. (1975), 'Mineurs, tullistes, métallurgistes: le Nord sans la métropole (1919–1939)', in M. Gillet (ed.) (1975), *La qualité de la vie dans le Nord-Pas-de-Calais au XXe siècle*, Lille, PUL

Michelat, G. and Simon, M. (1977), *Classe, religion, comportement politique*, Paris, Presses de la FNSP/Éditions Sociales

Michelet, J. (1974), *Le Peuple*, Paris, Flammarion, 'Champs' series (reprint)

Ministère de la Culture (1982), *Les pratiques culturelles des Français*, Paris, Dalloz

Mitzman, A. (1964), 'The French working class and the Blum government 1936–1937', *International Review of Social History*, IX

Mizrahi, A. and A. (1977), 'Perte d'autonomie et handicaps: application au cas des personnes âgées résidant en institution', *Consommation*, April

Molinari, J.-P. (1981), 'Entretien avec un ouvrier de la construction navale nazairienne', *Norois*, October

Molinié, A.-F. and S. Volkoff (1980), 'Les conditions de travail des ouvriers . . . et des ouvrières', *Économie et Statistique*, January

—— (1981), 'Les contraintes de temps dans le travail', *Économie et Statistique*, March

—— (1985), 'Les accidents du travail', in INSEE, q.v.

Montgomery, D. (1979), *Workers' control in America*, Cambridge, Cambridge University Press

—— (1987), *The fall of the House of Labor*, Cambridge, Cambridge University Press

Montmollin, M. de and O. Pastré (eds) (1984), *Le Taylorisme*, Paris, La Découverte

Moscovici, S. (1961), *Reconversion industrielle et changement social: un exemple, la chapellerie de l'Aude*, Paris, Colin

Moss, B. H. (1976), *The origins of the French labor movement: 1830–1914: the socialism of skilled workers*, Berkeley, University of California Press

Mothe, D. (1959), *Journal d'un ouvrier (1956–1958)*, Paris, Éditions de Minuit

Mouriaux, R. (ed.) (1974), *Les Jeunes ouvriers: enquête sur leur insertion*, CGT/Centre national d'études économiques et sociales

Mouvements ouvriers et dépression économique, (1966) (collected work), Assen (Netherlands), Van Gorcum

Muel, F. (1977), 'Les instituteurs, les paysans et l'ordre républicain', *Actes de la Recherche en Sciences Sociales*, November

Murard, L. and P. Zylberman (eds) (1978), 'Le soldat du travail (guerre, fascisme et taylorisme)', *Recherches 32/33*, September

Nadaud, M. (1976), *Léonard, maçon de la Creuse*, Paris, Maspero

Navel, G. (1945), *Travaux*, Paris, Stock

Naville, P. et al. (1971), *L'état entrepreneur: le cas de la régie Renault*, Paris, Antropos

Néré, J. (1959), 'La crise économique de 1882 et le mouvement boulangiste', 2 vols, Paris, doctoral thesis

Nerpin, N. (1984), 'L'alimentation des ouvriers urbains', *Revue Française de Sociologie*, no. 1

Noiriel, G. (1982), 'Les ouvriers sidérurgistes et les mineurs de fer dans le Bassin de Longwy pendant l'entre-deux-guerres', Université de Paris VIII, doctoral thesis

—— (1984), *Longwy, immigrés et prolétaires (1880–1980)*, Paris, PUF

—— (1984a), 'L'histoire de l'immigration: note sur un enjeu', *Actes de la Recherche en Sciences Sociales*, September

—— (1985), 'Les ouvriers au XIXe siècle', *La Documentation Photographique*, October

—— (1988), 'Du "patronage" au "paternalisme": la restructuration des formes de domination de la main-d'œuvre ouvrière dans l'industrie métallurgique française', *Le Mouvement Social*, July–September

—— (1988a), *Le creuset français, histoire de l'immigration (XIXe–XXèeme siècle)*, Paris, Éditions du Seuil, 'L'Univers Historique' series

Nord, P. (1981), 'Le mouvement des petits commerçants et la politique en France de 1888 à 1914', *Le Mouvement Social*, January

O'Brien, P. and C. Keyder (1979), 'Les voies de passages vers la société industrielle en Grande-Bretagne et en France (1780–1914)', *Annales ESC*, September

Offerte, M. (1984), 'Illégitimié et légitimité du personnel politique ouvrier en France avant 1914', *Annales ESC*, July

Office du Travail (1893), *Enquête sur les salaires et les conditions de travail*, Paris, Imprimerie Nationale

Oualid, W. (1928), 'L'immigration ouvrière en France et ses causes', *Revue d'Économie Politique*

Oury, L. (1973), *Les Prolos*, Paris, Denoel

Ozouf, J. (1966), '*L'Humanité* et les journées de février 1934 (1945–1964)', *Le Mouvement Social*, January

Parize, R. (1981), 'Le paternalisme et son influence politique au Creusot (1899–1939)', Toulouse, typescript thesis

Peneff, J. (1979), 'Introduction' to 'Autobiographies de militants CGTU–CGT', *Les Cahiers du LERSCO*, December

Perdiguier, A. (1982), *Mémoires d'un compagnon*, Paris, Maspero

Perrot, M. (1960), 'Les rapports entre ouvriers français et étrangers (1871–1893)', *Bulletin de la Société d'Histoire Moderne*, no. 12

—— (1974), *Les ouvriers en grève (France 1871–1890)*, 2 vols, Paris, Mouton. Reprinted in a shorter form under the title *Jeunesse de la grève 1871–1890* Paris, Éditions du Seuil, 1985

—— (1976), 'L'éloge de la ménagère dans les discours des ouvrières françaises au XIXe siècle', *Romantisme*, pp. 105–21

—— (1978), 'Les ouvriers et les machines dans la première moitié de la XIXe siècle', in Murard and Zylberman (eds), q.v.

—— (ed.) (1983), 'L'espace de l'usine', *Le Mouvement Social*, October, (special issue)

—— (1985), 'Sur la formation de la classe ouvrière en France', in Katznelson and Zolberg, q.v.

Peteers, A. (1975), 'Les plantes tinctoriales dans l'économie du Vaucluse', *Étude Rurales*, pp. 41–54

Pétonnet, C. (1979), *On est tous dans le brouillard*, Paris, Galilée

Peyronnard, L. (1981), 'Le charbon de Blanzy, la famille Chagot et Montceau-les-Mines', 2 vols, Le Creusot, Éco-Musée, typescript

Pialoux, M. and B. Théret (1980), 'État, classe ouvrière et logement social', *Cahiers d'Économie Politique*, nos. 9 and 10

Pierrard, P. (1965), *La vie ouvrière à Lille sous le Second Empire*, Brionne, Gérard Montfort

—— (1984), *L'église et les ouvriers en France*, Paris, Hachette

Pigenet, M. (1982), 'L'usine et le village: Rosière (1869–1914)', *Le Mouvement Social*, April/June

Pinçon, M. (1984), *L'aciérie Thomé à Nouzonville (Ardennes)*, Paris, CSU

Pitrou, A. (1977), 'Le soutien familial dans la société urbaine', *Revue Française de Sociologie*, no. 1

Polanyi, K. (1944), *The great transformation*, New York, Rinehart

Ponty, J. (1979), 'La communauté polonaise de 1936 à 1939', in Gillet and Hilaire (eds), q.v.

—— (1985), 'Les travailleurs polonais en France, 1919–1939', Université de Paris-I, thesis

Poull, G. (1982), *L'industrie textile vosgienne (1765–1981)*, Rupt-Sur-Moselle, G. Poull

Poulot, D. (1981), *Le sublime* (reprint, with 'Introduction' by A. Cottereau), Paris, Maspero

Pouthas, D. (1956), *La population française pendant la première moitié du XIXe siècle*, Paris, PUF

Prost, A. (1964), *La CGT à l'époque du Front populaire, 1934–1939*, Paris, Colin

—— (1966), 'Les manifestations du 12 février 1934 en province', *Le*

Mouvement Social, January
—— (1967), 'Les grèves de juin 36: essai d'interprétation', in P. Renouvin and R. Rémond (eds), *Léon Blum, chef de gouvernement, 1936–1937*, Paris, Colin
Punelle, P. (1969), 'Étude d'une mentalité patronale: le Nord industriel de 1930 à 1935', *Revue du Nord*, pp. 641–50
Rambaud, P. and M. Vincienne (1964), *Les transformations d'une sociéte rurale: la Maurienne, 1561–1962*, Paris, Colin
Rancière, J. (1981), *La nuit des prolétaires*, Paris, Fayard
Rancière, J. and A. Faure (eds) (1976), *La parole ouvrière*, Paris, UGE, '10/18' series
Réault, J. (1981), 'L' usine des Batignolles à Nantes: l'histoire d'une usine du XXe siècle', *Norois*, October
—— (1983), 'Ouvrier de l'Ouest', in R. and M. Vivant (eds), *L'Ouest bouge-t-il? Son changement social et culturel depuis 30 ans*, Nantes, R. & M. Vivant, pp. 115–57
Rebérioux, M. (1974), *La République radicale?*, Paris, Éditions du Seuil, 'Points Histoire, Nouvelle Histoire de la France Contemporaine' series
—— (1979), *Jaurès et la classe ouvrière*, (collection), Paris, Maspero
—— (1981), *Les ouvriers du livre et leur fédération*, Paris, Temps Actuel
Reddy, W. (1975), 'Family and factory: French linen weavers in the Belle Époque', *Journal of Social History*, pp. 102–12
—— (1981), 'Mode de paiement et contrôle du travail dans les filatures de coton du Nord', *Revue du Nord*, no. 1
Régourd, F. (1981), *La Vendée ouvrière*, Les Sables-d'Olonne, Le Cercle d'Or
Reid, D. (1981), 'The role of mine safety in the development of working class consciousness', *French Historical Studies*, no. 1
—— (1985), 'Industrial pattern: discourse and practice in 19th century French mining and metallurgy', *Comparative Study of Society and History*, October
Renolleau-Antoine, M.-C. (1978), 'Population et mono-industrie dans la haute vallée de la Meurthe: Plainfaing', *Société Philomatique Vosgienne*, pp. 77–105
Rerat, R. (1983), 'Vers une généralisation du travail d'OS: de l'éclatement des métiers à l'éclatement des emplois', *Société Française*, no. 8
Reybaud, L. (1977), *Le fer et la houille*, Brionne, Gérard Montfort, (reprint)
Reynaud, J.-D. (1972), 'La nouvelle classe ouvrière, la technologie et l'histoire', *Revue Française de Sciences Politiques*, no. 3
Ribeill, G. (1984), *Les cheminots*, Paris, La Découverte
Riccomard, J. (1934), *La bonneterie à Troyes et dans le département de l'Aube*, Paris, Hachette
Riché, J. (1964), *L'évolution sociale des mineurs de Ronchamp aux XIXe et XXe siècles*, Besançon, Impr. Jacques et Demontrond
Roche, D. (1981), *Le peuple de Paris (essai sur la culture ouvrière au XVIIIe siècle)*, Paris, Aubier
Roncayolo, M. (1959), 'Quelques données pour une analyse géographique de la class ouvrière en France', *Les Cahiers de la République*, September
Rosanvallon, P. (1985), *Le moment Guizot*, Paris, Gallimard

Rougerie, J. (1965), 'Composition d'une population insurgée: la commune', *Le Mouvement Social*, October

—— (1968), 'Remarques sur l'histoire des salaires à Paris au XIXe siècle', *Le Mouvement Social*, April

Roux, M.-C. (1972), 'Grande industrie en Vaucluse au XIXe siècle: l'usine de l'Oseraie (1843–1914)', *Études Vauclusiennes*, pp. 17–24

Sabel, C. (1982), *Work and politics*, Cambridge, Mass., Cambridge University Press

Sadoul, G. (1962), *Le cinéma français*, Paris, Flammarion

Sainsaulieu, R. (1979), *L'identité au travail*, Paris, Presses de la FNSP

Salais, R. (1983), 'La formation du chômage moderne dans les années trente', *Économie et Statistique*, no. 155

Salais, R., N. Baverez and B. Reynaud (1986), *L'invention du chômage*, Paris, PUF

Sandrin, J. (1982), *Enfants trouvés, enfants ouvriers (XVIIe–XIXe siècles)*, Paris, Aubier

Sauvy, A. (1965–1970), *Histoire économique de la France entre les deux guerres*, 4 vols, Paris, Fayard

Sayad, A. (1977), 'Les trois "âges" de l'émigration algérienne', *Actes de la Recherche en Sciences Sociales*, no. 15

Scardigli, V. and P.-A. Mercier (1978), *Ascension sociale et pauvreté: la différentiation d'une génération de fils d'ouvriers*, Paris, Éditions du CNRS

Schöttler, P. (1985), *Naissance des bourses du travail*, Paris, PUF, (French translation of *Die Entstehung der 'bourses du travail', Sozialpolitik und französischer Syndikalismus am Ende des 19 Jahrhunderts*, Frankfurt/Main, Campus Verlag GmbH)

Schumpeter, J. (1984), *Impérialisme et classe sociale*, Paris, Flammarion (reprint)

Schweitzer, S. (1982), *Des engrenages à la chaîne, les usines Citroën, 1915–1935*, Lyon, PUL

Scott, J. (1982), *Les verriers de Carmaux*, Paris, Flammarion (French edition)

Segrestin, D. (1984), *Le phénomène corporatiste*, Paris, Fayard

Sellier, F. (1979), *Les salariés en France*, Paris, PUF, 'Que sais-je?' series

Sewell, W. H. (1971), 'La classe ouvrière de Marseille sous la Seconde République: structure sociale et comportement politique', *Le Mouvement Social*, July

—— (1980), *Work and revolution in France: the language of labour from the Old Regime to 1848*, Cambridge, Cambridge University Press

—— (1981), 'La confraternité des prolétaires', *Annales ESC*, July

Seys, B. and M. Gollac (1984), 'Les ouvriers', *Économie et Statistique*, November

Shinn, T. (1978), 'Des corps de l'état au secteur industriel: genèse de la profession d'ingénieur, 1750–1920', *Revue Française de Sociologie*, no. 19

Shorter, E. and Tilly, C. (1974), *Strikes in France, 1830–1968*, Cambridge, Mass., Cambridge University Press

Simiand, F. (1932), *Le salaire, l'évolution sociale et la monnaie*, 2 vols, Paris, Alcan

Simmel, G. (1920), *Philosophie des Geldes*, Munich, Duncker und Humblot

(3rd edition)

'Société ouvrières et communisme français', (1987), *Communisme*, nos. 15–16 (special issue)

Stearns, P. (1978), *Paths to authority: the middle class and the industrial labor force in France, 1820–1848*, Chicago, University of Illinois Press

Sternhell, Z. (1983), *La droite révolutionnaire*, Paris, Éditions du Seuil, 'Points Histoire' series (reprint)

Suzuki, H. (1969), 'L'évolution de l'industrie du coton dans la région rouennaise au XIXe siècle (1789–1880)', Rouen, typescript thesis

Tanguy, L. (1983), 'Les savoirs enseignés aux futurs ouvriers', *Sociologie du Travail*, no. 2

Terraril, J.-P. (1982), 'Connaître le classe ouvrière', *Société Française*, no. 2

Thélot (1982), *Tel père, tel fils*, Dunod

Thiérvoz, R. (1954), 'L'industrie en Valdaine et ses conséquences démographiques, sociales et électorales', *Revue de Géographie Alpine*, pp. 81–105

Thiesse, A.-M. (1980), 'L'éducation sociale d'un romancier: le cas d'Eugène Sue', *Actes de la Recherche en Sciences Sociales*, April

—— (1984), *Le roman du quotidien: lecteurs et lecture populaires à la Belle Époque*, Paris, Le Chemin Vert

Thompson, E. P. (1974), 'Patrician sòciety, plebeian culture', *Journal of Social History*, Summer

—— (1975), *The making of the English working class*, London, Penguin Books (reprint)

Thuillier, G. (1966), *Aspects de l'économie nivernaise au XIXe siècle*, Paris, Mouton

Tilly, C. (1972), 'How protest modernized in France: 1844–1855', *The Dimensions of Quantitative Research in History*, pp. 192–255

Tilly, C. and L. Lees (1974), 'Le peuple de juin 1848', *Annales ESC*, October

Tirat, J.-Y. (1963), 'Problémes de methode en histoire sociale', *Revue d'Histoire Moderne et Contemporaine*, July

Tollet, A. (1970), *Classe ouvriére dans la Résistance*, Paris, Éditions Sociales

Toubeau, A. (1882), *Le prolétariat agricole depuis 1789*, Paris, La Philosophie Positive

Touraine, A. (1955), *Évolution du travail aux usines Renault*, Paris, Éditions du CNRS

—— (1966), *La conscience ouvrière*, Paris, Éditions du Seuil

Touraine, A. and O. Raggazi (1961), *Les ouvriers d'origine agricole*, Paris, Éditions du Seuil

Toutain, J.-C. (1963), 'La population de la France de 1840 à 1959', *Cahier de l'Institut de Science Économique Appliquée*, no. 3

Trempé, R. (1971), *Les mineurs de Carmaux*, 2 vols, Paris, Éditions Ouvrières

Truquin, N. (1977), *Mémoires et aventures d'un prolétaire à travers la Révolution*, Paris, Maspero

Turgan (1866), *Les Grandes Usines*, 6 vols

UIMM (1928), *Documents*, May

Valdour, J. (1909–34), *La vie ouvrière: observations vécues*, 18 vols, Paris,

various publishers
—— (1923), *Ateliers et taudis de la banlieue parisienne*, Paris, Spes
—— (1925), *Le faubourg*, Paris, Spes
—— (1927), 'L'ouvrier français', *Les Cahiers de la Corporation*, no. 2
—— (1928), *Sous la griffe de Moscou*, Paris, Flammarion
—— (1934), *Ouvriers de Lyon et de Troyes*, Paris, Nouvelles Éditions Latines
Veltz, P. (1982), 'Travail, société, politique dans une région ouvrière: le Valenciennois 1830–1980', Paris, EHESS, thesis
Verret, M. (1979), *L'espace ouvrier*, Paris, Colin, 'U' series
—— (1982), *Le travail ouvrier*, Paris, Colin, 'U' series
Verry, M. (1956), *Les laminoirs ardennais*, Paris, Éditions Ouvrières
Verry, S. (1954), 'Évolution de la condition ouvrière dans le textile sedannais (1646–1952)', Paris, typescript thesis
Videlier, P. (1982), 'Vénissieux entre les deux guerres', Université de Lyon-II, thesis
—— (1984), 'La restructuration de la main-d'œuvre: le cas de Vénissieux: une banlieue au début du siècle', Research report, Université de Lyon-II, typescript
Videlier, P. and Bouhet, B. (1983), *Vénissieux de A à V*, Lyon, PUL
Vigier, P. (1963), *La Seconde République dans la région alpine*, 2 vols, Paris, PUF
—— (1975), 'Les paysans dans "Le Peuple" de Michelet', symposium on Michelet et Le Peuple, Université de Nanterre, February, typescript
—— (1982), *La vie quotidienne en Province et à Paris pendant les journées de 1848*, Paris, Hachette
Villac, M. (1985), 'Les familles mono-parentales', in INSEE, q.v.
Villermé, L.-R. (1840), *Tableau de l'état physique et moral des ouvriers employés dans les manufactures de coton, de laine et de soie*, 2 vols, Paris, J. Renouard
Villey, E. (1927), 'Le problème du salaire dans l'industrie', *Bulletin de la Société d'Encouragement*, April
Vrain, P. and G. Gautier (1979), *Les ouvriers vieillissants de la région parisienne: activité professionnelle et conditions de travail*, Paris, PUF, Cahiers du CEE
Weber, E. (1983), *La fin des terroirs*, Paris, Fayard (French edition)
Weber, M. (1969), *Économie et société*, Paris, Plon (French edition)
—— (1969a), *L'éthique protestante et l'esprit du capitalisme*, Paris, Plon (French edition)
Weil, S. (1951), *La condition ouvrière*, Paris, Gallimard
Willard, C. (1965), *Les Guesdistes*, Paris, Éditions Sociales
Willard, J.-C. (1984), 'Conditions d'emploi et de salaires de la main-d'œuvre étrangère', *Économie et Statistique*, January
Winock, M. (1971), 'La scission de Chatellerault et la naissance du Parti Allemaniste (1890–1891)', *Le Mouvement Social*, April
Wisner, A. (1972), *Conséquence du travail répétitif sous cadence sur la santé des travailleurs et accidents du travail*, Laboratoire de Physiologie de Travail et d'Ergonomie, CNAM
Woronoff, D. (1984), *L'industrie sidérurgique en France pendant la Révolution*

et l'Empire, Paris, EHESS

Zarca, B. (1983), 'Survivance ou transformations de l'artisanat dans la France d'aujourd'hui', 3 vols, Paris, IEP-EHESS, thesis

Zylberberg-Hocquart, M.-H. (1978), *Féminisme et syndicalisme en France*, Paris, Anthropos

Index

Index

Index